Achieving Results from Training

Robert O. Brinkerhoff

Achieving Results from Training

*How to Evaluate
Human Resource Development
to Strengthen Programs
and Increase Impact*

Jossey-Bass Publishers

San Francisco   •   London   •   1988

ACHIEVING RESULTS FROM TRAINING
*How to Evaluate Human Resource Development to Strengthen
Programs and Increase Impact*
by Robert O. Brinkerhoff

Copyright © 1987 by: Jossey-Bass Inc., Publishers
350 Sansome Street
San Francisco, California 94104
&
Jossey-Bass Limited
28 Banner Street
London EC1Y 8QE

Library of Congress Cataloging-in-Publication Data

Brinkerhoff, Robert O.
    Achieving results from training.

    (The Jossey-Bass management series)
    Bibliography: p.
    Includes index.
    1. Employees, Training of—Evaluation. I. Title.
II. Series
HF5549.5.T7B65   1987   658.3′12404   86-46331
ISBN 1-55542-044-3 (alk. paper)

Manufactured in the United States of America

The paper in this book meets the guidelines for
permanence and durability of the Committee on
Production Guidelines for Book Longevity of the
Council on Library Resources.

JACKET DESIGN BY WILLI BAUM

FIRST EDITION
        First printing: May 1987
        Second printing: September 1988

Code 8708

The Jossey-Bass Management Series

Consulting Editors
Human Resources

Leonard Nadler
Zeace Nadler
College Park, Maryland

Contents

Preface

The practice and profession of human resource development is rapidly expanding. Human resource development (HRD) is an increasingly important part of virtually every organization. HRD is sometimes known also as "training," or "training and development," or "staff development." In a typical large company today, for example, HRD activities include job training programs for employees, executive seminars, internships for minorities, health and wellness workshops, exercise classes, tuition-reimbursement programs that enable employees to take courses at local universities, and so on and on. In short, the modern organization's investment in HRD is tremendous—and it is growing. But, while the practice, needs, and opportunities for HRD are expanding, so too are the expectations for its effectiveness, power, and worth. HRD professionals are being asked to do more—and are promising more results as well. If these promises are to be kept, HRD practitioners must continue to develop and refine their art. Despite the increasingly important role HRD is playing in organizations, however, there is little evidence that the evaluation of HRD efforts is likewise increasing. A recent poll of HRD leaders in major corporations (Meigs-Burkhart, 1986) found, for example, that less than half of all HRD programs are evaluated in any way.

    This book is based on the premise that the HRD profession ought to be more aggressive and proactive in using evaluation in all HRD efforts. Evaluation can be a powerful tool in improving the likelihood that HRD will yield benefits to the organization; and evaluation can be used to demonstrate and prove HRD's payoff. *Achieving Results from Training* presents a systematic evaluation model, with guidelines for implementation, that can give HRD practitioners what they need to make their programs work as well as possible and, in the process, furnish the evaluation data needed to present solid, credible arguments about the efficiency, effectiveness, and worth of HRD efforts.

The genesis of the book lies also in my experience in two major "camps" influencing evaluation of HRD. One is the extensive work done in evaluation of public education and social programs during the late 1960s to about 1978. The other is the evaluation approaches developed by business and industry and instructional design practitioners for application to training programs in business settings. These two influencing streams developed almost completely independently, but my entire professional life has been spent between and within these two camps. The specific settings in which I have worked include defense and social welfare programs, university-based professional preparation programs, and business and industry and public agency training efforts. As diverse as my assignments have been, a theme common to all of them is the use of evaluation concepts and procedures to help practitioners improve their efforts.

A wealth of program evaluation models and approaches grew from the United States's tremendous investment in social and educational programs that developed rapidly during the Johnson "Great Society" era and the following decade. Because those programs were meant for widespread use, and because of the speed with which they were put together and adopted, program evaluation approaches developed for them were heavily oriented to "formative" purposes. A major function of evaluation was to help school and agency personnel develop and "debug" these emerging programs. Emphasis, too, was placed on evaluation as a means of assessing installation of programs to determine whether and how they diverged from their designers' intent. If, for example, a school district was installing a new districtwide reading program, it was likely that the program would differ considerably from classroom to classroom. Until the program was developed and stabilized to the extent that everyone was implementing it in similar ways, its overall impact could not be judged. Nor could one expect that it would make much difference to the whole district until the whole district was, in fact, using the program according to the program designers' specifications.

And so, these many evaluation models (Stufflebeam's 1971 CIPP model, Provus's 1972 Discrepancy Model, and Stake's 1973 Countenance Model, for example) served a major and valuable function: they helped busy and sometimes unprepared staffs implement, develop, and refine hastily designed programs. Just as a key benefit of evaluation was program improvement, an implicit premise of these evaluation approaches was that without careful and systematic evaluation most programs would fail. Emphasis in these evaluation models was on process; they helped practitioners refine and improve processes as they investigated program procedures and activities.

Evaluation in business and industry programs is geared more to the "bottom line." The four-step model developed by Donald Kirkpatrick (1976) and broadly adopted by business and industry focuses completely on outcome. Kirkpatrick identified four levels of training outcome: (1) reactions, (2) learning, (3) on-job behaviors, and (4) impact on the organization. These four levels are sometimes paraphrased as "Did they *like* it? Did they *learn* it? Did they *use* it? Did it make a *difference?*" Hamblin's (1974) model, developed in England and considerably more extensive than Kirkpatrick's approach, also focuses on HRD results and impacts. Later writing by Kearsley (1982) and Phillips (1983) stresses cost/benefit methods and other "hard data" approaches to assessing the effects and value of training. There are several data-based "front-end analysis" models and approaches (see especially Rummler, 1976; Gilbert, 1978; and Mager, 1984) that pay careful attention to needs analysis and help forecast the eventual worth of HRD payoffs. These are excellent models but, like the other business and industry approaches, they focus on results of HRD programs alone and do not emphasize, as do the educational evaluation approaches, the "shepherding" of a program to a successful conclusion. In short, much of the evaluation development over the past three decades and nearly all of today's books and articles from the business and industry arena have a strong bottom-line, results-oriented emphasis. Except where careful instructional design technology has been emphasized, the implicit assumption is that the HRD program itself does not merit inquiry, or that evaluation, at least, should not concern itself with tinkering with HRD processes and systems.

Each of these two major areas of influence, business and industry and the education/social program arena, has a valuable perspective to offer. The effects of programs must be assessed and accounted for. The results of training and their value to the organization must be identified, and HRD that does not pay off should be changed or eliminated. But it is worthwhile recognizing, too, that HRD is like any other human activity—it is fraught with error, it is based on incomplete knowledge and understanding, it is difficult to control, and it is as likely to run off course as it is to succeed, if not more so. And so, this book blends the two major evaluation approaches together. It presents a comprehensive evaluation model that incorporates the strong results-oriented aspects of the business and industry models and also the strong formative, improvement-oriented aspects of the educational and social program models.

To my knowledge, no other book or evaluation developer has created such a hybrid. Yet the content of the book seems badly needed. How to evaluate the proliferation of HRD programs and efforts remains a problem. Success cannot long be gauged solely by HRD's current success at surviving and spreading; inevitably, days of reckoning will come.

The Six-Stage Model presented in this book has been used successfully in a number of settings. I have trained HRD practitioners from a variety of settings in the United States and Europe, and in New Zealand, Australia, and other countries in its use. This model also forms the conceptual base for the graduate programs in human resource development at Western Michigan University in Kalamazoo and is used consistently by myself and my colleagues in our consulting work.

Who Should Read This Book?

Achieving Results from Training is meant primarily for HRD professionals and others who are charged with responsibility for HRD in organizations. Because it deals systematically and comprehensively with HRD design, operation, and evaluation, it will also be of equal value to graduate students and others who are seeking to learn more about how to do their work well. While it is largely oriented to HRD in business and industry settings, the Six-Stage Model is readily applicable and has been applied widely in school, government, agency, and other settings. Thus, program managers in other areas, or evaluators of non–HRD programs, should find the book useful. The book is nontechnical and requires no prerequisite knowledge of statistics or quantitative research methods. It will prove valuable to the very experienced and sophisticated HRD professional as well as to the new and inexperienced trainer.

For all audiences, the book is intended to develop greater understanding of the HRD process and to empower readers to design and conduct better programs and collect data to demonstrate the impact, value, and worth of HRD functions.

Overview of the Contents

The need and rationale for the Six-Stage Model are presented in the Introduction, along with a brief overview of the model's elements. Chapter One presents a thorough overview and discussion of the model, which is designed to provide the reader with a solid grasp of the model and how it can be used.

Each of the next six chapters (Chapters Two through Seven) treats one of the model's six stages in detail. Offering full discussion, guidelines for use, and examples of applications, these chapters provide practical information in easy-to-follow steps. In each chapter, readers learn more about the underlying concepts, assumptions, and limitations of the stage under discussion and find out how to proceed with planning an evaluation that is responsive to the stage. How to use evaluation data from that stage to improve the overall HRD process is also covered. Each of these chapters closes with a listing of useful data collection procedures keyed to the stage it treats, and lists sources (keyed to data collection methods) where readers can learn more about each particular method.

Chapter Two shows how Stage I evaluation approaches can be used to assess HRD needs. The descriptions of different HRD "beginnings" in this chapter will help practitioners avoid the narrow constraints of typical approaches to needs assessment. The chapter also explains how to identify the diverse values that inevitably impinge on deciding whether HRD is likely to pay off or not, and readers are given guidelines to help establish criteria for the ultimate success of HRD efforts.

Stage II evaluation, presented in Chapter Three, focuses on methods for evaluating HRD programs *before* they are implemented to ensure maximum payoff. A special feature of this chapter is a detailed checklist for assessing the adequacy of HRD programs at the design stage. This checklist can be modified to allow HRD audiences and stakeholders to become involved in evaluating HRD programs before they are delivered.

Chapter Four presents a systematic approach to evaluating the operation of HRD programs—Stage III evaluation. It focuses on dimensions of HRD programs that are relatively easy to measure. Although evaluation at this stage yields numerous paybacks, it is frequently not attended to as carefully as it should be.

Stage IV, the evaluation of immediate learning results, is addressed in Chapter Five. Relatively well-known procedures, such as testing and competency ratings, are used at this stage. The chapter includes guidelines for these more familiar approaches and presents methods and suggestions for expanding the utility of learning assessment.

The durability and application of HRD results in the workplace—Stage V evaluation—are the topic of Chapter Six. Typical HRD evaluation approaches fall well short of the recommendations included in this chapter, and this chapter explains how such failure drastically reduces HRD's payoff. The chapter also includes guidelines and strategies for Stage V evaluation of such hard-to-evaluate functions as management training.

Chapter Seven addresses the final evaluation stage in the Six-Stage Model, which focuses on HRD's ultimate payoff. Strategies for assessing the results of virtually every sort of HRD program are described in this chapter. Also, this chapter provides special and essential practical guidelines for dealing with the problem of *valuation* in HRD, particularly the typical organizational assessment by stakeholders whose perspectives and values differ.

Chapters Eight and Nine explain how to conduct comprehensive evaluation that incorporates all six stages of the model. Like the other chapters, these employ examples and scenarios to clarify the content and help readers identify applications in their own settings.

Acknowledgments

The federally sponsored Evaluation Training Consortium (ETC), which I directed for eleven years, provided me with an opportunity and a setting in which to develop the comprehensive and self-help evaluation approaches I use in the Six-Stage Model. The ETC project ran from 1972 through 1983 and was the government's single largest investment in evaluation of training projects. ETC developed evaluation approaches to enable training project directors to design and conduct their own evaluations using a minimum of expert consultation. Many of the concepts presented in this book grew directly from this challenging and satisfying experience.

I owe a debt of gratitude to my colleagues Dale Brethower, a psychologist, and Kenneth Dickie, an instructional designer. They graciously shared their solid professionalism and expertise, and our work together in a number of consultation efforts helped the Six-Stage Model emerge as a practical and powerful HRD development tool.

Vivian Welke's careful and painstaking manuscript typing

was indispensable and is gratefully acknowledged. My thanks also to Edgar Kelley, my department chair, who encouraged me in this project and who helped me find the time to complete it.

This book is dedicated to my wife, Stevie, whose love and support I cherish.

Kalamazoo, Michigan   Robert O. Brinkerhoff
March 1987

The Author

Robert O. Brinkerhoff is professor of educational leadership at Western Michigan University, where he co-coordinates the graduate program in human resource development. He received his B.A. degree (1964) in English literature from Colgate University. He earned his M.A. degree (1971) in educational foundations and his Ed.D. degree (1974) at the University of Virginia.

Brinkerhoff's training experience began in the U.S. Navy where he served as a training officer from 1965 to 1969. Following a brief hiatus during which he conducted sailing charters in the West Indies, he directed a number of training grants for disadvantaged workers funded by the National Alliance of Business "JOBS 70" program and the Neighborhood Youth Corps. His experience with evaluation studies began with Malcolm Provus in 1972 at the University of Virginia where he conducted evaluations of a number of federal education and training projects. From 1978 to 1984 he was associate director of Western Michigan University's Evaluation Center where he directed evaluation research and service projects. From 1972 through 1983 Brinkerhoff directed the Evaluation Training Consortium, the largest ever U.S. Office of Education evaluation training program.

Brinkerhoff is a regular contributor to the American Society for Training and Development (ASTD) *Training and Development Journal,* and has conducted sessions at the ASTD national conference. He is the author of four books on evaluation, including *Program Evaluation: A Practitioner's Guide for Train-*

ers and Educators (1983, with D. M. Brethower, T. Hluchyj, and J. R. Nowakowski) and *Conducting Educational Needs Assessments* (1985, with D. L. Stufflebeam).

Brinkerhoff has consulted on training and evaluation with dozens of companies and agencies in the United States and Australia. During 1986–87, he was on sabbatical leave as a consultant to the Upjohn Company, assisting with the evaluation of corporate units and the development of productivity measures for corporate training and development functions.

Achieving Results
from Training

Introduction:
How Evaluation
Strengthens HRD Programs
and Increases Impact

For some time, Blue Sky Airlines had been losing money. An analysis of operations revealed the culprit: ticket counter salespersons were miscalculating fares at an alarming rate—20 percent of all fares were in error. Sometimes, customers were not charged enough, and the airline lost. In other cases, customers were charged too much. When an attentive travel agent caught the error and Blue Sky was asked to refund the difference, it cost the company $100 to make a simple $5 refund. The problem was serious: several hundred thousand dollars a year in losses from only one major Midwest terminal.

An outside firm was hired to develop a training program for all counter clerks. The training was carried out with great success, and tests showed that 100 percent of the clerks could calculate even the toughest fares with perfect accuracy. But the problem persisted. Fares continued to be miscalculated, and more money was lost.

One day the Blue Sky training officer was at the airport and noticed that a few Blue Sky clerks had long lines of complaining customers who made

1

rude comments to the clerks when they were finally served. Other clerks' lines were shorter and moved with ease and dispatch. Curious, the training officer jotted down the numbers of the positions that were moving slowly. Later, a check of positions revealed a startling clue: the few slow-moving lines were staffed by clerks who almost never made fare calculation errors; the fast-moving lines with happy customers were staffed by the error makers.

A few minutes' thought and some further checking disclosed the cause of Blue Sky's fare problems. All the clerks were fully capable of calculating fares correctly, as the expensive and unnecessary training program had showed. But, on the job, when things got busy, most fare clerks resorted to inaccurate, but quick, means of fare calculations, thus moving their lines quickly and avoiding customer harassment. A few thicker-skinned and more careful clerks used the laborious calculation methods and endured the customers' nasty comments. When Blue Sky simplified its fare calculation procedures and provided all clerks with a one-page chart to remind them of procedures, the problem went away within a week. Of course, it took a long time to earn back the huge amount of money wasted on the unneeded training program.

This story is fiction, but it is based, as many readers will recognize, on painful facts. Sometimes, perhaps often by some estimates, HRD programs are designed and run when HRD is not needed at all, or, as in the Blue Sky case, when real problems exist but the wrong solution—training—is used.

Unfortunately, there are many ways that HRD programs can go wrong! Sometimes, HRD is truly needed, but it doesn't solve the problems it was meant to. Consider the example of a manufacturing firm that has been experiencing a high and costly accident rate among machine operators. To deal with the problem, operators are trained in safety procedures and safety skills. Yet, when they return to the job, production pressures from supervisors wash out the effects of training, and operators revert to the unsafe but familiar and quicker procedures. Thus, unless training outcomes are supported on the job, they will wither and die.

Consider another example of HRD gone awry. Simple Tools Inc. had developed a new modular training program for supervisors. The old classroom method was very expensive and time consuming. The new, individual modules would, it was thought, both save time and be more convenient. An outside firm worked closely with the management of Simple Tools to develop the modules. Tryouts conducted in the training office showed that the modules were easy to read and could teach the required content. Simple Tools published the manuals and distributed them companywide. But tests conducted a year later, along with analyses of supervisor performance appraisals, showed a drastic slippage in supervisory effectiveness. Further inquiry showed that very few people used the modules in the way intended. Users did not follow the recommended sequences, and most skipped over the module tests to move on to the next piece. A well-designed and well-intended training program had not been properly installed and managed.

In other cases, human resource development programs may be implemented correctly but may not be needed in the first place. Or HRD might be needed but not done well. Programs might be needed and done well, but then, because conditions in the workplace are inhospitable to HRD outcomes, the learning never gets used. Sometimes, HRD is not wanted even though it is needed, and its value is not recognized by trainees. And even when HRD goes well and serves real needs, it might be excessive, or inefficient, taking too long and costing too much money.

Evaluation and HRD

In sum, HRD programs do not always work. And when they do work, they sometimes do not work as well as they should. A major tool for making HRD work better is evaluation. Evaluation, if done well and at the right time, could have helped turn all the training failures discussed in the forgoing paragraphs into successes.

In the Blue Sky Airlines case, for example, an evaluation

of the current level of fare calculation knowledge and skill of counter clerks would have immediately shown that the problem was not caused by knowledge or skill deficits. Further inquiry into working conditions and activities would have quickly turned up the fact that sometimes some clerks calculated fares correctly and that at other times all clerks calculated fares correctly. The real cause for the problem, and an obvious solution, would not have remained hidden had the correct inquiry been followed. And, it might be added, the evaluation needed to figure things out would have been a great deal less costly than trying to fix the problem with an inefficient and ineffective training program.

Yet the Blue Sky case is not unusual. HRD is often looked at as a quick fix. Trainers and others in organizations often seize on training solutions for almost any and all performance problems. Quick fixes that do not really fix anything, however, must be avoided. When evaluation is done according to the concepts and procedures contained in this book, HRD leaders will be able to claim, and back up their claims with convincing data, that their programs

- are aimed at important and worthwhile organizational benefits.
- use the best available and most cost-effective designs and plans.
- operate smoothly and efficiently and are enjoyed by participants.
- achieve important skill, knowledge, and attitude objectives.
- are used effectively on the job.
- produce valuable and cost-effective organizational benefits.

But not all evaluation can make claims such as these. Just as HRD programs do not always work as well as they should, evaluation inquiries can also be faulty. The typical evaluation of HRD programs consists of collecting opinions of participants about the quality of the program they have just received. Most often, the dimensions of the program they are asked about—or the dimensions that affect their responses regardless of what they are asked about—relate to the entertainment value of the program and to how well organized it was and how smoothly it ran. All this is fine as far as it goes. Good programs ought to be well run, and if participants find them entertaining and enjoyable, the chances are greater that learning will occur.

But HRD leaders will have to do better, when called on the corporate carpet to account for themselves, than argue that their programs are entertaining and smoothly administered. The business of HRD is to serve the needs of the organization. This means that HRD can only be justified and can only be demonstrated to have value if it meets some worthwhile organizational need. Training might, for instance, have helped an organization achieve a better safety record and thus have created a safer work environment, thereby also enhancing productivity and profitability. Again, a program might have helped people do their jobs more accurately and efficiently, thus creating more profit for the company. Or HRD might have made employees more committed and satisfied, thus reducing turnover and grievances.

Human resource development can take many forms. It might entail a single workshop or consist of a multiyear development effort. It might include a tuition-reimbursement program or a system of encouraging and supporting attendance at meetings of professional associations. But while HRD can take a wide variety of forms and encompasses a wide range of subject matter, intended results, and delivery means, all HRD is alike in that it approaches improving individual or organizational performance through learning. The central theme of HRD is that people can learn; that is, they can acquire new skills, knowledge, or attitudes. Human resource development must, however, go beyond mere learning. Learning must somehow translate into real and valuable benefits to the organization.

Chapter One will demonstrate that training must meet two crucial criteria. First, of course, it must produce learning changes with efficiency and efficacy. But it must also satisfy a second criterion, since in all fields of human endeavor there is an unfortunate tendency to do well what is not worth doing. A person can be taught a useless skill very efficiently, effectively, and even enjoyably! If HRD does not pay off, if it does not result in some benefit to the organization, then it has no worth. Worth is defined as the extent to which HRD produces value to the organization at a reasonable cost.

Human resource development, therefore, must be carried out effectively and efficiently, and it must create worth. The evaluation model presented and discussed in this book is aimed at ensuring that HRD will meet both these criteria.

The evaluation model presents six stages of program development and operation. Each stage is crucial to either the efficiency or worth of training, and each stage has specific evaluation strategies and methods associated with it. This model—the Six-Stage Evaluation Model—helps HRD practitioners identify and systematically respond to information needs vital to each stage of training's development. As information pertaining to each stage is collected and used, the probability for successful training—training that will pay off to the organization—is increased.

A basic assumption of the Six-Stage Model is that the primary payoff from evaluating HRD is the improvement of programs. While accountability data are needed and virtually every HRD operation could use data to better justify its existence, "proving" the value of HRD is not the main reason to evaluate it. When evaluation data are systematically collected and used to make programs work better, the "proof" argument tends to take care of itself. HRD programs that are systematically evaluated will be more successful, and systematic evaluation will create a data base from which the proof argument can be readily constructed.

Making programs work, and making them work better, requires information. It is clear, for example, that for programs to be worthwhile they must address valued and important organizational needs. But what is valued and needed varies from organization to organization and even varies over time within the same organization. It is impossible to know what is needed, and how much it is needed, without accurate and detailed information from and about the organizational context. The first stage of the Six-Stage Model addresses this information need and shows how the intended goals of HRD programs can be evaluated against organizational needs.

Program designs and plans are always flawed, because they are based on inadequate research and knowledge bases and because things never work quite the way they are supposed to. The most expensive way to find out what is right and wrong, weak and effective, about a program plan is to just run it and see what works and what does not. Stage II of the model discusses how program plans and designs can be evaluated *before* a program is put into operation so that many of the bugs can be removed while the design is still only on paper. A major benefit of this kind of evaluation is that it creates stronger plans through building consensus and a spirit of teamwork and commitment.

Stage III focuses on the operation of programs, and evaluation at this stage aims to keep programs on a successful track through successive control and feedback cycles. Stage III also builds the data base from which future revisions to programs can be most productively made.

Stages IV through VI investigate the impact of HRD, from individual learning through interaction in the workplace to eventual organizational benefit. Programs succeed, when they do, through a complex network of causally related events. Human resource development practitioners must understand this complex sequence, measuring and nurturing those changes that are positive and intervening when indications are that results may be negative.

As a whole, the Six-Stage Model helps conceptualize good programs and guides systematic inquiry to create the information needed to make them work and pay off as best they can. Data about program contexts, plans, operations, and results are necessary to doing HRD well. And these data, when combined with the sort of systematic inquiry that the model prescribes, keep programs in a self-improving mode. A basic assumption of this book is not just that HRD can and ought to be better but that HRD must be continually seeking improvement. It will be a good thing when the HRD leader can say, "Our training was aimed at a real need, had a good plan, was run efficiently, and produced real learning that was used to create cost-effective

value to the company." But it will be a better thing (and perhaps a necessary thing) for the HRD leader to be able to amend
the first statement with this: "Here are data collected to show
how we will get these same or better results the next time a little more quickly and a little more efficiently!"

The Six-Stage Model will enable HRD leaders to make
such statements with confidence and with a base of information
to back them up. But we must also recognize that tying HRD to
real and valued organizational benefits requires a much tighter
weaving of training programs into the organizational fabric than
is typically the case. Human resource development cannot be
viewed as an add-on function or an employee benefit or given
any other sort of separate role. The function of HRD must be
closely tied to business goals, strategy, and performance. Making this tie may require HRD leaders to reperceive their own
roles and function, and almost always requires that the consumers of programs—potential participants and organization leaders
alike—be educated as to the real function, goals, and "logic" of
HRD. Thus, the Six-Stage Model emphasizes strategies and
methods for getting HRD into the mainstream of the corporation and for turning potential beneficiaries of HRD into more
educated consumers and critics. What the HRD profession de-
cidedly does *not* need is evaluation done and decisions made
about HRD by uninformed and misled consumers. But unless
HRD takes on the evaluation role, and takes it on proactively,
that is exactly what the profession will get.

The stance of this book is that the HRD office should not
wait for the phone to ring, with corporate headquarters calling
and asking for HRD to send up some data to justify its existence. Rather, HRD should be ringing up corporate leaders on a
regular basis to provide them with data about program needs,
plans, operations, and results and to show them on a regular
basis what training is doing to further corporate goals and values.
The Six-Stage Model that follows in the remaining chapters of
this book should provide HRD leaders with the conceptual and
procedural tools to meet these crucial evaluative information
needs.

1

The Six Stages of Effective HRD Evaluation

This chapter sets the stage for understanding and using the Six-Stage Model. It does this by first presenting and discussing the "logic" of HRD. To think about how to evaluate HRD so that you can do it better requires first that you consider what HRD *is* and how it is supposed to work. The logic of HRD is used to construct a six-step decision model showing how all HRD, in order to pay off, must be guided successfully through a series of logically connected decision points. The presentation of the Six-Stage Evaluation Model builds directly on the decision steps. Finally, some key characteristics and features of the model are discussed.

How HRD Works to Produce Value

All HRD programs share a basic logic: HRD is meant to produce something of value to the organization, something that will help the organization to better meet its goals. Supervisory training, for example, is meant to improve the quality and effectiveness of supervision, thereby increasing productivity. Or a fitness program might aim to improve employee health, thereby increasing productivity through a reduction in illness, sick leaves, and so forth. The point is that any HRD program intends to

9

create value for the organization. Thus, HRD cannot be defined without taking the organization into account, and the "logic" of any particular instance of HRD would include a description of the particular value that a particular HRD event was meant to produce.

Human resource development can take several forms. As Nadler (1980) explains, HRD can be construed as "training" when its primary purpose is to improve current job performance, as "education" when its primary purpose is to help personnel advance to a different job, or as "development" when it aims to strengthen the organization through benefiting individuals or organizational units. Regardless of its form (training, education, development, or some combination or variant of these types), all HRD is alike in that it is not meant to be done for its own sake but rather to benefit the organization.

The logic of HRD is most clear in the instance of training programs. As Figure 1 shows, participants are provided some sort of learning experience, such as a workshop, on-job training, self-instructional resources, or an external course. They acquire some new skill, knowledge, or attitude (SKA) from this intervention. Then—and here comes an important part—they return to the workplace and put the new SKA to some use. And, more important yet, the use of the new SKA has some positive result for the organization: it enhances a strength or reduces a deficit or problem. In sales training, to take a simple example, trainees might learn about the new XYZ sales method in a workshop. They then return to their territories and *use* the XYZ method. As a result, the organization benefits from increased sales and profits.

Figure 1. The Logic of HRD.

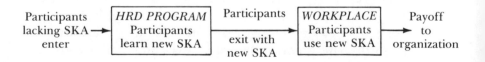

This causally related sequence of events—learning a new skill or attitude, using it, and benefiting the organization—represents the structure of classical training. That is, with training, the "route" to impact of value to the organization is through changes in job behavior; for example, participants acquire a new skill, they use it on their job, and, as a result, the organization benefits in some way. But this classic behavioral route is not the *only* avenue by which HRD may achieve organizational benefits.

For many types of HRD, the route to organizational benefits is neither direct nor clear. For example, consider the matter of cardiopulmonary resuscitation (CPR) instruction for employees. Here, participants acquire a skill that many will never have to use. Now, clearly, when people do use their CPR skills correctly, it is easy to see how the organization benefits, for a life is saved. But there are benefits even if the skills are never used. CPR-trained employees may feel more confident and thus be more productive, or they may come to respect their organization more, for it has demonstrated a respect for their well-being by providing this kind of training. Or, for another example, consider retirement seminars and counseling provided to employees as they near retirement age. Again, the simple fact that such programs are available at all probably reaps benefits in terms of morale and commitment to the organization. Such programs are also intended to reduce the time that employees might otherwise spend worrying and fretting over the vagaries of impending retirement. Sessions provided to employees to help them avoid personal credit and indebtedness problems have a similar intent, as it is hoped that persons so trained will have more productive time to spend at work.

Sometimes HRD programs are provided as a reward, for example, when an employee is rewarded with a trip to a professional convention. Here, certainly, the HRD activity must meet at least some criteria to establish itself as genuine HRD, but it need not result in newly acquired skills that are applied in the workplace. Programs provided as a reward are intended to create greater loyalty, commitment, and dedication in the recipient. And these attributes, it is assumed, will pay off to the organization in increased productivity of recipients and even their subordinates, lower turnover, and the like.

The point is that *any* HRD activity is meant to benefit the organization. In the case of skill training and many instances of education and development, the route to benefit is through behavior change in the workplace. But this is not always the case. And, very often, a single HRD intervention may have some intended benefits that do not require on-job behavioral changes as well as some that do.

Table 1 contains a three-part format for representing the three levels of HRD outcomes (new SKA or reactions, on-job behavior changes, and organizational benefits) and provides several examples of the logic of HRD applied to different sorts of HRD efforts. The reader will note that not all the examples shown represent the classic behavior-change route. *All*, however, show organizational benefits, for these are required by the logic of HRD; and, certainly, some routes from HRD programs to eventual payoff are less direct and more complex than others. To evaluate HRD's outcomes, it is necessary to dig out and write down (as in Table 1) the logic of the program to be evaluated.

While Table 1 portrays the basic logic (the planned sequence of causally related outcomes) for several examples of HRD efforts, it is not a complete explanation for any of the programs shown. That is, any HRD effort would likely have multiple outcomes at both the immediate results (learning) level and the organizational benefits level. And most HRD efforts would also have multiple outcomes at the job-usage (or personal-usage) level. The HRD program cannot be properly planned, understood, or evaluated until the logical sequence and connections among the three levels are identified regardless of the complexity of that sequence—and this would take considerably more space and description than found in Table 1.

Consider, for example, a training program in performance appraisal for new supervisors that is to lead, eventually, to increased worker productivity. Once supervisors learn the necessary skills, knowledge, and attitudes required to do good performance appraisal, the sequence of on-job behaviors planned

Table 1. Different Routes to Organizational Payoff.

Training Intervention	New SKA or Reactions	Behavior Change	Benefits to Organization
Safety training	Awareness of, and skill in following, safety procedures	Greater adherence to procedures	Reduced injuries and lost time
Conflict resolution for supervisors	Skill and knowledge in methods	Use of techniques when called for	Reduced grievances; more productivity
CPR training	Skill in CPR	Use of CPR when called for and greater feelings of security at all times on job	Increased morale, productivity, commitment to organization; lives saved (maybe !)
Personal finances and credit control workshops	Skill and knowledge in handling personal finances; feeling that organization cares	Reduced time on job spent in personal matters or worrying	Increased productivity; more commitment to organization
Retirement training and counseling	Skill and knowledge in retirement planning; feeling that organization cares	Reduced time on job spent in worrying and personal planning	Increased productivity and morale
After-work classes in French cooking	Skill and knowledge in French cooking; feeling that company cares	Maybe none!	Increased morale; reduced employee turnover
Attendance at convention or conference	Feeling that organization cares; maybe a new skill or knowledge	Maybe none!	Increased morale; reduced employee turnover

for eventual productivity gains might be that supervisors will analyze job needs and then redefine and clarify worker expectations, so that workers will understand and adopt improved work standards. Next, supervisors will accurately discriminate between instances and noninstances of worker behavior and accurately record worker behavior, so that they can provide constructive feedback to workers. As a result, workers will modify their job behavior, and the organization will benefit from increased productivity. But while the complex causal connections across the three levels of outcome—from immediate learning to organizational benefit—might involve more detail, the structure of Table 1 provides the format needed to analyze HRD's logic. Any program could be analyzed in terms of this structure, showing expected (or accomplished) results at the several levels, from immediate skill, knowledge, attitude, or reaction outcomes to ultimate organizational benefits.

Making the HRD Process Pay Off

Human resource development programs take many forms: workshops, seminars, tuition-reimbursement programs, apprenticeships, on-job instruction, seminars, and conferences, to name but a few. HRD can occur in many different ways, at different levels in the organization, at different costs, and with different outcomes in mind, from manual skills to management abilities, from simple job guidelines to complex human interaction skills. Despite all these differences, however, all HRD programs are alike in that they aim at eventual organizational benefits.

But all HRD is alike in another important way. Sometimes it pays off, and sometimes it does not. Programs do not pay off when participants complete their training without having acquired intended SKA or reactions; programs do not pay off when SKA are meant to be, but are not, transformed into on-job behaviors; and programs do not pay off if new behaviors or reactions do not, in fact, lead to the expected organizational benefits. But almost all programs can be *made* to pay off. Doing this involves making correct decisions about HRD needs, design, operation, and effects. To develop a process model for making HRD programs pay off, we can extend the logic of training to create a training decision-making cycle, as shown in Table 2.

Table 2. The HRD Decision Cycle.

The Logical Steps	Some Key Decisions
1. Goals for HRD that will be worthwhile to the organization are established	• Is there a worthwhile problem or opportunity to be addressed? • Is the problem worth solving/addressing? • What organizational benefits could HRD produce? • Can HRD help? • Is HRD the best solution? • Who should receive HRD? • What SKA are needed?
2. A workable program design is created	• What learning processes will best produce needed SKA? • Is a design already available? • Can an effective design be created? • Is it likely to work?
3. A program design is implemented and made to work	• What is really happening? • Has the design been installed as planned? • Is it working? • What problems are occurring? • What changes should be made?

(continued on next page)

Table 2. The HRD Decision Cycle, Cont'd.

The Logical Steps	*Some Key Decisions*
4. Recipients exit with new SKA; enough HRD has taken place	• Who has and has not acquired SKA? • What else was learned? • Are SKA sufficient to enable on-job usage?
5. Recipients use new SKA on the job or in personal life; reactions to HRD are sustained	• Have HRD effects lasted? • Who is using new SKA? • Which SKA are/are not being used? • How are SKA being used? • How well are SKA being used?
6. Usage of SKA benefits the organization; original HRD needs are sufficiently diminished	• What benefits are occurring? • What benefits are not occurring? • Are any problems occurring because of new SKA use/nonuse? • Should HRD be continued? • Should less be done? More? • Are revisions needed? • Was it worth it?

Table 2 forms the basic structure for the Six-Stage Evaluation Model that will follow and shows that program design and operation move through a series of steps, each of which is accompanied by several decisions.

First, there must be a legitimate need or opportunity for HRD. That is, there must be some intended benefits to the organization (for example, reduced waste, improved morale, greater productivity) that a program could produce. At this point, the HRD practitioner looks forward, envisioning a potential program design, participants with new SKA, participants using the new SKA, and so forth, to decide whether (1) a problem/opportunity is worth addressing and (2) whether HRD could possibly be worthwhile in addressing that problem or opportunity. This step is typically known as *needs assessment*, which means determining whether there is a sufficient need for HRD and deciding what the goals of a program ought to be. This step might begin with problem solving, such as figuring out why a production problem is occurring, why grievances have increased, or why sales are down. Or this step might begin with considering why a particular strength exists. Sometimes HRD programs can help maintain organizational strengths (for example, good morale, high sales, low accident rates). Programs might even begin with a special opportunity, such as a training grant, a resource newly available, or a new program on the market.

Step 1 finishes with deciding not just that training can make a difference but that the difference will also be worth making. An airline company, to refer to an earlier example, may have noticed a sharp increase in errors made by ticket counter clerks in calculating fares. Given that considerable money is involved in the form of lost revenues and refund expenses, the problem warrants a solution. Further inquiry reveals that counter clerks are motivated to calculate fares correctly and that other job factors (supervision, job design, and so on) are *not* causing poor performance; rather, the cause of the problem is that counter clerks are unfamiliar with new fare programs and calculation steps. Thus, learning (giving clerks more knowledge) appears to be a good solution; potential training costs will be much less than the increased profits to be gained by reducing errors and refunds. Finally, it would have to be determined that a training solution (giving clerks new skills or knowledge) would be a better alternative than any other potential solutions, such as simplifying the fare structure.

The second step involves deciding *how* to produce the needed new SKA in the potential trainees. There may be training "packages" on the market that could be reviewed and assessed to determine their suitability. Or vendors might be available, likewise requiring review and assessment to decide which, if any of them, to hire. As is often the case, it may be that a program design must be created, because no suitable package or vendor-with-package is available. This step involves also, of course, a host of logistic and planning questions: when to schedule a program, how long it should last, what delivery methods and materials to use, and so forth. To return to the airline example, a decision would have to be made as to whether to conduct on-the-job training, workshops, self-instructional materials, or some other type of learning intervention.

Once these many decisions have been made and a program design has been arrived at, it then remains to put it in place and make it work. Anyone involved in HRD knows that this is no easy trick. As the poet noted in the case of cups and lips, there is many a slip 'twixt program plan and program operation. In fact, two harsh realities of HRD life rear their ugly heads at this point. First, no program design is perfect; all program designs have some flaws. Second, no program works exactly as it was designed; something always goes wrong and needs changing.

Knowledge of participant needs and characteristics is always partial, and education and learning theory is always incomplete. Thus, HRD designs are "best guesses"—compromises between theory and practicality that will inevitably need tinkering with as they are installed and operated. Likewise, even good plans can go wrong in operation. Problems always come up. On-the-spot revisions and control are needed to adapt programs to their environment and make them work. So, the third step is aimed at getting the program design installed, monitoring its operation to make revisions, and keeping the program on track so that it can meet its objectives.

The fourth step, once programs are in place and running reasonably smoothly, involves finding out who is learning what. Where appropriate learning is occurring, it must be recognized and reinforced. But if learning is not taking place, this must also be noticed so that corrective action can be taken. Or the "wrong" learning might accrue. Recipients might be developing bad attitudes, acquiring sloppy habits, or learning inapplicable skills; this must be corrected or accounted for. This fourth step is aimed at deciding whether a program has accomplished its *immediate intended learning outcomes* and asks whether participants are ready to return to the workplace.

Step 5 decisions focus on the transfer and endurance of learning to be sure that the program is headed toward payoff. The training-acquired SKA must be used on the job, or the intended organizational benefits will not happen. Returning again to the airline counter clerks example: The clerks may have, as step 4 would have shown, mastered the new skills and knowledge needed to calculate fares correctly. But, for some reason, job conditions keep them from doing it correctly. Perhaps long lines of complaining customers force them to return to old, but quicker, methods of calculation. Perhaps supervisors do not notice errors or do not reinforce accurate work. Maybe the clerks just forget, as time goes by, how to make correct calculations. (But, it should be noted, thorough inquiry at step 1 should have identified many of these job-site conditions that could impede the application of training. There is no sense undertaking training that does not have a good chance of working!) If such usage is not occurring or is occurring incorrectly, corrective action is necessary. Sometimes additional training or training of other persons (for example, of superiors) is called for.

In other instances, unanticipated (good *or* bad) usage of training-acquired SKA occurs. These instances may represent opportunities to extend and augment HRD content and designs, or they may indicate other revisions. In any type of HRD program, enduring, noticeable results in people and their behavior on the job are anticipated. The aim of the step 5 decisions is to determine when HRD results are working and enduring and when they are not.

Step 6 decisions focus on the organizational benefits that were initially expected to occur. When HRD has fully "worked," the SKA usage or endurance (step 5) has produced the sought-after benefits. But it sometimes happens that conditions have changed and that the SKA usage is no longer sufficient to make a dent in the problem that initially inspired a program. Or maybe only *some* SKA usage has resulted in benefits. Perhaps the program was based on invalid assumptions, and it is learned through painful experience that the SKA transfer, no matter how enduring, correct, and pervasive, just does not make a worthwhile difference.

Step 6 decisions conclude with deciding whether the whole effort was worth the costs and whether the initial need has gone away. At this point, step 6 returns (or "recycles" in systematic language) to step 1; that is, needs must be *re*considered. Maybe new programs are called for if initial needs were not sufficiently remediated, or, often, new needs have emerged and "old" needs have only been partially addressed.

In summary, designing and conducting HRD programs to make them pay off require a series of decisions, as outlined in the six-step "HRD Decision Cycle" of Table 2. Each of these decisions must be made, and made well, if good programs are to result. The Six-Stage Evaluation Model is intended to help HRD practitioners collect the information (data) needed to make these decisions accurately. The checklist for "good HRD" that follows presents criteria against which training decisions can be assessed, forming the basis for the Six-Stage Model.

While the checklist poses a series of declarative sentences, it is important to note that these are not yes-no dimensions. Probably no program would ever earn an unqualified "yes!" to each checklist item. Rather, responses are a matter of degree. The surer one is of a positive response, the more certain one is of a good HRD effort. Likewise, uncertainty or answers tending toward the negative indicate problems. Lastly, the ability to respond at all to the checklist criteria requires information—a great deal of information. Each item on the checklist is accompanied by some notes about information needed to achieve that checklist criterion. Without information about HRD contexts, plans, operations, and effects, the checklist questions cannot be responded to at all. Getting the information needed is the job of the Six-Stage Model, as we will see in the discussion following the checklist:

| | INFORMATION
NEEDED TO |
CRITERIA	JUDGE CRITERIA

Stage I—Goal Setting and Needs Analysis

A. HRD aims to go beyond producing immediate reactions and changes in SKA to achieving worthwhile organizational benefits	• Specifications of objectives at (1) immediate, (2) job-place, and (3) organizational benefit levels
B. Intended organizational benefits are	• Data about organizational values, goals, mission
1. important	• Judgments of value of HRD goals by key individuals from several levels
2. compatible with organizational mission and goals	• Judgments of research data and/or expert opinion concerning validity of logic of HRD objectives
3. valued by the organization	
4. worth as much or more than projected program costs	• Data about job-place values, constraints, and climate
C. Reaction and SKA: organizational benefit connections are valid if	• Data about causes of problems to be addressed by HRD
1. SKA changes would lead to intended job-behavior changes	• Judgments of HRD's cost effectiveness to address problems and goals
2. Intended reactions and SKA objectives would be re-	• Judgments about acceptability of HRD (especially job-place) objectives

CRITERIA	INFORMATION NEEDED TO JUDGE CRITERIA
inforced and supported, not extinguished, by the job place	
3. Intended reaction and job-behavior objectives would lead to intended organizational benefits	

Stage II—Program Design

CRITERIA	INFORMATION NEEDED TO JUDGE CRITERIA
A. Designs are complete and specify	• Specification of intended program inputs, processes, and outcomes
1. inputs needed (for example, facilities, media, staff, entry levels)	• Judgments of completeness of design information
2. procedures and processes (for example, selection of participants, learning activities, social activities)	• Judgments of theoretical adequacy of design; research data about designs; instructional design technology and learning theory
3. intended outcomes (immediate reactions and SKA; job-behavior changes; organizational benefits)	• Judgments of extent to which activities reflect good practice and instructional design technology
B. Planned activities are potent and theoretically sound; that is, they are likely to work	• Data comparing selected plan features to features of alternative plans

CRITERIA	INFORMATION NEEDED TO JUDGE CRITERIA
C. Planned activities reflect best educational and instructional design principles	• Comparison of plan to data about values preferences, work demands and constraints, and corporate culture
D. Planned activities are superior to available alternatives	• Comparison of plan to ethical and legal guidelines
E. Program activities are compatible with existing schedules, organizational climate, and individual and organizational values	• Data about participant and consumer opinions
F. Program activities and procedures are ethical and legal	• Judgments about feasibility and economy of plan
G. Program plan is perceived favorably by participants and consumers	
H. Program plan is practical and economical	

Stage III—Implementation and Operation of HRD

A. Program adheres to specifications for inputs, costs, procedures, and enabling objectives except when divergence is necessary	• Data on actual program inputs, activities, and achievement of enabling objectives
B. Program operation responds to participant and con-	• Judgments of suitability of actual inputs, activities, and enabling objectives achieved

CRITERIA	INFORMATION NEEDED TO JUDGE CRITERIA
text problems and opportunities by diverging from plan when necessary to further sound HRD progress	• Recognition and assessment of problems and opportunities • Judgments about suitability of discrepancies between actual and intended operation

Stage IV—Immediate Outcomes

A. Participants achieve satisfactory exit levels on intended reaction and SKA objectives	• Data about actual reactions and SKA achievements of participants
B. Unanticipated reaction and SKA outcomes are suitable and compatible with the HRD plan	• Judgments of suitability of SKA and reaction achievement

Stage V—Endurance and Application of Immediate Outcomes

A. Reaction and SKA achievements endure long enough for application	• Data about endurance of SKA and reactions achieved
B. Participants correctly apply SKA in intended usage behaviors	• Judgments of suitability of SKA applications in on-job and off-job behavior
C. Unanticipated SKA applications are compatible with training plan and organizational values and goals	• Data about unanticipated SKA usages; judgments of suitability

CRITERIA	INFORMATION NEEDED TO JUDGE CRITERIA

Stage VI—Organizational Benefits

A. Intended organizational benefits are achieved at satisfactory levels	• Data about actual organization impacts
	• Judgments of suitability of impacts
B. Unexpected organizational impacts are compatible with organizational values, goals, and mission	• Data about HRD costs and value of organization impacts
C. Worth of all organization impacts is equal to or greater than HRD costs	• Judgments of cost-benefit of HRD effort

In looking back over the checklist, it should be obvious that response to the checklist is impossible without a great deal of accurate information. To decide, for example, whether immediate program efforts have been sufficient (checklist item IV A.) requires information about the nature and extent of actual recipient SKA gains. Without such information, step 4 decisions cannot be legitimately made. Or, for another example, to determine whether program schedules are compatible (checklist item II E.) requires information about the planned schedule, organizational demands, when participants have available time, when they would like to attend training, and so on.

In sum, effective and efficient HRD must build from a base of systematically collected information about program contexts, plans, operation, and outcomes. It is a further premise of this book that, to be good, HRD must also systematically revise itself. Revision is inherent in good programs, and HRD must actively pursue improvement or it cannot be deemed worthy. So, not only is information necessary to make the best possible plans and assess their operation, but the ongoing effort of col-

lecting and using information to revise programs is part and par-
cel of good HRD itself. Programs that are not getting better are
probably getting worse.

The Six-Stage Evaluation Model

The model derives directly from the cycle of key training
decisions. The Six-Stage Model responds to the decisions necessary for programs to proceed productively and defensibly
through the stages, enabling and facilitating quality efforts. The
six stages of the model correspond directly to each of the steps
in the training decision cycle, as shown in Table 3.

Table 3 names each stage of the model and gives a few
key questions and some common procedures that characterize
each stage. Figure 2 pictures the model as *circular.* The final
stage "returns" to the first stage, beginning the process anew
and showing that new HRD inquiry builds on the results of past
efforts.

The arrows drawn in Figure 2 between the evaluation
stages depict the general sequence of training decisions, as well
as a series of causal connections:

1.   Stage I evaluates the value and importance of problems
      and/or opportunities that may be responsive to HRD inter-
      ventions. Stage I also assesses whether a program might
      make a difference more worthwhile than some other inter-
      vention would and helps determine whether the process
      should proceed further with the selection or creation of a
      program design. Stage I seeks data that will "predict"
      whether on-job behavior can and should be changed, wheth-
      er specific SKA changes would be sufficient for changed be-
      havior, and whether SKA changes are achievable through a
      training intervention. Stage I includes all the evaluative data
      that will help decide whether HRD will produce worth-
      while results and whether it is likely that HRD's promises
      can be kept.
2.   Stage II aims at the production of a defensible HRD pro-
      gram design and might assess a given design's practicality,

Figure 2. The Six-Stage Model as a Cycle.

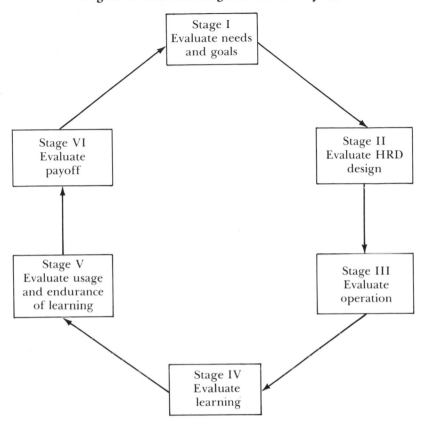

theoretical soundness, and responsiveness or the relative merits of competing alternatives. Stage II determines whether HRD can, finally, move beyond the design stage to implementation. Is the design good enough to be put into operation? Is it better than alternative designs?

3. Stage III, which assumes that the design was good enough to "go," is concerned with whether the design is, in fact, being installed and operated according to plan. Stage III assesses the significance of unplanned departures from the design and helps determine where departures from the design are necessary. The key question of Stage III is, "How is it going?" Stage III consists of monitoring training activi-

Table 3. Six-Stage Model for Evaluating HRD.

Evaluation Stage	Some Key Evaluation Questions	Some Useful Procedures
I. Goal setting (What is the need?)	• How great is the need, problem, or opportunity? • Is it amenable to HRD solutions? • Would the HRD difference be worth making? • Would HRD work and be likely to pay off? • Are criteria available to judge whether it paid off or not? • Is HRD better than alternative approaches?	Organizational audits; performance analyses; records analysis; observation; surveys; study of research; document reviews; context studies
II. Program design (What will work?)	• What kind of HRD might work best? • Is design A better than design B? • What is wrong with design C? • Is the selected design good enough to implement?	Literature review; expert reviews; panels; checklists; site visits; pilot tests; participant review
III. Program implementation (Is it working?)	• Has it been installed as it is supposed to be? • Is it working on schedule? • What problems are cropping up? • What really took place? • Did trainees like it? • What did it cost?	Observation; checklists; trainer and trainee feedback; records analysis

IV.	Immediate outcomes (Did they learn it?)	• Did trainees learn it? • How well did they learn it? • What did they learn?	Knowledge and performance tests; observation; simulations; self-reports; work-sample (product) analyses
V.	Intermediate or usage outcomes (Are they keeping and/or using it?)	• How are trainees using it? • How well are they using it? • What part(s) of it are they using?	Self-, peer, and supervisor reports; case studies; surveys; site visits; observation; work-sample analyses
VI.	Impacts and worth (Did it make a worthwhile difference?)	• What difference does using it make? • Has the need been met? • Was it worth it?	Organizational audits; performance analyses; records analysis; observation; surveys; document reviews; panel reviews and hearings; cost-benefit comparison

ties, gathering feedback about the reactions of trainees and others, and implementing other process evaluation procedures. There is often considerable recycling back to Stage II decisions, because very frequently things do not go the way they were planned.

4. Assuming that it (the design's implementation) in fact went satisfactorily, that necessary revisions were made, and that training was completed, recipients should exit programs with some new SKA and/or the positive reactions intended. Stage IV tests this assumption, assessing the nature and extent of reactions and/or acquired SKA. If SKA were *not* acquired, then the question of whether they are being used or whether progress toward benefit to the organization is being made is moot. If Stage IV reveals that sufficient SKA were in fact acquired by recipients, then usage, or intermediary results, can be expected.

5. Stage V assesses how much and how well acquired SKA are being translated into intended on-job behavior changes. Or, in the case of HRD efforts with no on-job behavior intended, Stage V assesses the durability of acquired SKA and their translation into the expected intermediary results posited by the logical plan for the program. When such usage or intermediary effects are achieved, organizational effects can be expected.

6. The value of organizational effects and their relationship to training as documented through Stages III to V are the focus of Stage VI. This stage presumes that HRD has "worked" thus far: people learned something and are in fact using what they learned. Thus, if Stage I results were valid, Stage VI evaluations should now discover positive organizational results of value. In practice, Stage VI evaluation is much like Stage I evaluation—it collects and uses the same, or similar, data. Stage VI also involves making an estimate of the *worth* of HRD so that recycling decisions can be facilitated. Worth is determined by comparing what was gained (the Stage VI results) with what the program cost. Where HRD has returned benefits equal to or greater than

its costs, it has positive worth. The actual worth of HRD is a relative attribute, however. Say, for example, that a given program produced benefits valued at $10,000 for a cost of $5,000. This sounds like a good deal; HRD costs yielded a 200 percent return. But if some *other* solution to the problem (redesign of the job, for example) would have yielded the same return value ($10,000) at a cost lower than the HRD program, then HRD was clearly not the best investment. Programs must not only produce value greater than their costs but must cost less than alternative routes to the same value yield.

The Six-Stage Model shows an arrow connecting Stages VI and I, indicating the general recycling function of the model. If the problem that a program initially attacked has been solved, then perhaps this program has yielded all the value it can and ought to be discontinued. But if the problem exists elsewhere, or has grown, then perhaps the program ought to be continued or even extended. Recycling decisions also must consider whether the program worked as well as it could have. Are revisions called for? Could the program have worked more efficiently? Because the recycling decisions involve questions of need (is there still a need?) and design (could it have worked better?), the model "returns" to Stages I and II. Recycling HRD begins the decision cycle all over again. The circular configuration of the model emphasizes that HRD is a continuous process within the organization and that HRD decisions always should build on knowledge of previous HRD experience.

Why the Model Is Not Linear

Though the model follows a logical developmental and decision-making sequence, it is not strictly linear. That is, each stage is not simply accomplished once and then abandoned for the next stage, never to be returned to. The several stages interact with one another, there is recycling among the stages, and sometimes stages are "nested" in one another.

A pilot test of a program, for example, involves an extensive Stage II evaluation. A pilot program is conducted as an experiment to test and revise a given design. But though a pilot is explicitly aimed at a Stage II decision (that is, "Is this design any good?"), it would involve working through all six stages. In other words, the design would be assessed in operation, and there would be a check to see whether participants learned, followed by a test for on-job usage, benefit to the organization, and so forth. In a pilot test, all six stages are nested within the larger Stage II purpose. This book argues that most HRD ought to be developmental; thus almost all programs should become informal "pilots" and the six stages should aim at drawing Stage II conclusions about the effectiveness and efficiency of training designs. Similarly, all six stages are nested in Stage I, because Stage I inquiry will look at variables in job behavior, the potential relationship of SKA and reactions to organizational benefits, and so forth. Decisions about whether HRD is likely to work and whether it is likely to produce worthwhile benefits require knowledge of how HRD programs can, do, and will work; that is, they require knowledge of all six stages.

Cycling and Recycling

There is cycling back and forth among the stages as well. Stage III inquiry (how are programs going?) looks "ahead" to the later stages, asking whether the current operation seems to be leading toward participant learning that will produce results. In a skill training workshop, for example, trainers use interim tests and other means to check learning progress. These look ahead to Stage IV, as well as check back to see how well various exercises and examples have worked to produce interim learning. Likewise, as Stage III inquiry discovers problems with a design, new design alternatives will be generated about which Stage II questions must be raised. When we discover that something does not work, we often "go back to the drawing board" and outline and assess new ideas. A typical Stage III evaluation method is to assess trainee reactions, learning, and opinions partway through the training. These checks may indicate that a unit was not understood, an exercise was not engaged in, or a presentation offended some trainees. Stage II questions (should the plan be changed? how?) are immediately implied.

When evaluation discovers a breakdown at any stage, the accuracy of results at preceding stages is automatically questioned. For example, here are some typical results:

1. *"They didn't learn it!"* (Stage IV) Did the design in fact get carried out (Stage III)? Was it a bad design after all (Stage II)? Did the trainees really need to learn it (Stage I)?
2. *"This design isn't going well; it can't be carried out after all!"* (Stage III) Is it a good design (Stage II)?
3. *"They're not using it!"* (Stage V) Did they really learn it (Stage IV)? Do they still need to do it (Stage I)?
4. *"We can't come up with a feasible design that anyone thinks will work!"* (Stage II) Is this problem worth solving? Is training really the answer (Stage I)?

In fact, it should not require a breakdown in training to make "returns" to earlier stages sensible. Continuing to check out assumptions is a characteristic of good practice.

Recycling among the stages of the model is not chronologically bound or constrained. Stage I questions can and should be asked, for example, at any point in the chronology of programs. Asking them, in fact, facilitates revisions to the program design. Good HRD deliverers also automatically ask themselves many questions from several stages as they move ahead. A "huddle" among the staff might be called during a lunch break to make some quick Stage II decisions about the afternoon's plan on the basis of facts and intuition about participant reactions to activities (Stage III), indications of learning (Stage IV), discussion of potential uses (Stage V), revelations of additional needs (Stage I), and so forth. In the same way, good trainers continually do needs assessment while a program is being conducted and when it has been completed. Such simple queries to participants as "Is this example pertinent?" or "What else could we have included in this session?" are good examples of Stage III practice, but they reflect and are useful for making Stage I decisions about the need, relevance, and likely utility of a particular program.

Addressing Merit and Worth

As was noted in the Introduction, merit derives from how well programs are done, and worth derives from the results of the program. Making the distinction between merit and worth clear can help HRD practitioners avoid an unfortunately common pitfall: doing well what was not worth doing in the first place! The merit of HRD is assessed as a function of Stages II, III, and IV; that is, meritorious HRD has a theoretically sound design that makes economical use of resources, is efficiently conducted, and results in learning. Worth, however, pertains to the value of what was learned. Was it the "right" stuff? Can, and do, participants use it? Does it make a valuable contribution to the organization?

Good HRD must seek both merit *and* worth. Merit is necessary, but not sufficient, for worth. The HRD function and profession cannot survive (and *should* not) if worth arguments cannot be legitimately made. Programs have to make, and should be able to prove that they have made, valuable contributions to an organization. Doing well what is not worth doing cannot and should not be tolerated. But seeking merit should not be denigrated. Human resource development professionals must be equally well prepared to make good arguments for merit. There should be solid evidence that a program is efficient, that it does not use more resources than necessary, that it is carried out quickly with the least disruption possible, that it achieves learning gains in proper and enjoyable ways, and so on. A training program that no one likes, that takes too much time, that is costly, and that wastes time and resources on unnecessary components should be revised *even though* it may currently be paying off to the organization. To fail to do something better simply because it works today (to ignore merit in the cause of worth) should not be tolerated. The HRD function must be equally concerned with merit and worth.

Outcomes Versus Process

Evaluation methods have typically focused on HRD out-comes. This makes practical sense, of course, for it is results that HRD is after. Did participants learn? Is the program making a difference? These are important questions for evaluation. But the proof-is-in-the-pudding approach by itself is not sufficient. There are two very good reasons why HRD evaluation must be equally concerned with a focus on the process of programs: (1) accountability pressure will demand data about HRD activities and transactions (process data), and (2) programs cannot be improved without such data about processes.

To consider the accountability argument, assume that the HRD operation in a corporation is sophisticated enough to be able to produce convincing data that its programs do, in fact, make a worthwhile difference:

Corporate Boss: Say, HRD, I just wanted to let you know how we all appreciate the good job you are doing for our organization.

HRD Manager: Gee, thanks, CB! I was hoping you'd notice.

Corporate Boss: Why, of course, we notice. The data you've given us show your program really works. I mean, people learn, they use what they learn, and their new behavior pays off in ways we really care about. Yes . . . you certainly do good work.

HRD Manager: Golly, that's sure nice of you to say so. I'm glad our data can tell our story. But, uh, say, CB . . . I really appreciate your appreciation, but, uh . . . is there something else on your mind?

Corporate Boss: Funny you should ask, HRD. Actually, there is. Now that we know you really do make a difference, some of us were talking in the boardroom the other day . . .

HRD Manager: Yes, CB?

Corporate Boss: We wondered if you might get the *same* results with a little *less* cost? Or maybe a little quicker?

I am fairly certain that this kind of conversation could take place and I am sure that it *should* take place. That is, HRD might be required not only to prove its worth but to prove its merit—to demonstrate that it strives for results in the most cost-effective way possible. Accountability data must, then, go beyond the assessment of outcome. Data are also needed to demonstrate a quest for efficiency—getting the optimum results with the minimum expenditure of time and resources and the least disruption of ongoing activities.

In addition to the accountability argument, improvement of HRD cannot take place without process data. At the most simple level, programs must be monitored to document what actually takes place in any given intervention. It will do the improvement effort little good to discover that positive results (outcomes) were achieved if no one knows how (process) those outcomes came about! Similarly, when HRD does *not* achieve its intended results, what really took place in the program must be documented and known or mistakes will necessarily be repeated. The outcome focus of evaluation is well represented by a familiar slogan: "You can't tell if you have gotten there if you don't know where you're going." Turning this around a bit, we can represent the equally important process truth: "You can't get there again if you don't know how you got there in the first place!" Much of the improvement effort will be realized by recycling between Stages II and III—recycling between decisions about what to do (Stage II) and decisions about whether the process is going satisfactorily (Stage III). This recycling is the heart of process evaluation and helps a great deal with improvement of both knowledge and the practice of training.

How Process Evaluation Works

A training design is created and is then evaluated to see whether it is *good enough to go with* (not perfect, mind you). Following that, the design is installed and begins to operate. Sometimes Stage III inquiry will show that things are going just fine—activities are running smoothly and trainees are learning. But problems almost always occur. Sometimes there will be "control" problems. That is, the design for an activity will be good, but problems (for example, lack of learning, confusion, lack of interest, no engagement in tasks) have come up because the plan was not adequately followed. In other words, the idea was all right, but its implementation ran afoul. Sometimes, however, the plan itself is no good. The design will be adhered to, but there is still a problem, and thus the plan must be reassessed and revised. When this occurs (as it often does), recycling to Stage II is necessary; that is, new plans for action (designs) will have to be considered and assessed.

In summary, outcome evaluation alone cannot serve HRD improvement needs; it can account for program impact, and it can certainly indicate a need for process evaluation when results have not been achieved. But outcome data alone will not yield a sufficient basis for the inevitable improvement needs of HRD practice. It was also noted that HRD ought to be engaged in a continued quest for more efficient designs. Practicing careful and systematic process evaluation will yield the data needed for improvement. Documenting the practice of evaluation and demonstrating that it has resulted in revised programs constitute further evidence of its value. When HRD can show systematic collection of data aimed at revision and improvement *and* data about the worthwhileness of its results, the HRD manager can proudly say, "Yes, I have here some data that show how we have provided a worthwhile return on our HRD investment. And I have *here* some data that show how we have done some evaluation and changed our practice several times to get even better results for less investment."

In summary, the Six-Stage Model is meant to help clarify and inform the many decisions that must be made if HRD is to succeed. Information must be collected for each of these decisions. Information collection begins at Stage I when decisions about whether to do HRD at all are made. At this point, HRD problems or opportunities are analyzed, needs are assessed, and tentative training goals are assessed in terms of their potential for worthwhile organizational benefits. Stage I concludes with a decision as to whether HRD is the right solution and has targeted worthwhile results. Stage II evaluation creates the information needed to produce and judge design ("solution") alternatives. This stage answers the question "Is the HRD plan (design) good enough to go with?"

Implementation comes next. Successful implementation of HRD designs requires close monitoring and on-the-spot problem solving. Thus, Stage III guides process evaluation and asks the general question "How is it going?"

Stages IV, V, and VI track the results of programs. Stage IV assesses the immediate reactions and learning outcomes that occur as a result of HRD efforts. Stage V might measure on-job usage of HRD-acquired learning or otherwise check to see whether learning outcomes are enduring and surviving on the job. Stage VI evaluation asks whether HRD's promise to the organization has been met and whether the whole effort was worth it.

Recycling among the six stages is inevitable and is the process by which HRD builds on its own experience to improve. While proving HRD's impact and worth is a goal of evaluation, the real payoff of evaluation—and the real basis of the Six-Stage Model—is improving HRD.

2

Assessing
Whether the HRD Investment
Will Meet Organizational Needs
and Pay Off

Stage I evaluation focuses on the *why* of HRD. Its purpose is to evaluate the intentions of potential HRD programs to be sure they will meet realistic, feasible, and worthwhile needs.

It is important to note the "evaluation" component of Stage I. This stage includes the analysis of organization problems and contexts to identify *potential* HRD needs. These potential needs must be evaluated to assess their importance and priority. Moreover, the potential gains to the organization if the needs were addressed must also be assessed. Human resource development needs should not be conceived of as discrete, tangible entities embedded somewhere in the organization awaiting some measurement process to dig them out. Rather, Stage I inquiry assesses organizational problems, situations, strengths, and opportunities to assess their importance and the urgency with which they must be addressed. Evaluative judgment is then applied to the information (data) produced from this inquiry. The evaluative component of Stage I inquiry comes when the HRD needs that have been identified are assessed to decide: (1) Are they real HRD needs? (2) Are they worth addressing? (3) How important and urgent are they?

How HRD Begins

Some HRD practice and literature distinguish needs analysis (the identification of a target group for possible HRD intervention) from needs assessment (the assessment of the SKA deficits of the target group). The Stage I concepts and procedures presented in this chapter do not make this distinction. Stage I includes analysis of both organizational conditions and individual states and conditions to assess HRD needs and opportunities. Thus, the end point of Stage I—evaluating the potential worth to be achieved if the HRD program is pursued—is always the same. But the beginning point of Stage I inquiry typically varies. Following are some common starting points for HRD programs.

The "Problem" Beginning. Often, the HRD cycle begins with a problem somewhere in the organization that someone thinks could be solved with training or other HRD efforts:

- "Employees are unmotivated and unproductive. Let's start some supervisor training."
- "People keep ignoring the safety rules. Let's start some safety training."
- "Sales are down. Let's train our salespeople."
- "People keep breaking their tools. Let's have maintenance training."

When problems like these are presented as the stimulus to begin the HRD cycle, Stage I inquiry begins with problem-solving approaches, moving from problem definition and assessment (is the problem worth solving?) through analysis of causes to final assessment of the potential worth and appropriateness of a general HRD solution to all, or parts, of the initial problem.

The problem initially presenting itself is often a *performance* problem: employees are not doing their job well enough, there are such symptoms of organizational ill health as high absenteeism, unacceptable employee turnover rates, excessive grievances, and so on. Or problems may be people centered, such as impending retirement bulges, substance abuse, or rampant personal financial entanglements. In any of these instances, Stage I evaluation would first assess the problem itself to decide whether it is worth solving. Assuming that the problem is worth solving, evaluation inquiry would next aim to determine what, if any, HRD-solvable problems underlie the presenting problem, so that the potential worth of HRD solutions could be assessed.

The "Change" Beginning. Impending organizational change (for example, hiring new employees, introducing new products or equipment, implementing new management approaches, reorganizing) can also stimulate the beginning of the HRD cycle. These instances are dealt with by Stage I inquiry in a way very similar to the problem-focused approaches discussed above. But, of course, when an impending change stimulates HRD, problems are forecasted or projected rather than existing at present. For example, let us say that the HRD leaders in a large organization suspect that changing demographic patterns (the "baby bust") will create a diminished labor supply and greater competition for talented professionals. Will this situation create problems with future staffing in the organization? What divisions and units are most likely to be affected? How capable of dealing with potential problems are the employee relations staffs in each division? Will there be retraining needs and, if so, how important and urgent will they be?

In the "change" beginning, Stage I inquiry is similar to the problem-solving approach but must be modified because the problems do not yet exist. Efforts are made to project and predict, collecting information from sources both inside and outside the organization to try to envision the future and then to determine whether HRD needs will arise and require any present action. As in the problem beginning, determination of the worth of dealing with the projected problem must be made, and the feasibility of a possible HRD solution must be assessed.

The "Opportunity" Beginning. An HRD program might be considered because a particular opportunity presents itself. A new training program, consultant, or firm might become available. The HRD manager might read about an appealing new program. A training department, as a result of company accounting decisions, might receive additional financial resources. In the American automobile industry, recently, new labor contracts mandated huge amounts of training funds, and new HRD centers were immediately constructed. In instances such as these, a particular problem has not yet become apparent. Rather, it is a matter of thinking of HRD as a "solution in *search of* a problem"! In the opportunity circumstance, Stage I involves identifying potential HRD goals (or "investments"), then assessing their relative potential payoff to the organization. Stage I procedures might focus on incipient, projected, or emerging problems, in which case procedures similar to the "problem" beginning would be employed. Or Stage I activities could aim to assess personnel values, preferences, or opinions regarding possible training goals by using surveys, discussion groups, or other opinion-gathering techniques. In this instance, Stage I inquiry might entail evaluating preferences and opinions, asking people how they think the training resources should be invested.

The "Strength" Beginning. Training does not have to be deficit oriented. That is, training need not be perceived solely as a means to "fix what's broke" or to solve existing problems. Indeed, training that only concerns itself with putting out fires or fixing problems will never help move an organization ahead beyond the status quo. Stage I inquiry might, rather than asking what is *wrong,* ask what is especially *right.* There may be performance areas or organizational characteristics that are especially strong and that would, if training were directed to them, extend strengths to others, increase strengths, or otherwise continue to be strengths. A sales company noticed, for example, that sales records from a particular unit were especially and consistently high. Further investigation revealed that the rise in sales performance coincided with the district manager's institution of bimonthly breakfast meetings in which salespersons discussed problems and shared new approaches and other experiences using brainstorming techniques and referring to "diaries" that the district manager had them keep on a regular basis. The HRD manager in this scenario might have invested resources in this sales unit to nurture this new practice or might even have extended the practice to other units where it looked as if the strong performance might be extended. Or, for another example, I have worked extensively with an organization that has a tradition of high morale and extraordinary employee loyalty. The HRD function works hard through a variety of programs to maintain this valuable human resources asset.

Using the "strength" beginning, Stage I inquiry would first identify areas of strength and assess their worth to the organization. Then, inquiry would proceed to assess the potential worth of HRD as it could be applied to these areas. Could HRD make a worthwhile improvement to a worthwhile strength? Could HRD programs extend, nurture, or ensure the continued existence of important strengths?

The importance of recognizing the validity of the "strength" beginning should be emphasized. Needs do not have to be currently unmet to be important needs. The relationship of stress to performance exists, for example, regardless of whether current worker stress levels are high or low; that is, there is a need, if performance is to be maintained at optimum levels, to regulate stress levels. Thus, in a situation where stress levels of workers are currently within acceptable limits, there might be need for the organization to do something to help maintain the stress levels within those acceptable limits. The implication for Stage I practice is to consider strengths as well as weaknesses in the search for and evaluation of HRD needs. Spending HRD resources to address a given deficit need (a weakness) means those resources cannot be spent elsewhere, and perhaps there is a current strength to be maintained with those resources that represents a greater need.

The "New Direction" Beginning. In some instances, HRD may be quite proactive, seeking to move an organization beyond current problems or even strengths to new or greater levels of performance. The Sperry Corporation's institution of companywide programs in listening skills, in which employees from all levels were trained to be better listeners, is a good example of this sort of beginning. This beginning point for the training cycle is, in fact, a variant of the "opportunity" conceptualization, and thus Stage I inquiry would be very similar to the approach recommended earlier for the opportunity beginning. In the new direction beginning the HRD practitioner would seek out potential HRD goals and investments, then assess their relative potential payoff to the organization.

The "HRD Is a Given" Beginning. While it does not represent ideal practice, it certainly happens that the HRD program will be done because someone *said* it will be done. Training might be mandated by a manager, a chief executive officer, or some external authority. Just because someone decided, whether by intuition, revelation, or even "divine right," that a program will be done, this does *not* relieve HRD of its responsibility to have some worth to the organization. Thus, Stage I inquiry must go on. To be sure, Stage I will have to proceed with political astuteness and perhaps even wear kid gloves. But go on it must. The preferred approach is for Stage I inquiry to seek out the problem or other situation that motivated a superior to decide there would be HRD and then to proceed as with the "problem" or "strength" scenarios described earlier.

But it may be that a decision *not* to initiate the HRD program is precluded for political or other reasons. When this is the case, then Stage I should focus on assessing the employee groups, organizational areas, or performance dimensions where the HRD effort is likely to have the greatest yield (or, in worst case scenarios, have the least disruptive effects). I was once asked to serve as a consultant to a company to help design training in long-range planning techniques for managers and executives. Why was such training needed? The president had a friend whose company ran similar training programs, the president liked the idea, and so on. It was clear that the training would be implemented. But this was not sufficient license to skip Stage I altogether and proceed immediately to make Stage II decisions, such as where to conduct the sessions, whether to use films or slides, and so on. Rather, Stage I inquiry was conducted (in close contact with the president) to help decide the particular long-range planning topics, examples, and applications that would have the greatest potential payoff to the organization. From the president's point of view, Stage II planning was well under way: his training staff was buckling down to the task he had assigned it. From my perspective, however, Stage I work was under way—narrowly constrained, to be sure, but Stage I nonetheless. Given the fact that long-range planning is going to take place, I asked, how can I make it address the most important problems and/or strengths of this organization?

A note of caution must be added here. While the "HRD-is-a-given" situation clearly exists and perhaps has even become common, the HRD profession cannot allow it to become the norm. In the long run, HRD will survive only if it continues to add value to the organization. While it may be expedient in certain instances (as in the long-range planning example cited) to forgo complete Stage I analysis and accept the HRD-as-a-given circumstance, this should not become standard operating procedure. Stage I should always seek assessment of worth beyond the "given" boundaries and ask (1) what alternatives *to* HRD might be more worthwhile and (2) what alternative HRD goals might be most worthwhile? Asking whom to train and when, where, and how to train might help make HRD more valuable than if these questions were not asked at all. But to ask *only* these questions evades the worth issue and contributes to undermining the HRD profession.

Table 4 summarizes the several kinds of problems or conditions that can precipitate HRD. Obviously, HRD programs in today's organizations serve multiple and complex purposes. A narrow, deficit-oriented model of HRD needs is clearly inadequate. Stage I inquiry (needs analysis) is a complex process and cannot rely on single or simplistic approaches. When a performance problem exists (for example, sagging sales), problem-solving, analytic approaches are called for in Stage I. But where HRD is a given or will be provided as a staff benefit, opinion surveys or other value-clarification procedures will be required to make Stage I decisions. While the overall Stage I purpose is constant—to decide what, if any, HRD ought to be initiated—

Table 4. Summary of HRD Needs and Beginnings.

Kind of Need	Typical Examples	Key Stage I Questions
Problem or deficit	Performance problems; low productivity; poor organizational health	• What *is* the problem? • Is it worth solving? • Why is it a problem? • What contribution (*if any*) can HRD make? • Should HRD be pursued?
Impending change	New hiring; new products and new equipment; change in organization	• What problems will the changes bring? • Will the problems be worth solving? • Will HRD work to solve the problems?
Opportunities	Training monies received; new training package available	• Are there problems or strengths HRD could address? • Are the problems/strengths worthwhile? • Could HRD make a worthwhile contribution?
Strengths	High performance incidences; exceptionally strong organizational health indicators; key market entries; good productivity	• What *are* the strengths? • Are the strengths worthwhile? • Could HRD increase these strengths, make them last longer, or make them more widespread?

New directions
Growth in a particular area is desirable or predicted; greater virtuosity is possible; changes in organization or mission would be valuable

- What is the current status?
- What new directions are available?
- Would changes be worthwhile?
- How could HRD stimulate change?
- Would HRD make worthwhile contributions to change?

Mandated training
Someone decides HRD will be done; HRD will be provided as a reward or employee benefit

- What problems or opportunities could HRD address?
- Where could HRD make the most worthwhile contribution?
- What sort of HRD is preferred?
- What kind of HRD would have the biggest payoff?

Stage I procedures will vary according to the kind of need presented, as outlined in Table 4.

Value Component of Needs Analysis

Needs are not absolute. They are relative and vary in nature and degree according to organizational and individual values. What is a problem to one organization or individual might not be a problem, or could even be a strength, to another. A 5 percent absenteeism rate among assembly line workers in an auto plant might be typical and thus not really present a problem, while the same absenteeism rate in a hospital emergency room could precipitate a crisis. Human relations skills might be crucial in one setting, and nearly irrelevant in another; one organization might value participatory management styles very highly, while another might discount them.

Given this reality, HRD professionals must realize that Stage I evaluation is a value-laden activity in which subjective judgments will frequently be needed and absolutes are few. Scientifically derived data are important and will provide insight into current problems and situations. Whether or not HRD ought to be initiated always involves a judgment call by human decision makers. The should-HRD-be-done decision is never the predetermined output of some data collection and analysis procedure. In the best cases, data about current problems, causes, conditions, opinions, and contexts will be provided and used by decision makers. But these data will not make the decision for the HRD leader.

Disentangling HRD Needs

Training problems do not present themselves in neat, simple, easy-to-solve units. Problems, as well as strengths and opportunities, are always embedded in the organization. And they often have non-HRD as well as HRD aspects. A company's sagging sales, for example, might be caused by several factors. New competition, outsized territories, inadequate commissions, insufficient communication about new prospects, a poor overall economy, and too many salespersons can all affect sales performance, yet only a few aspects of these factors can be impacted by HRD. Stage I analysis may need to go through several cycles of inquiry, data collection, and analysis before those few HRD-susceptible factors can be isolated and assessed.

Typically, no single data collection effort will accurately assess an HRD need. Rather, several rounds of inquiry must occur. In most instances, Stage I inquiry begins with some general "probing around" activities: talking to people, reading reports and memos, and following other familiarization procedures. Then some general questions are formulated (for example, "Is the problem people's motivation?"). These initial questions form the basis for data collection efforts, after which analysis results, not in firm answers, but in more informed and astute questions. Then, more data collection, analysis, thinking, discussing, and probably more data collection will be needed until the situation becomes clear, and HRD needs are (or are not) firmly established.

Good Stage I practitioners also recognize the existence of differing *levels* of analysis. Sometimes, Stage I inquiry begins at a very general level with very few limiting assumptions. At other times, it begins at a very specific discrete level and is limited by many assumptions. Stage I inquirers need to be able to recognize at what level they are operating and to understand the assumptions that limit their work. Consider the following brief series of potential "need" questions:

1. We have some resources that could be used for capital expansion, HRD, new technology, or something else. Do we have any problems that need attention or opportunities that should be addressed? Let's decide where and how to invest these resources. Maybe HRD is one alternative.
2. We have some HRD resources—some funds, some expertise, some equipment. Let's see what our HRD needs and opportunities are so that we will know where and on what kind of HRD goals to spend these resources or whether to do any HRD at all.
3. We have several programs, one on listening, another on time

management, still another on financial problem solving, and so on. Let's find out who is having difficulty with what, so that we can determine who should get which program.

4. We have a workbook that can help a supervisor define performance standards. Let's see which, if any, of our supervisors could use it.

5. The boss says we have to use this workbook about performance standards with some unit. Let's figure out which target group will get the biggest payoff from this workbook.

These five need questions are all legitimate, as each seeks to maximize potential payoff. But they obviously imply different assumptions. Expression 4, for instance, has already identified a given treatment and asks only who, if anyone, needs it. Alternative treatments are not considered by this limited expression. Expression 3 is a bit broader and includes assessing alternative HRD goals. Likewise, expressions 1 and 2 are increasingly broad, and each carries successively fewer limiting assumptions. Expression 5, at the other extreme, says someone will get a given treatment, regardless, and has many limiting assumptions.

Decision making at Stage I will always be bound by some assumptions. It is always critical to identify and understand these assumptions, and sometimes it is necessary to question them, bringing attention to them so that better decisions can be made. Very often in HRD practice, problems initially identified as training problems turn out not to be problems at all or to have only some aspects that are solvable by training. A local division of a cereal manufacturing company once called its HRD department and requested that the packing equipment operators be trained to perform their jobs more carefully because an inordinate number of packing boxes had been popping open during shipping. In the plant manager's mind, the problem and solution were clear: boxes start popping open; operators must not be performing correctly; therefore, let's train operators! The HRD officer correctly decided to do a little Stage I detective work. She did *not* leap immediately to Stage II and begin to choose among different training programs and schedules. The assumption that operators were at fault was questioned, and problem solving soon discovered the real cause of the popping boxes—a shipment of faulty glue!

Assumptions bearing on Stage I inquiry and problems initiating HRD should always be identified and assessed. This of course must be done with appropriate political and organizational sensitivity. Programs that will not solve real, worthwhile problems should not be conducted. In this respect, it would have been professionally irresponsible for the HRD officer in the popping-boxes story to design and deliver training to the operators until limiting assumptions had been carefully checked out. HRD practitioners must recognize, too, that sometimes checking out assumptions will require tactful, though dogged, efforts. The desire for quick and easy fixes is strong and dies hard.

Stage I Sets Evaluation Criteria

Because Stage I analysis aims to establish the potential worth of HRD, it is closely tied to the later evaluative stages that determine whether training has been transferred to the job (Stage V) and the actual worth of that training to the organization (Stage VI). Stage I is not complete until it has developed a definitive answer to the question "How will we tell if the HRD has been worthwhile?"

Let us return briefly to the popping-boxes example. First, Stage I inquiry could have assessed the worth of solving the problem—for example, by considering facts and figures such as these:

1. Six percent, or 360 boxes, of the 6,000 boxes shipped each week pop open.
2. The damage estimate of a popped box is $8 per box.
3. $2,880 (360 boxes × $8) each week would be saved by solving the problem.

Assume further that Stage I analysis has removed competing alternative causes (for instance, bad glue, sabotage, inadequate communication of performance standards) from consideration and has identified the low, but correctable, skills of box-sealing operators as the cause. Training success criteria might be set as follows:

1. Pretraining conditions were documented, showing persistent (5 to 15 percent) errors in operation of a sealing lever, resulting in improper sealing in an average of 6 percent of all boxes among a specific group of operators.
2. Posttraining usage objectives were to reduce average sealing lever operation error to a 0 to 3 percent range, with an expectation of savings of $2,200 to $2,800 per week in damage costs after training.
3. Training costs of $6,000, when compared to an expected annual return of $120,000 ($2,200 × 52 weeks), appear to make training a wise investment.

As this case shows, criteria for training were expressed in terms of (1) (Stage V) job behavior for operators and (2) benefit to the organization (Stage VI) as total savings and damage rates. While this skill training case is admittedly simplistic, it demonstrates the emergence of Stage V and Stage VI criteria as a natural consequence of Stage I inquiry. This identification of criteria for the worth (Stage VI) of training should occur in any case, regardless of the nature of HRD programs. In skill training applications, criteria will most often be identified in terms of changed job-behavior targets and cost savings or profit increases (or such related phenomena as sales increases and scrap decreases). With other sorts of HRD that intend no on-job behavior changes, criteria for organizational worth may be expressed in other terms, such as reduced absenteeism, increases in job satisfaction, changes in promotion and turnover rates, endurance of learning results, endurance of reactions, and so forth. The point is that the nature of Stage VI expectations for change (criteria for training) will, and should be, the same as those variables, dimensions, and so on that were the focus of Stage I inquiry. Or, in simpler language, the reasons for doing the HRD in the first place should be the basis for judging whether it worked or not. This Stage I to Stage VI relationship is pictured, for several kinds of programs, in Table 5.

Table 5. Some Examples of Stage I to Stage VI Relationships.

Stage I Needs (Reasons) for HRD	Stage VI Benefits (Criteria for Success)
Production problems due to skill deficits	Behavior changes with concomitant changes in productivity indexes
Morale problems as evidenced by critical behaviors	Changes in morale-related behaviors (absenteism, for example)
Management/supervisory problems as evidenced by subordinate behaviors	Changes in supervisory behaviors with concomitant changes in subordinate behaviors (for example, fewer grievances, less turnover, and so on)
Commitment to organization; involvement	Changes in expressions of commitment and involvement behaviors (for example, turnover, volunteerism)
Low rates of involvement in development and learning	Increased involvement in self-development activities

As is obvious in Table 5, there is congruence between Stage I needs (or reasons) for HRD and the criteria by which HRD's success will be assessed at Stage VI. More accurately, there *should* be congruence, and this congruence is best established before a program begins. When all parties to HRD can agree on Stage VI criteria, then the training plan has the greatest chance for success. But if HRD consumers or initiators cannot agree on these criteria, then it is likely that Stage I has not

been completed or is inaccurate. Thus, a good test of the suffi-
ciency of Stage I analysis is to check for agreement to Stage VI
criteria. If criteria for deciding whether HRD paid off or not
cannot be identified, or when identified are not agreed to or valued, an immediate "red flag" is raised: either more Stage I
work is needed, or perhaps no HRD need exists at all.

Levels of Stage I Effort

The amount of effort that goes into Stage I inquiries will
usually vary widely. The Meigs-Burkhart (1986) poll cited in the
Preface reported that less than half of all HRD programs are
preceded by a needs analysis. While this degree of Stage I practice certainly should not be considered the ideal, it is reflective
of the usual state of affairs; because of time and resource limitations HRD practitioners do not regularly and systematically
conduct Stage I evaluations. It is my contention, however,
that at least some Stage I evaluation ought to precede all HRD
effort. Just how much Stage I evaluation is required or appropriate will necessarily and legitimately vary. The scenarios that
follow demonstrate differing degrees of effort in Stage I inquiry.

Scenario 1: Flyrite Airlines had received several citations
from a regulatory agency concerning maintenance procedure
violations and had been put on probation; if further violations
occurred in the next six months, the airline's operating license
might be suspended. Flyrite first placed overtime inspectors to
monitor all maintenance operations to catch and correct mistakes. Then, to get at causes and to find solutions, it decided to
conduct an immediate inquiry into the nature and causes of the
violations and therefore hired a consulting firm to study all procedures, guidelines, practices, and employee attitudes and skills.
The firm surveyed personnel, observed and interviewed supervisors, tested the knowledge of maintenance operators, and reviewed all procedural guides and job aids. As the inquiry pro-
ceeded, it became increasingly clear that the nature and degree
of supervision were probably the root problems. Worker skills
and knowledge were adequate, and resources and guidelines
were comparable to those at airlines that were not having prob-

lems. But morale and motivation were low, and workers complained of lack of feedback and inconsistent monitoring. Hence, a supervisory training program was recommended, and specific behavioral objectives for improved supervisor job performance were defined and agreed to by supervisors and their bosses.

Scenario 2: The HRD manager at Multinational Services received a request to conduct a supervisor orientation program for a newly acquired operation. This program, regularly provided to all other units in the corporation as demand arose, had been developed and evaluated several years earlier. Rather than agree over the telephone to specific program delivery dates, the HRD manager suggested that she and the new operation's manager meet for coffee. Over coffee, the HRD manager asked about the number of supervisors in the new operation, explained the program's content, and told the manager what objectives the session could be expected to achieve. The new operation's manager replied that those objectives were just what the supervisors needed; they then moved on to plan a convenient time for the program.

Scenario 3: The managing director of the research unit in a pharmaceuticals firm suspected, on the basis of grapevine reports and observations, that supervisory practices in his unit were slipping. He called the HRD manager and requested that workshops be set up for supervisors. The HRD manager met with the director and talked over some of the perceived problems. Agreeing that the situation sounded serious, the HRD manager suggested a survey of employee attitudes and organizational conditions, to be followed by some focus group interviews, wherein small groups of employees would discuss problems from their perspectives. The training would be much more effective, the HRD manager explained, if they could target it on critical needs and problems. The survey was conducted and followed up with group interviews. All division units appeared to be quite "healthy," with the exception of a small but critical lab unit. On review, the division director recalled that many of the complaints and concerns he had heard emanated either from this small lab unit or from units that dealt closely with it. A meeting between the director and the lab supervisor revealed that the supervisor was severely depressed over some personal problems; counseling and vacation leave were recommended.

Scenario 4: Hardaz Nails Company experienced a banner year, as construction was booming and was expected to remain strong for some years to come. All company budgets were secure, and some had even been increased. But the HRD manager, in the course of browsing through trade journals, had repeatedly noted articles on the development of new kinds of fasteners and fastening systems. He met over a long breakfast with the managers from sales, production, and product development. They all agreed that while the company was doing very well, its product line was limited and none of them was really well versed in future trends and emerging technology. All present agreed to prepare memos for their next meeting that would list future trends and conditions from their various perspectives, the sorts of impacts they projected for each of their areas, and the key personnel that would be most involved with the changes to come. The HRD manager reviewed and analyzed these memos to produce a set of expertise goals for several key Hardaz personnel. At their next meeting, they decided that the HRD manager should look for seminars and other learning opportunities that would enable them to update their thinking about future fastening systems and building trends.

Scenario 5: A mid-level manager at Gotham Life, a large insurance company, became frustrated over the seemingly endless stream of meetings that she found herself attending. Assuming that things were just as bad for her staff, she had them keep informal time logs for the next few months of company meetings and the time they spent attending them. Over lunch with the HRD director, she shared her staggering results: nearly 40 percent of all her staff's time was spent in one meeting or another. Later, the HRD manager prepared a brief survey that he sent to a stratified sample of all Gotham employees. The results were similar: members of professional and staff units spent an average of 40 percent of their time in meetings. Spurred on by these findings, the HRD director and the mid-level manager designed an experiment and a meeting productivity study for her unit that would keep track of all meetings and would require participants to complete a brief evaluation form at the end of each meeting assessing its efficiency and value. At the same time, all meetings in the unit would be reduced in either time or frequency anywhere from 20 to 50 percent. A graduate student intern from the local university was hired to conduct the study. Unit productivity records (already maintained) were analyzed to create a "before" base line and were then monitored over the experimental period. After eight months, unit productivity had increased significantly, meetings were consistently rated as more efficient, and group interviews with all involved personnel and unit customers showed no reduction in work quality. Based on this study, the HRD manager convinced top management that there was a need at Gotham to reduce time spent in meetings, and a simple training program in how to increase meeting efficiency was designed and conducted for all management personnel.

Scenario 6: The HRD manager at Jaques Custodial Supplies was told by the chief executive officer that the company needed a program in time management for supervisors. In fact, the chief executive officer had already arranged an appointment for the HRD office with a program vendor for the next day and wanted training to begin as soon as possible. The HRD manager met briefly with small groups of the company's twenty-six unit managers. At these meetings, she asked questions about time pressures and interest in time management. She was able to identify five managers who admitted to some time management problems and were willing to try out the program. She then prepared a training schedule that included conducting the new time management workshop for these five units over the next eight months for the chief executive officer's review. That officer was happy to see such an immediate response to his "suggestion" and happily approved the schedule.

The preceding scenarios demonstrate a wide range of Stage I efforts, from a twenty-minute discussion over coffee to complex and multimethod studies. All represent legitimate and conscientious Stage I efforts aimed at evaluating the need for, and projected worth of, potential HRD goals. At the briefest end of the spectrum was the meeting over coffee in scenario 2.

In this scenario, the HRD manager was asked to institute a training program that was very likely needed; supervisors brand new to the company were almost surely going to need orientation to the culture, procedures, policies, and structure of the organization. Thus, the briefest of Stage I inquiries was called for, and the informal discussion over coffee was sufficient to confirm the need for the program. In other circumstances—for instance, if the new supervisors had been experiencing severe performance problems—a more systematic, problem-solving Stage I analysis might have been necessary. But given the context (the acquisition of a new business with supervisors foreign to the home company), the HRD manager's experience, and a training program of previously established value, the informal, brief, and seemingly casual meeting filled the Stage I bill.

The situation at Flyrite Airlines (scenario 1) was of a very different order. Here, there was a serious operational problem that theatened the company's existence. The need for an immediate and potent solution was great, and the margin for error was slim. Thus, a comprehensive and accurate picture of needs was required; the company could not afford a wasteful or weak HRD effort. In contrast, scenario 4 (Hardaz Nails) involved a far more leisurely context. Here, all was going well, and HRD was looking to the future in an effort to maintain the organization's health. The Stage I method in this scenario was highly systematic but incorporated opinions and conjectures about the future rather than data about current performance.

Scenario 3 was similar to the Flyrite example in that a performance problem was apparent. In this instance, however, the problem was isolated in one unit, and recognition of the potential need came from informal observation and hunches rather than from an external agency. And the identified problem (potential supervisory deficits) was more narrowly restricted, thus allowing a less ambitious and more focused Stage I inquiry.

Scenario 5 was similar to 3 in that recognition of a potential problem again came from the hunch of a manager. Here, the HRD director was confronted with a potentially serious companywide problem; fortunately, however, there was a manager with considerable motivation to work on the problem. In this scenario, a relatively comprehensive action research method was used to validate the need for reducing time spent in meetings. The level of effort was relatively great, but so was the potential payoff in terms of productivity gains and employee morale.

Scenario 6 represented a valiant effort to make the best of a relatively bad situation. Here, the "need" for time management training was mandated, and the HRD manager had little choice but to deliver the program. But the Stage I ball was not immediately punted away. Rather, the HRD manager decided that the best way to get the mandated training to pay off was to provide it for those who wanted it most and were most likely to adapt it to meet some important needs. The HRD manager knew, too, that in the course of conducting the program she would be able to use the later stages of the Six-Stage Model to modify the training for even greater payoff. While the Stage I context in this scenario permitted no assessment of alternative needs (was something else more important than time management?), there was at least the opportunity to provide the training to a target group that was very likely to use it to meet *some* needs.

The scenarios also represented a variety of Stage I methods. Scenarios 1, 3, and 5 employed quantitative procedures such as surveys and analysis of productivity data. Other scenarios used more subjective approaches and relied not on broad samples of data but on individual, informed opinion. Such ranges of methods are entirely appropriate in evaluation of HRD. As the final chapter will show, it is highly important to match information collection methods to the questions and information needs that precipitate an evaluation. The levels of effort also varied as appropriate to the situation. In cases where there was relative certainty as to the existence of needs and the consequence of a wrong needs decision was not particularly threatening, then a less ambitious Stage I effort was called for. By contrast, in situations where there was uncertainty as to what needs might really exist and it was crucial that a correct HRD solution be found, a greater investment in Stage I was required.

Useful Stage I Procedures

This section describes, in alphabetical order, some common and especially useful procedures for implementing Stage I evaluation. Each procedure is accompanied by one or more references to sources that will offer readers more information about it. This listing is not exhaustive, but it is meant to be relatively broad and includes alternatives that I hope will suit readers' varied circumstances.

Action Research Studies. Action research studies combine research inquiry with "action" taken to solve a problem or confirm or address a need. Action research embeds specific and tightly focused research efforts in the planned operation of ongoing activity. The purpose of action research studies is to try out new approaches and to solve problems in ways that will have direct application to the work setting. Action research is directly relevant to an actual situation in the work environment. It is empirical in the sense that it relies on actual observation and behavioral data, not on subjective opinions or data from past experience.

The kinds of problems that may be investigated using the action research methodology range in scope from general problems involving an entire plant or company to specific problems involving a small number of employees in one unit. Some examples would be (1) meeting the personal and professional needs of newly recruited staff, (2) evaluating the training experiences provided for beginning telephone operators, and (3) improving company productivity through a training program for production employees (Argyris, Putnam, and Smith, 1985; Cook and Campbell, 1979; Shumsky, 1958).

Assessment Centers. Assessment center methodology is a highly structured and formalized approach to assessing individuals' abilities in different domains, usually management and supervision. "Centers" of performance, that is, sets of critical competencies or abilities, are identified and defined through careful research and review. Multiple, standardized measures (for example, in-basket simulations, tests, role plays, and performance tasks) are designed and administered, sometimes over a period of several days. Specially trained observers score each individual's performance and rate abilities on the several competency domains. Assessment center methods are especially useful for accurately assessing a range of key abilities and can be used for a variety of HRD purposes. Since it is expensive to develop and administer assessment center methods, smaller organizations may pool resources, form or join professional associations using assessment centers, or purchase assessment center services.

Because of the expense involved, assessment center approaches are useful when the skills of large groups of people need to be assessed or the need to assess skills will be present over a long period of time. In cases where supervisory or management training is institutionalized, assessment center approaches can make diagnosis and prescription highly accurate and precise. Over the long run, it is likely that start-up costs will be recovered from more efficient management, selection, and training of personnel (Bray, 1976; Finkle, 1976; Phillips, 1983; Thornton and Byham, 1982).

Attitude Surveys: Employees. Questionnaires are developed or selected (a large number of surveys are commercially available) that contain items to assess individual characteristics and/or opinions that have been previously identified from reviews of pertinent research and literature, or are otherwise perceived to be important. These questionnaires are then administered to all employees or to samples of them. Once tallied, responses to questionnaire items can then be analyzed according to employee or organizational characteristics. Finally, inferences are drawn to make generalizations about the characteristics, opinions, values, morale, and so on of the responding groups or subgroups.

When specific data about groups, especially large groups, of persons are needed, surveys are a relatively cheap and quick way to collect these data. Surveys of employees can be used to collect a wide range of data, including their preferences for training topics, their work habits, their attitudes toward the organization, their personal habits and characteristics, and so on. Respondents are, of course, reluctant to divulge certain sorts of information or may even misrepresent true feelings and behaviors, so caution is advised. Following up surveys with individual or group interviews is highly recommended; otherwise, it is very difficult to interpret survey data (Babbie, 1973; Wexley and Latham, 1981).

Behaviorally Anchored Rating Scales. The Behaviorally Anchored Rating Scales (BARS) usually measure the subject's job performance and are a useful mechanism for conducting a needs assessment. In the BARS, a continuum scoring scheme is used, and the subjects are individually rated. Most BARS will use between five and ten separate scales. Typical behaviors found on BARS include knowledge of work, initiative, quality of work, quantity of work, and so on. These findings can then be measured against the requirements of the position to determine training needs. The rating scales would have individual descriptions for each of the behavioral traits. For example, if the trait to be rated is job knowledge, the top rating might require "complete awareness of the latest techniques and their application to the operations." The lowest rating might be described as "no awareness of current practices and using outdated methods." Intermediate steps on the scale for this behavior would have different but vividly descriptive phrases that would guide the appraiser in identifying the proper rating. BARS are sometimes used in performance appraisal, and most needs analysis applications would require a boss to rate a subordinate's job performance (Sashkin, 1981; Fogli, Hulin, and Blood, 1971).

Case Studies. Here, particular groups, individuals, or events are selected and then studied by means of a variety of data collection methods. The subjects for study are carefully selected to make sure that they will represent the variables and dimensions under investigation. Case studies usually produce both narrative and quantitative data, are conducted over a relatively long period of time, and require exhaustive analysis.

Often, cycles of data collection and analysis are repeated, as new variables or hunches emerge from analysis that require further information collection.

Case studies are most useful when (1) the questions or phenomena to be studied are complex and likely to be highly influenced by the context, and (2) there is uncertainty as to what the specific variables, causal events, or phenomena might be. Case studies require considerable time and money but can yield rich information.

For example, let us take a company that noticed erratic performance in its technical sales efforts. Some salespersons had exceptional sales records regardless of territory, other territories had high sales regardless of salespersons, and some salespersons did poorly no matter where they worked. To try to figure out what salesperson and territory attributes were associated with high performance, the company selected a few of the high and low performers for study. After it had looked into research on sales performance, data were collected about the salespersons themselves—their previous training, knowledge of product, and so forth. Salespersons, their major buyers, and district managers were interviewed and queried about behaviors, attitudes, and reactions. The HRD department studied those data, then returned to the field to accompany high performers on some sales calls to observe, question, and take notes. A team of HRD staff and a sales consultant then studied all the data, from which they identified several initial factors related to sales performance. Some factors were clearly not "trainable" but implied changes in district management procedures and salesperson selection. But a few factors emerged that implied potential training for both salespersons and their district managers (Borg and Gall, 1983; Guba and Lincoln, 1981; Patton, 1980).

Critical Incident Technique. The critical incident technique is helpful as a needs assessment mechanism in that it provides an index of critical behaviors that may then be assessed in terms of their effectiveness in the given situation. The technique consists essentially in the collection of reports of behaviors that were critical in the sense that they made the difference between success and failure in the observed work situation. The individual observing and reporting the behavior is most typically a supervisor or an associate of the person involved in the incident. The incident is acceptable as a critical one only if, in the observer's judgment, it relates to an important aspect of the work and indicates behavior that is outstandingly effective or ineffective with respect to the situation. The critical incident is principally characterized by its reference to actual behavior in a defined situation rather than to assumed traits. Critical incident methods can be very useful in identifying crucial job skills and knowledge that may represent training needs (Flanagan, 1954; Patton, 1980).

Delphi Technique. The Delphi technique is useful in Stage I evaluation for gathering and investigating opinions of key individuals and groups. Like the nominal group technique (a variant), this method is especially useful for Stage I inquiry when consensus and group commitment are a priority. It was designed to generate group consensus in order to minimize the following disadvantages:

1. The bandwagon effect of a majority opinion
2. The power of a persuasive, prestigious individual to shape group opinion
3. The vulnerability of group dynamics to manipulation
4. The unwillingness of individuals to abandon publicly stated positions

This procedure employs groups to generate opinion, but also elicits opinions from individual group members and provides a forum for a systematic review of the emerging consensus. Individuals can reconsider their initial positions in light of the group trends and make any adjustments felt to be appropriate. The final result is an informed consensus insulated from the forces of face-to-face group interaction (Helmer, 1967; Isaac and Michael, 1981).

Expert Reviews. One or more persons with exceptional expertise in a given area are chosen, and their opinions and ideas are then systematically obtained. There are several means of garnering their ideas: correspondence, person-to-person or telephone interviews, visits, responses to questionnaires or other structured instruments, written reactions to reports, panel discussions, and so on. The expert opinions are then used to help make decisions about needs.

Expert opinions are useful in a broad range of situations and can be quite narrowly focused ("given these data, what do you think of this particular training need?") or quite open ended ("where might we head in the future, given our current status?"). Because experts have in-depth knowledge of particular content, they represent helpful shortcuts and can make it unnecessary to conduct lengthy literature reviews or use other knowledge-gathering methods. Experts are especially helpful in identifying training needs in new or novel situations where previous standards for performance do not exist. Experts must be carefully chosen, of course, and must also be well informed about the particular context, requirements, and so on (Doyle and Straus, 1976; Schindler-Rainmann and Lippitt, 1975).

Front-End Analysis. Front-end analysis refers to the steps and procedures used in determining if there is need for a training program and whether training efforts will be worth the costs involved. Front-end analysis is a generic term and includes a variety of analytic and problem-solving methods. When a problem has been identified, front-end analysis is used to develop alternative solutions to it. Sometimes the most feasible answers are better materials, methods, and machines or more money rather than a training program. The following are the main steps involved in this kind of analysis:

1. Identifying deficiencies in people's performance
2. Determining the costs involved in meeting the deficiency or not meeting the deficiency
3. Deciding which deficiencies to meet and which to ignore
4. Listing the deficiencies to be met in order of priority

A deficiency in people's performance can be identified by asking these questions:

1.   What skills, knowledge, and/or attitudes are required?
2.   Which of these do they have already?
3.   Which are they lacking?

In other words, in the context of a specific job, is there a gap between what people can do and what they cannot do? Then, is that difference significant? Next, is it more expensive to do something about it or to leave it alone? Finally, if we decide to do something about it, what should we do? (Harless, 1981; Mager and Pipe, 1984; Rummler, 1976).

Interviewing. Interviewing can range from highly structured to quite "loose" and open-ended conversations. At the highly structured end of the continuum, an interview is more like an orally administered survey questionnaire. More loosely structured interviews use "probe" questions to stimulate thought and responses. Regardless of their degree of structure, interviews are an excellent means of gathering trainee reactions to and opinions about the operation and design of training programs. Interviews are especially useful because they permit interpretation of gestures, expressions, and so forth, and they allow an interviewer to follow up and gain more detailed explanations of responses. Interviews can be conducted with single individuals or with groups of trainees (Guba and Lincoln, 1981; Henerson, Morris, and Fitz-Gibbon, 1978; Patton, 1980; Payne, 1951; Sudman and Bradburn, 1982).

Knowledge Tests. Possible participants for a training program can be given a test to determine their training needs. This test yields a score derived from their response to the test items. Test items are selected or constructed to effectively sample the domain of knowledge being assessed (for example, supervisory techniques). Test item formats may vary but typically are multiple-choice or short-answer (completion) items. Knowledge tests can be constructed to yield highly accurate and valid measures, and numerical scores allow extensive statistical analysis and reporting. Such information could prove quite useful in determining the extent of a problem and the need for a training effort (Gronlund, 1982).

Literature Review. The purpose of research is to discover relationships among variables and phenomena of interest. Research studies have discovered how motivation affects learning and performance, how feedback reinforces behavior, how incentives increase performance, and so forth. While it is unlikely that an organization's HRD department can afford to conduct its own research efforts (though this is not impossible), research *literature* can be used to help identify key variables and traits that affect performance and thus might be the target for training. Using experts is a shortcut for getting at research knowledge. But when one wants direct access to the wealth of research knowledge (or cannot afford experts), then a library visit is appropriate. At present, there are many information search and retrieval services available that can save dozens of hours chasing down appropriate references. One begins by looking up (or asking a retrieval service to find) references dealing with the phenomena of interest (say, performance appraisal skills). Successive reading, refinement of questions, and more reading will turn up relevant research that has identified the skills, knowledge, or attitudes relevant to the behavior or phenomena of interest. This sort of knowledge of causality (or simply of relationships) is helpful in discovering or refining training needs (Borg and Gall, 1983).

Nominal Group Technique. An effective participative approach for diagnosing training needs involves use of the nominal group technique. The nominal group process is begun by having members first write their ideas on a slip of paper without discussing them. A period of five to fifteen minutes is usually required for this. Then each member is asked in turn to contribute one of his or her ideas. As an idea is suggested, it is written on a blackboard or flip chart by the leader. No evaluation or discussion of ideas is permitted during the posting. As the round robin continues, some members may pass if they have no ideas to offer that differ from those already posted. However, a person may suggest ideas not on the original list, and members are encouraged to build on each other's ideas. After all ideas are posted, the leader goes down the list and asks if there are any questions, statements of clarification, or statements of agreement or disagreement about the relevance of the ideas. Subsequent rounds of voting will identify, and lead to agreement on, those problems or topics perceived as most important. This procedure works well with groups of up to nine persons, but it should not be used in larger groups unless carried out within subgroups first, followed by a pooling of ideas from the differing subgroups (Delbecq, Van de Ven, and Gustafson, 1975; Harrison, Pietri, and Moore, 1983).

Performance Audit. The performance audit is a technique for performance problem analysis. It is a framework for viewing human performance problems and a set of procedures for systematically determining the worth of correcting the problem, finding the causes of the problem, and designing solutions to the problem. An evaluation system for determining the impact of the solution on the problem is inherent in the procedures. There are two dimensions to the performance audit: behavior and economics. The audit examines behavior and the impact of behavior on the economics of the organization by analysis of five components:

1. The job situation or occasion to perform
2. The performer
3. The behavior (action or decision) that is to occur
4. The consequences of that behavior to the performer
5. The feedback of the consequences to the performer

This model discriminates between problems or deficiencies that can be best corrected through training and those that require changes in the "environment." For the latter, it also helps determine what changes are required to correct the deficiency or to support the recommended training.

An economic analysis tells whether a problem is worth solving and defines organizational consequences that are intended to result from changes in behavior. The economic analysis is concerned with the payoff question: Is it worth it? This question could be addressed from the organizational level, from the work-unit level, and from the proposed program level. These three levels form the bases for the total performance analysis (Gilbert, 1978; Rummler, 1976).

Work Sample Tests. Work sample tests measure job skills by taking a sample of behavior under realistic, joblike conditions. Actually, the performance may not be measured at the job station but on a standard test machine and with a standardized task. For example, applicants for the job of sewing machine operator might be given a standard set of tasks reflecting the various techniques required on the job. Or a prospective unit supervisor may be asked to provide responses to a series of issues that form part of a regular work schedule. Work sample tests could be based on any work output—mechanical, written, and so forth—for which criteria for the quality of the work sample are available or could be produced. A trainer, for example, would assess supervisors' writing skills by rating the quality of memos and letters that the supervisors have actually written. These tests are intended to test present skills or achievements, not aptitude or potential. They would therefore be of greatest use in situations in which one needs to measure on-the-job skill levels (Ghiselli, 1966; Jewish Employment and Referral Service, 1966).

3

Deciding
What Program Design Alternatives
Will Achieve the Best Results

Stage II evaluation focuses on the HRD design itself. It begins
with the assumption (assessed in Stage I) that it is a good idea
to do HRD in the first place; thus, the focus of Stage II is not
whether to use HRD but the *how* of HRD programming. The
basic guiding question of Stage II is, How good is the HRD
plan?

There are several purposes that Stage II evaluation can
serve. Most often, a particular HRD design or strategy has already been decided upon. Given slumping sales performance
and apparent skill deficits in salespersons (a Stage I conclusion), for example, a company might decide upon a particular
HRD design strategy, such as conducting a series of skill workshops. At this point, Stage II evaluation could be used to assess the adequacy of the design(s) for the skill workshops. That
is, a tentative or "draft" design would be written up, describing
intended activities, participant selection procedures, learning
objectives, schedules, and so forth. This design would then be
evaluated, perhaps through use of a checklist, a panel review, or
a group discussion. The primary function served by this sort of
Stage II evaluation would be to identify strengths and weaknesses in the design so that revisions could then be made to the
design.

But other Stage II strategies could also be pursued. Referring to the same example, it could be that two or three alternative designs for remediating salesperson skills would be drafted—for example, a workshop, self-instructional materials, and a mentoring program. Using previously established criteria, Stage II evaluation could then be applied to systematically compare these three alternative plans to select a "winner." Or, in a variation on this theme, the evaluation might identify the relative strengths and weaknesses of each plan, not to select a winner, but to construct a *fourth* plan consisting of the best elements of each of the original three.

Still another Stage II strategy is possible. It might be that, in our sales training example, one design is selected as a pilot. In this case, Stage II evaluation would consist of a complete test of the training model under actual operating conditions. This try-out could be a full-blown experiment in which rigorous tests of causal hypotheses were conducted or a less expensive effort that collected participant reactions, learning data, and cost data. As another possibility, two or more alternative pilot strategies might be experimentally compared.

Thus, a variety of specific Stage II strategies and procedures can be used. Each employs different methods and varies in its costs and the kinds of questions it addresses. While the overarching Stage II purpose is the same—to evaluate the adequacy of the HRD design—HRD practitioners will want to consider a range of Stage II alternatives, basing their chosen approach on the setting and needs at hand. At this point, therefore, let us review some typical Stage II evaluation questions:

- Among several different HRD approaches, which is best?
- Is plan X any good?
- What are the strengths and weaknesses of training plan Y?
- What would work best: HRD method A or B?
- Should this workshop have a presession orientation?
- Is HRD method Y likely to achieve objective X?
- Which of several approaches is the most efficient?
- What are the best training methods for achieving training objective Z?

- Which HRD package should we purchase: A or B?
- Which would be best: a "homegrown" plan or an off-the-shelf package?
- How feasible is HRD strategy C?

While these evaluation questions obviously differ, they are similar in some important ways. First, each of the questions has a common object—to arrive at some particular plans, methods, strategies, or designs. Second, these questions do not ask whether HRD is needed or whether HRD is, or has been, effective. They are future oriented. They ask what will work or is likely to work. They represent crucial questions that designers of programs must ask *after* they have decided to initiate HRD but *before* they actually do it. In other words, they are evaluation questions typically encountered at the HRD design stage. They are Stage II questions.

A third common feature of the questions listed is that "answers" to them would be largely a matter of professional, expert judgment. In other words, people with considerable training experience and expertise could probably give helpful responses to questions such as those listed. Research on learning and teaching also provides a Stage II referent base.

In a nutshell, Stage II involves deciding on the important evaluation questions to ask in a particular HRD design situation. Then, whatever information is needed to arrive at satisfactory answers to those questions is gathered, weighed, and considered. Following that, the HRD plan is finalized. Stage II closes when the HRD practitioner can say, "There, that's enough consideration of alternatives. We've got a plan here that we know is pretty good—let's get on with doing our program!"

Because any HRD plan will always contain uncertainty and hidden flaws, it would be theoretically possible to remain permanently at Stage II. Ideas and recommendations for refining and improving a training plan, like ideas for decorating and improving a home, can flow in an endless stream. But at some point, the new home is ready to move into, even though not all the curtains are up and not all the trim has been painted. Likewise, the HRD plan, though not yet perfect, is good enough to go with. The HRD practitioner will know full well that flaws remain and that there are further adjustments to be made. But the HRD plan has undergone sufficient inquiry and development to have a reasonable chance to succeed, so practicality dictates that it be implemented.

There is in fact a reason beyond practicality to move a training plan from the drawing board and place it into operation. It is often only during actual implementation that certain flaws, strengths, and improvement needs will be discovered. To return to the new home analogy, many families have learned that it is best to leave some decorating and improvement jobs until later, when the family has had a chance to live in the house for a while and get a feel for the new space and how they operate in it. The family may know, for instance, that the new playroom lacks enough electrical outlets but waits to see just how the room actually gets used before completing the wiring. Program designs, like the final arrangements of house elements and decorations, most often will attain their final shape and specifications only after a "live-in" period, during which a watchful eye is kept for emerging strengths and problems. And, just as most homes continually evolve (my eighty-year-old parents commented, after yet another move last year, that they think they are now beginning to get a handle on just how they like things arranged in their home!), HRD designs should be continually tested and revised as they are implemented over and over again. Evaluation is HRD's "watchful eye" and reminds us that even the training program that has been repeated for years and years is still being tried out.

Levels of Stage II Effort

Just how much evaluation a design needs before implementation varies from instance to instance and depends on a variety of factors. Using our new home example once again, we can note that one family's budget, creative abilities, social and job needs, tolerance for disorder and upheaval, and yet other characteristics and circumstances will require an extremely finished and complete home environment. Another family, by contrast, happily lives with plywood floors, trimless doors, and dangling light fixtures, decorating and redesigning as they go. The correct approach, for new houses and HRD programs alike, depends on several factors. Moreover, a range of alternative approaches is available. Not every situation calls for elaborate Stage II evaluation. In fact, in many cases quite simple "armchair" approaches can be used. A trainer, for example, who has been given a particular training need to address and then, while driving home, mulls over some different alternatives is doing Stage II evaluation. Following are a few typical Stage II vignettes—some, to be sure, more elaborate and systematic than others but all, nonetheless, Stage II efforts:

- "Hmmm," muses a trainer relaxing at home in a favorite chair. "I wonder if role playing might work. No, probably not. We'll have a mixed group, and there will be too much reluctance to really open up in front of all the bosses."
- The Schwartz Company conducts a two-month pilot test of a new supervisory training manual that is being considered for adoption.
- Pat shows Joe, who works in a different division, a new HRD plan and asks for some critical feedback.
- The Downfield Corporation hires an expert in skill training to review its skill-training program and write a summary report detailing its strengths and weaknesses and making recommendations for improvement.
- The HRD officer convenes a meeting of floor supervisors to review and discuss plans for a new set of job aids.
- Using a checklist, several experts rate the adequacy of XYZ Company's new plan for management development.
- The training officer and her assistant visit a neighboring organization to see how its highly rated computer training program works, then compare notes to assess whether their own organization's efforts are up to par.
- The Uptown Company hires a university research team to conduct an experimental study aimed at assessing which of two statistical-control training programs produces the best results.

Such vignettes reveal not only that Stage II involves different methods but that the overall level of effort also differs considerably. On the one hand, pilot studies, experimental comparisons, even visits by experts can be quite expensive and time consuming. On the other hand, a visit down the hall to get a second opinion, a trip to the library to read a research report, or a meeting with an employee group are all relatively cheap and quick methods for gathering evaluative information. When conducted systematically, however, even these simple and inexpensive techniques can pay off handsomely.

Is Stage II evaluation always necessary? The inevitability of flaws in HRD plans has to be confronted, and this is, of course, the major reason for conducting Stage II evaluation. Any and all designs can be improved, and very often revisions and improvements can be made prior to a plan's implementation. Any Stage II effort, then, is likely to have a positive payoff. The question is not whether to do Stage II evaluation but how much of it to do. How good does the HRD effort have to be? If the risks of putting even a slightly flawed plan into operation are great, then the need for Stage II inquiry is also great. Table 6 shows some indications of when high investments in Stage II evaluation should be seriously considered.

Additional Benefits of Stage II Evaluation

The primary reasons emphasized thus far for Stage II evaluation are (1) to assess a given design in order to improve it prior to its implementation or (2) to select a "winning" design from alternative designs. But even when the potential benefit from these two primary reasons suggests a low investment in Stage II evaluation, there are usually good reasons to dedicate significant effort to a systematic evaluation of the design. These additional benefits, with a brief discussion of each, are listed below. Each of them is related directly to HRD's opportunity to create worthwhile impact on the organization, and thus each potential benefit warrants careful attention as Stage II evaluation investments are considered.

1. Commitment and "buy in." Human resource develop-

Table 6. Indications for Varying Investment in Stage II Evaluation.

When:	Higher Investment	Lower Investment
Program design is . . .	Very experimental, unique, innovative, controversial	Usual, tried and true, proven, guaranteed
HRD costs are . . .	High, big proportion of budget, under careful scrutiny, hard to justify	Low, a drop in the bucket, part of an obscure surplus
HRD needs are . . .	Crucial, life or death, highly visible, widespread	Minor, low incidence, very indirectly tied to performance, obscure
Participant groups are . . .	Volatile, influential, high level, demanding, diverse	Docile, easy to please, insignificant, homogeneous
Opportunity to repeat or recycle HRD is . . .	Low	High
Decision to do HRD in first place was . . .	Difficult, controversial, very visible	Easy, routine, mundane, obscure

ment involves change efforts in an organization. It is supposed to make a difference, and that inevitably means that one or more employee groups will have to change in some way. Theory and research on change efforts indicate that the degree of "buy in" by employees plays a key role in whether change will last or even take place at all. A systematic Stage II evaluation that solicits opinion and advice from those persons in the organization who will be most affected by the HRD program engenders the "buy-in" phenomenon and increases the commitment to change that is required if change is to occur. A needs analysis, for example, might indicate that senior male executives need to change their decision-making and supervisory behaviors when dealing with newly hired female managers if affirmative action and equal opportunity programs are to be improved. Allowing, even "forcing," these executives to become involved in the program development process will enhance their commitment and thus enhance the opportunity for success of training. Stage II procedures might engage them, for example, in reviewing the needs data and then critiquing preliminary program designs for both the female managers and themselves. As their input shapes, and as they *see* their input shaping, the final HRD plan, their sense of commitment and ownership will grow. The plan will become "theirs" rather than remaining some bizarre invention of the HRD department, and it will thus stand a better chance for success.

2. *Customer accountability and concern.* Much of the current writing and discussion about "excellence" and productivity stresses accountability to customers. Providing a product that meets the customer's expectations for quality is seen as a major organizational goal. A Stage II evaluation can be conducted to identify the expectations for and reactions to proposed program designs of such HRD "customers" as trainees and their immediate superiors. Representatives of HRD audiences could, for example, be asked to review and critique the draft design for a program. Or a similar group of individuals might be asked to construct a checklist of elements that they think a high-quality HRD effort should have. Then, they or another group could assess a tentative program design using that

checklist. These Stage II approaches demonstrate and operationalize a concern for customer accountability and likewise assure
that customer concerns are considered before HRD takes place.
Involving HRD groups in Stage II should not be viewed as a sign
of weakness or uncertainty by HRD leaders. Rather, it should
be seen as a sign of honest concern, sensitivity, and commitment
to quality.

   3. *Using and modeling participation.* Stage II evaluation
involving HRD groups yields the kinds of direct results that
only participation can produce. It also affords an opportunity
to model participatory methods, which are often an HRD subject in organizations. Participation by HRD groups in the program design process is likewise a valuable aim. To begin with,
learning theory mandates that program designs should be as
compatible with participant interests, needs, abilities, preferences, values, and culture as possible. Carefully and systematically gathering trainee reactions to program designs and plans
is one of the best and most direct methods of meeting this compatibility criterion. Such efforts almost always yield ideas on
how to make critical revisions to a design. But there are participation benefits beyond these revisions. Even if a design is already known to be highly compatible, it is a good idea to systematically involve trainee representatives and groups in Stage
II reviews, critiques, and so on. Such involvement breeds political support and enhances commitment to and "ownership" of
the program among trainees. These efforts democratize HRD
and tend to diffuse its control to increasingly lower levels in the
organization.

   4. *Facilitating transfer of training.* Most experienced trainers are sadly familiar with cases in which training effects were
"washed out" because trainees' superiors (or even subordinates)
did not support on-the-job application of program-acquired
skills. In most of these instances, had the key groups of superiors and subordinates been better informed about the training
needs and purposes, then the washout of effects would have
been greatly reduced. Stage II evaluation approaches can be
used to systematically involve these key groups in the training
design process, soliciting and using their input to revise designs.

The payoff for transfer of training effects to the job place is twofold. First, these groups will inevitably have good ideas on how to revise the training to make it more usable on the job. Second, and perhaps more important, the process of soliciting their input is a sort of covert training that creates knowledge and awareness crucial to transfer of training effects.

5. *Shaping expectations for success.* Almost always, the organizational and performance problems that precipitate HRD are larger and more complex than HRD alone can completely solve. A program's impact is likely to be marginal, and it will be difficult to prove with any high degree of certainty what that impact amounted to. Again, Stage II evaluation that involves key audiences for the program (particularly officers at high levels who want to see HRD's payoff) in a critical review of designs will be better able to inform those audiences about how the HRD program is supposed to work, the problems it will face, and what it hopes to accomplish. Such Stage II procedures, because they stimulate dialogue about HRD, will help articulate and shape expectations for HRD's performance. Previously hidden expectations might be brought to the surface and, when they are unreasonable, can then be resolved. Or expanded expectations might stimulate revisions that otherwise might not have been incorporated in a plan. In such instances, expectations become clarified and resolved, and HRD's chances for meeting expectations, a major key to its survival, are enhanced.

6. *"Marketing" training in the organization.* Most HRD practitioners and theorists agree that HRD must be firmly embedded in and responsive to the overall organization or it will not survive. All the benefits listed above share a common educating-the-consumer or marketing function. Human resource development leaders who make sincere and systematic Stage II evaluation efforts that involve, over time, key audiences from all levels in the organization are marketing the HRD function in a legitimate and productive manner. These efforts make HRD visible, keep it responsive to organizational needs and interests, and educate consumers as to its functions, problems, and benefits. In brief, these efforts improve HRD and help assure its success and future in an organization.

Documenting the HRD Design

A program design must be documented in some format or another or it cannot be evaluated. There are, of course, many styles and formats in which a program design can be documented, and likewise many reasons for documenting the design. But Stage II evaluation requires a special sort of documentation so that those persons asked to evaluate the design will be provided with a clear and complete portrayal of just how the HRD program will operate and what results it is intended to accomplish. Again, there may be several formats for documentation that could be used during Stage II evaluation. I have chosen to explain one such documentation method here—a method that has proved useful in a number of instances.

This method for documenting an HRD design uses three worksheet formats. Each of these describes a different aspect of the design, and the three as a whole portray the entire design in a manner that facilitates careful Stage II evaluation.

The first worksheet is a participant/outcomes analysis (Table 7).

The participant/outcomes worksheet shows, for any particular HRD program or component, (1) who will receive the program, (2) what immediate learning outcomes the program will achieve for those participants if it is successful, (3) the job-usage objectives that will be achieved if learning endures and/or is successfully transferred, and (4) the organizational benefits that will accrue if the job-usage objectives are successfully achieved. Or in the language used in the first chapter of this book, this worksheet portrays the logic of the training for a particular group of recipients of HRD.

The participant/outcomes worksheet is presented here as a format to be used for Stage II evaluation. But it can also be used when conducting needs analysis, in which case analysis of HRD needs would begin in the far right-hand column (social/organizational benefits) and then proceed from right to left to determine what on-job behavioral changes would be required to produce such benefits and what learning outcomes would need to be produced for which groups of employees. This worksheet

Table 7. Example of Participant/Outcomes Analysis.

Who is to receive HRD?	What skills, knowledge, or attitudes will be changed as a result of HRD?	How will recipients use the new SKA—what on-the-job behaviors will change?	What social/organizational benefits will accrue?
Cafeteria line servers	• Awareness of results of customer waiting	• More pleasant and accurate response to customer questions	• Decreased customer waiting
	• Knowledge of replenishment guidelines • Serving skills	• Speedier replenishment of dishes	• Increased customer satisfaction
		• Adherence to serving guidelines	• Increased cafeteria usage
	• Knowledge and skill in responding to customers		
Supervisors	• Awareness of line-server supervision needs	• Increased supportiveness in interactions with line servers	
	• Awareness of actual working conditions	• Increase in appropriate and timely supervisory actions	
	• Knowledge and skill in supervision techniques		

is also useful for communicating, in a brief and concise way, the intended results of an HRD program to interested audiences, such as trainees, managers, executives, and so forth. And lastly, as will be considered in detail in later chapters, this format is useful for planning evaluation measures to assess whether immediate, job-usage, and organizational benefit objectives have actually been achieved from HRD efforts.

The next two worksheet formats are used to describe the "how" of HRD. The first of these worksheets is a components-network. It shows the major process components in a program design and also shows (with arrows) the intended relationship among the several components and subcomponents. A sample components-network for a program for cafeteria workers is shown in Figure 3.

Figure 3. Sample Components-Network for a Program for Cafeteria Workers.

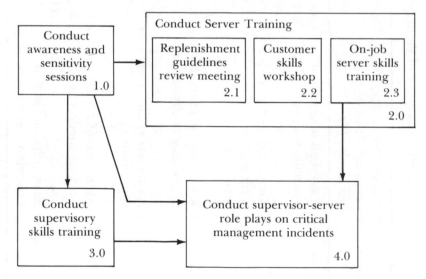

The components-network provides an overview of an entire HRD function's activities. Each component represents a major activity and may be subdivided further (see component 2.0 in Figure 3) into subcomponents. The arrows represent functional dependencies, in which one component relies on an-other for one or more of its necessary inputs. For example, component 4.0 (role playing) requires as inputs supervisors with newly learned skills (an output of component 3.0) and servers with newly learned skills (an output of component 2.3).

The third and final documentation worksheet is the input-process-output (IPO). The IPO is used to depict the de-tailed operation of a component or subcomponent and shows the inputs (resources) the component needs, the process by which it will achieve its outcomes, and a listing of each intended outcome that the component will produce if the process is suc-cessful. Inputs, processes, and outputs are described for each component or subcomponent in the design. A sample IPO for one of the components (component 3.0) in the training design shown in Figure 3 is given as Table 8.

Together, all three worksheet formats—the participant/outcomes analysis, the components-network, and the IPO—pro-vide a complete picture of an HRD program's intended opera-tion, including how it will operate and, if it is successful, what learning objectives will be accomplished by the end of the pro-gram, how they will be used on the job, and how the organiza-tion will thereby benefit. This complete portrayal of the HRD program's intended operation provides the documentation needed for Stage II evaluation to take place. Completed work-sheets for an HRD program or function could, for example, be given to a group of training experts, potential trainees, trainees' supervisors, or others, who would then be asked to evaluate the adequacy or soundness of that design along some critical dimen-sions. The trainees' supervisors might be asked, for instance, to assess the appropriateness of the intended job-usage objectives, or an HRD expert might be asked to review the design and pro-vide opinions about the potential effectiveness of the training exercises and procedures.

In summary, Stage II evaluation depends on complete and accurate description of HRD's intended operation and out-comes. It is this description that then becomes the referent for evaluative judgments about the HRD design. Such judgments, of course, derive from expectations, opinions, and values that

Table 8. Example of a Completed Input-Process-Output Worksheet.

Input	Process	Output
• Fourteen cafeteria supervisors • Supervision skill manual and workbooks (one per participant) • Qualified supervisory skills trainer • Projector and screen • Use of seminar room (two days) • Funds for overtime pay • Supplies and materials • Learning-style inventory (one per participant) • Training design reviewed by supervisor representatives • Feedback and skill assessment instruments • Three trained observers • Films	Component 3.0 "conduct supervisory skills training." Supervisors will attend a two-day workshop scheduled over weekend and holiday period (with overtime pay) at company conference center. Supervisors will first complete a learning-style inventory to aid their participation and learning in group sessions. They will then view and discuss several training films. Following discussion, supervisors will engage in several small-group training sessions using the supplied manual. Performance in a series of simulated incidents requiring supervision will be observed and rated by assessors. Small-group manual sessions will be repeated as needed prior to final session performance observations.	Supervisors who meet criterion level in: a. performance assessment and charting skills b. coaching techniques skills c. knowledge of motivation and feedback principles

are held about the HRD function itself. In the next section, therefore, we will turn to some general criteria that can be used to facilitate the judging of HRD designs.

Important Stage II Criteria

As already noted, Stage II inquiry might compare alternative approaches, assess a given design, or yield additional benefits and improvements. In all these instances, however, the general aim of Stage II inquiry is to ask questions about the "goodness" of HRD designs, methods, and strategies. Given this general aim, there are several key criteria, or dimensions, of HRD plans that need to be assessed. What makes a particular HRD design good for a given purpose and situation is, of course, variable. Lecture methods, for example, might be good for communicating information about new accounting procedures but not at all appropriate for building communications skills. Participatory training might work well for one group of trainees but might be a disaster with another, less experienced or less interested group. Specific instances, then, require the identification and consideration of specific Stage II criteria. But these specifics derive from more generic categories of criteria that HRD practitioners can use to work out their own Stage II criteria and methods.

Design Criterion 1: Clarity and Definition. Program plans and designs must be clearly and explicitly defined and communicated. It is difficult, if not impossible, to assess the goodness of an HRD design on any dimension (except that of clarity!) if those who are trying to assess it cannot understand it. Stage II inquiry requires clear definition of (1) HRD needs, goals, and objectives at immediate learning, usage, and organizational benefit levels, (2) HRD processes and methods, and (3) the resources and inputs planned to support the program.

Design Criterion 2: Theoretical Adequacy of the HRD Design. Training designs must be theoretically sound. They should incorporate sound learning theory and reflect the current knowledge and research base about how people learn best. These criteria for theoretical soundness cover a wide range of dimensions, including such aspects as the structure of a learning activity, the format (and even the color) of materials, the extent of interaction and feedback incorporated, and the adequacy of facilities. The fields of instructional psychology and design are especially pertinent to this criterion. This knowledge base is constantly changing and being added to, requiring HRD practitioners to keep up with current literature (see, for example, Gagne and Briggs, 1979; Esseff, 1982; Hunter, 1982; Reigeluth, 1983). Moreover, the lessons and guidance found in the literature on training and learning are rarely absolute and certain. Thus, assessing the theoretical adequacy of training designs requires not only knowledge of the current research, but knowledge of the particular training context and needs under consideration.

Design Criterion 3: Compatibility. A design must "fit" its environment and the culture of the organization of which it is a part. This criterion honors the fact that what worked in one setting with one group of people cannot necessarily be transported to another locale and group and be expected to work as well. Judgment about a design's compatibility requires, of course, detailed knowledge of the culture and environment of the intended host organization; use of independent, external experts to judge this criterion, then, is probably not possible. The compatibility criterion is broad and will vary in its significance and specification from setting to setting. But even though it is somewhat difficult to define precise compatibility needs for a particular program, compatibility is nonetheless an important criterion. Considerations of compatibility would include such questions as:

- Is the program consistent with other training programs and organizational priorities? In a recent case, I found it necessary to redesign a company's new training program in performance appraisal because the procedures and terminology used in the proposed training were not consistent with a major productivity measurement project that the company had also recently undertaken.

- Is the program consistent with corporate culture, policy, and values? For example, a training program that contained activities that required persons from different organization levels to work together in small groups might need to be redesigned for a culture with rigid and strict boundary lines.
- Are program content and procedures compatible with trainee educational and social levels, values, and expectations? Many programs contain references, materials, and activities that would be appropriate for one group but not for another.
- Is the program consistent with the schedules, work demands, and personal practices of trainees?

Design Criterion 4: Practicality and Cost Effectiveness. An HRD design must be economical and feasible. Programs can be theoretically sound but make such unreasonable demands on personnel, trainee, and other resources that they stand little or no chance of survival. Included in this criterion are such questions as the following: Are required resources readily available? Are processes and procedures practical and economical? Have briefer, less costly procedures been considered? Is the projected payoff of HRD worth the likely expense? Note that care must be taken to identify and account for *all* direct and indirect projected costs for the program.

Particularly costly elements and components can usually be designed in a more economical way. Thus, Stage II evaluation for the cost criterion should be directed at each component in the program design and should seek out and compare less costly alternatives and their potential consequences for the HRD's overall objectives.

Design Criterion 5: Responsiveness to Needs. As noted in the chapter on Stage I evaluation, a decision that HRD will respond to worthwhile needs has already been made *prior to* consideration of program designs (Stage II evaluation). The goals that HRD should address, regardless of just how the programs will be carried out, have been identified. Experience tells us, however, that any design is more or less a compromise; the realities of what can actually be done, given time, budget, and other constraints, almost always dictate that the objectives HRD will *actually* achieve will be slightly less than, or at least different from, the *initial* expectations held for it. And so, as a program design is nearing its final shape and specifications, it is wise counsel to "revisit" the initial goals and ask whether *this* HRD program is likely, in fact, to meet the goals initially set. Further, when dealing with off-the-shelf program packages, it is likely that objectives in addition to the initial goals might be achieved. And any program is likely to produce some unantici-pated results. Given the likelihood that one or more of these three phenomena—compromise objectives, additional objec-tives, and unanticipated effects—will occur, Stage II evaluation should carefully identify the objectives that a given design will probably achieve, then compare these against the initial expec-tations to assure that real and worthwhile needs are likely to be addressed.

Design Criterion 6: Superior to Alternatives. It is particu-larly true of HRD that there is frequently more than one way to get the job done. Further, while there are always several alterna-tive approaches for any given HRD goal, all will be flawed in one way or another. Finally, training resources are limited, meaning that the problem is rarely that of getting the best HRD that money can buy; rather, it is usually that of getting the best HRD that the *least* money can buy. To put it briefly, alterna-tives must be considered and systematically compared during Stage II. Human resource development professionals should be prepared to argue not only that one particular design is good but that it is *better* than contending alternatives.

Design Criterion 7: Adult-Learning Practices. There is a substantial body of literature (Knowles, 1984; Lenz, 1982; McKeachie, 1978) concerning "best practices" for adult learn-ing and teaching. While some of this literature is based on con-jecture and some on traditional practice, there is considerable research evidence and even more anecdotal evidence to support these practices. Program designs should reflect state-of-the-art practice when possible and should certainly avoid obsolete or outmoded methods. This criterion should not be construed to mean that HRD should try to be "stylish" or keep up with the latest fads and foibles of the profession. Above all, thoughtful and careful construction of programs should never be sacrificed for the appearance of modernity.

Design Criterion 8: Legality and Ethics. This criterion is obvious, but too important not to be stated explicitly or to be omitted from Stage II evaluation. All HRD settings, but particularly those in public agencies and regulated industries, are subject to many laws, rules, guidelines, and policies, not to mention principles of fairness and humane treatment. Whereas trade-offs and compromises among the preceding seven criteria are possible and often necessary, the criteria regarding ethics and legality are absolute and must not be compromised. Trainee selection procedures should not, for example, violate employment opportunity laws. These criteria as they relate to laws, policies, and guidelines that impinge on such HRD procedures as selection, access to programs, testing, and reporting of evaluation are relatively obvious and can be readily assessed by experts. There are, however, more subtle processes and events within HRD that might infringe on basic human rights and courtesies. No HRD process, for example, should needlessly embarrass or humiliate participants. Participants' rights to privacy—for example, not being required by a training process to divulge personal or sensitive information—should be honored and protected. Program materials and exercises should recognize and respect ethnic and cultural diversity; no materials or exercises should be biased or discriminate on the basis of sex, race, or religious preference. And finally, of course, HRD designs should assure the physical safety of participants.

Useful Stage II Procedures

This section describes, in alphabetical order, some useful procedures for implementing Stage II evaluation. Each procedure is accompanied by one or more references to sources that will offer readers more information about it. This listing is not exhaustive, but it is meant to be relatively broad; specifically, it includes alternatives that I hope will suit readers' varied circumstances.

Advocate Teams. A design review and construction technique called *advocate teams* is a useful method for Stage II evaluation. In this technique, several teams of advocates (or adversaries) analyze, critique, and sometimes revise alternative program designs. These competing designs are then assessed, by means of a checklist of common criteria, to pick a "winner." Advocate teams are generally groups of people who are brought together to develop competing strategies for achieving a given set of objectives. Essentially, teams are developed through identification of experts in a particular area. Although each expert may have his or her own bias, the team as a whole will represent the entire spectrum of viewpoints. Upon obtaining these viewpoints, one could look for similarities and make choices among the differences. Some selection criteria for advocate team members are:

1. Credibility with peers and others
2. Evidence of innovative thinking
3. Task orientation
4. Ability to conceptualize broadly
5. Commitment to the needs of the organization

An agenda for an advocate team's orientation session might include the following:

1. A brief overview of antecedents. In sum, what is the problem?
2. A statement of the "charge" to the team. This will include goal statement, general objectives, statement of "givens" (if any), list of criteria, and format outline.
3. Discussion of the support services available to the teams.
4. Opportunity for team members to meet in individual teams.

Beyond this, team members should be encouraged to use their creative energies in developing alternative solutions for consideration by sponsors of the study (Reinhard, 1972; Stufflebeam and others, 1971).

Checklist Analysis. A subjective approach to the evaluation of a proposed program design can be obtained by using checklist analysis. Here the raters, who may be the program planners, previous or prospective trainees, independent judges, or supervisors, are typically given a list of statements, ratings, and objectives and asked to report on the value of these in the design.

Checklist analysis helps to "check over" an HRD plan or design document. A checklist is constructed that incorporates particular criteria, standards, or other expectations that the design should meet or address. Individuals (training experts, for example) are then provided with a copy of the design and a copy of the checklist and asked to assess the extent to which the design meets, or does not meet, the checklist criteria. Variations of checklist analysis would include having groups complete the checklists or having checklist respondents attend a presentation briefing on the design. And the checklist might ask for comments about inadequate elements of the design, as well as recommendations for strengthening them.

The source for checklist criteria is an important consideration, for this will affect the validity of the analysis and the credibility of its results. Checklists might represent company or HRD division training standards, standards derived from literature reviews and research, trainee expectations and criteria, or some combination of all these sources (Babbie, 1973).

Experimental and Quasi-Experimental Designs. Experimental or quasi-experimental designs are useful and thorough but expensive scientific approaches for determining the validity and reliability of a proposed program design. Experimental approaches are used to investigate possible cause-and-effect relationships by exposing one or more experimental groups to one or more treatment conditions and comparing the results to one or more control groups not receiving the treatment. Internal and external validity is the major objective of experimental methodology. It asks, Did the experimental manipulation in this particular program really make a difference (internal validity)? How representative are the findings, and can the results be generalized to similar circumstances and subjects (external validity)? The seven steps in experimental research are the following:

    I.   Survey the literature relating to the problem
   II.   Identify and define the problem
  III.   Formulate a problem hypothesis, deducing the consequences and defining basic terms and variables
  IV.   Construct an experimental plan:
        A.   Identify nonexperimental variables that might contaminate the experiment and determine how to control or account for them
        B.   Select a research design
        C.   Select a sample of subjects to represent a given population, assign subjects to groups, and assign experimental treatments to groups
        D.   Select or construct and validate the instruments to measure the outcome of the experiment
        E.   Outline procedures for collecting the data and possibly conduct a pilot test to perfect the instruments or design
        F.   State the statistical or null hypothesis
   V.   Conduct the experiments
  VI.   Reduce the raw data in a manner that will produce the best appraisal of the effect that is presumed to exist
 VII.   Apply an appropriate test of significance to determine the confidence one can place in the results of the study (Borg and Gall, 1983; Campbell and Stanley, 1966)

Group and Panel Reviews. In Stage II applications, this method is essentially a critical review of a given HRD design, or several alternative designs, by one or more groups. The groups could be composed of potential trainees or of persons expert in some area pertinent to the HRD effort. In any case, the task of the group or panel is to gather opinions and critical reactions about a design. Various degrees of structure might be employed. Groups could be given only the barest minimum of direction (for example, "Look it over; what do you think?") or provided with particular questions and criteria to guide their discussion. Additionally, structured rating instruments and checklists could be used. Regardless of the specific methods employed, the general idea is to stimulate thinking and open discussion about one or more designs (Doyle and Straus, 1976; Schindler-Rainmann and Lippitt, 1975).

Nominal Group Technique. An effective participative approach to program planning and evaluation of potential HRD design alternatives is the nominal group technique (see Chapter Two for a description of this technique). In Stage II applications, groups would work to identify strengths and weaknesses of design alternatives or would generate new HRD ideas (Delbecq, Van de Ven, and Gustafson, 1975; Harrison, Pietri, and Moore, 1983).

Pilot Study. A pilot study permits a preliminary testing of the proposed program that in turn can lead to further fine tuning. It may lead to changing some features, dropping others, and developing new methods. It also provides the HRD leader with ideas, approaches, and clues of which he or she may not have been aware prior to the pilot study. A pilot study may save the HRD practitioner from spending a large amount of time and money on a project with little potential value. Many HRD ideas that seem to show great promise are unproductive when carried out in the field. The pilot study almost always provides enough data to make a sound decision on the advisability of going ahead with the program. Finally, in many pilot studies, it is possible to get feedback from trainees and other persons involved that leads to important improvements in the design. Although the pilot study should follow the main design procedures for the most part, variations such as trying alternative instruments and procedures and seeking feedback from trainees on the methods, measures, and other aspects of the HRD design are usually desirable (Borg and Gall, 1983).

4

Monitoring
How Well Programs
Are Being Implemented
and Succeeding

Stage III begins when an HRD plan has been completed and a decision has been made to begin to implement that plan. The primary purpose of Stage III evaluation is to monitor the implementation of HRD and to provide data that will help "shepherd" the program to a successful conclusion. The basic question that guides Stage III evaluation is "How is it going?" The assumption underlying this question (and underlying Stage III evaluation itself) is that some parts of the program will go well and other parts will not go so well. Those parts that appear to be moving toward achievement of the HRD objectives should be recognized and nurtured. Those parts that are not progressing well should be monitored and changed.

The basic concept that characterizes Stage III evaluation comes from the Discrepancy Evaluation Model developed by Provus (1971). In Stage III evaluation, the program is observed to determine what is actually taking place. These observations of actual HRD performance are then compared to what is supposed to be taking place to see if there is a discrepancy between what is supposed to be happening and what is really happening.

The expectation for HRD—what is supposed to be happening—is set by the design for the HRD program. What is really happening ("reality") is discovered by observing and assessing the HRD program as it unfolds. In a training workshop, for example, it might be expected that participants will form small groups and try out a new consensus procedure they have been learning about. Observation (using, say, a previously developed checklist) might discover, however, that the groups are being dominated by one or two individuals and that the consensus approach is, in fact, not being used. In other words, there is a discrepancy between what is supposed to be happening (expectation) and what is really happening (reality).

Information about discrepancies between expectations and actual performance engenders problem solving, so that discrepancies can be resolved, thereby making HRD work and eventually pay off. To return to the previous example, once the discrepancy (participants are not trying out the consensus procedure) has been identified, problem solving can begin. Why aren't participants trying it out? Perhaps the directions were not clear; perhaps the composition of the group is such that an authority figure (someone's boss, say) is hampering participation; or perhaps the participants did not learn how to use the procedure in the earlier part of the training. In any case, the trainers will isolate one or more possible reasons for the discrepancy, then decide what to do about it. They might, for example, decide to intervene and repeat the directions, or they might redesign the exercise to simplify it.

The Discrepancy Model posits two alternative routes to removing a discrepancy. An effort may be made to resolve the discrepancy by controlling what is happening (reality) so that the expected performance can be achieved. In the case of our earlier example, this could mean repeating the directions. Other control options could, of course, be tried. The trainers might reconstitute the groups, repeat the training meant to teach them how to use the consensus process, and so forth. These efforts to control performance could be tried with the current group of participants, or the trainers might wait for the next workshop to try out their remedy. In either case, the effort to resolve the discrepancy would be through control.

Another approach to resolving discrepancies exists, however. Sometimes efforts to control might not be feasible or they might be found to be ineffective. Again, it might be decided that the discrepancy is not important and can be ignored. In these instances, the approach to resolving the discrepancy is not through control but through redesign. That is, the expectation itself is modified so that what actually happens is acceptable. In other words, the design is changed to reflect reality; the trainers' "expectation" now equals the actual results.

Stage III evaluation repeatedly cycles through the problem-solving and decision-making process of diagnosis and control or redesign. Typically, HRD programs encounter many discrepancies between what is supposed to be happening and what is really happening. As these problems are noticed and considered, the program is modified to make it more effective. Sometimes, modifications will consist of implementing different or additional controls (simpler instructions, repeated learning activities, more frequent reviews, smaller task divisions, better resources, and so forth). In other instances, the modifications will be to the design itself and will change the expectations for performance of participants. Trainers might try out simplified instructions, yet still notice discrepancies; the next effort might be to reconstitute groups and then to assess the difference that this modification seems to make. In any case, the Stage III process is one of observing and assessing the program's progress, noticing discrepancies, making revisions, and trying it out again, then reobserving and reassessing to see if progress is now acceptable. This is the process that makes training work and move toward payoff.

Finally, this overview of Stage III evaluation would not be complete without repeating the major premise discussed earlier in this book that such evaluation is vital to the improvement of programs. Program plans are inherently flawed because we lack complete knowledge about the process of training and learning. And the real world we live in has a nasty way of fouling things up. Even the best-laid plans of mice and trainers go awry. Thus, Stage III evaluation is necessary. Sometimes, HRD leaders will want to stick to their designs, attempting control efforts in the face of the inevitable discrepancies that occur. Sometimes, however, they will decide that the world has taught them a lesson—that their design was in some way flawed and should be revised. But isn't that how we all learn?

Purposes Served by Stage III Evaluation

As is apparent from the preceding discussion, the overarching purpose of Stage III evaluation is to improve HRD. But this larger purpose is served in several ways by Stage III, and each of these ways has additional benefits.

Control. Human resource development programs, like all organized endeavors, require management. The more complex the program and the greater the number of people involved, then the more management control it will require. In one respect, Stage III evaluation is a matter of establishing a management information system for controlling the program and ensuring that it meets the schedule, cost, and performance specifications set forth in the program design. Thus, to carry out this management control purpose, the training design must be reviewed, and several key monitoring points and associated schedule, cost, or performance objectives must be specified.

It might be decided, for example, to administer a quiz to participants at a certain point in the program so that weak performance can be remediated. Alternatively, a date and time to check whether program enrollments are on schedule could be established, or a cost objective that identifies the amount of budget that should remain as of the midpoint of the program could be set. Data about actual progress would be collected at these points (a quiz would be administered, for example, or the actual number of enrollees counted) to determine if discrepancies exist. Typically, Stage III evaluation of this "control" type reaps two direct benefits. First, the establishment of the control plan itself helps communicate and clarify important objectives to HRD staff, and thus the probability that objectives will be achieved is enhanced. Second, carrying out the evaluation of these key schedule, cost, and performance objectives helps to identify discrepancies so that they can be resolved.

Documentation. Stage III evaluation serves the relatively simple, but very important purpose of documenting what really happens in an HRD program. Having a concise and accurate record of what actually takes place in HRD is important for a number of reasons. This record serves a management function in helping to track and chart the program's progress, so that budgets and other management records can be maintained and interpreted. When the inevitable problems crop up, a record of what has taken place in the program up to the point where the problem occurred is a great aid to problem solving and troubleshooting. Further, documentation of training programs is useful for accounting purposes and can also be helpful in training additional HRD staff. Finally, and most basic: When HRD pays off, as we hope it will, it is nice to know what was done so that it can be done again!

Research and Development. As was noted in the beginning of this chapter, the overarching purpose of Stage III evaluation is to improve HRD. In addition, it was proposed at the start of this book that all training be considered as developmental—that virtually any form of training can be improved. Human resource development programs afford a readily available "laboratory" in which action research and development efforts can be implemented. Consider a large supervisory training program, for example, that brings bosses and subordinates together for some joint learning activities. It might be decided to try out, with a subset of these activities, a procedure in which employees are trained to provide some training to their bosses. Particular evaluation attention, in a sort of "mini-research" style, might be focused on this approach to assess how well it works and whether it is more effective than the method already being used elsewhere in the training program. Such evaluation can discover important new approaches and techniques for HRD. These discoveries may reap benefits for other HRD programs in the organization and perhaps even for professional organizations.

Staff Development. Stage III evaluation usually necessitates broad involvement of HRD staff in the evaluation process. Typical Stage III evaluations might, for example, have trainers observe each other making presentations or leading groups, ask trainers to keep logs of problems and their perceptions of training's progress, or engage HRD staff in regular debriefing sessions to identify, discuss, and document the issues, problems, and strengths of an ongoing training program. These and other Stage III information collection approaches are important in that they yield useful evaluation data for decision making. But they also produce very worthwhile staff development and performance benefits. The HRD program benefits in an immediate way from increased staff participation in and awareness of program activities. But most importantly, involvement in Stage III evaluation promotes staff learning and development. Staff members learn about their own effectiveness and gain immediate insight into what works and what does not. Further, when Stage III evaluation is made a priority, this fosters a sense of accountability and engenders an atmosphere of inquiry and experimentation and encourages the use of feedback for improvement. These are worthwhile benefits, and alone they would justify significant investment in Stage III evaluation.

Levels of Stage III Effort

As in the previous stages of evaluation, there are varying degrees of effort that might be invested in Stage III evaluation. On the one hand, evaluation of implementation could be relatively simple and informal, assessing only a few dimensions of the program's installation. On the other hand, an extensive and formal evaluation during the installation phase might be necessary. The level of effort called for is dependent on the particular information needs and development requirements existing in a given HRD program. Following are several Stage III scenarios, each representing a different level of evaluation effort and each responsive to differing evaluation purposes and training program development needs. Each scenario is accompanied by a brief discussion that highlights its key elements.

Scenario 1: Pat Smith is conducting a three-hour workshop for supervisors to teach them how to implement the company's revised performance appraisal system. The workshop has been conducted many times, is highly developed, and is known to work well when properly implemented. Pat's Stage III evaluation uses several brief and simple procedures. She uses a checklist to go over all arrangements, as well as all facility, materials, and equipment needs, to see whether her department has completed the necessary preparatory steps. She has trainees sign in for the workshop, indicating their position and department or unit affiliation. This list is then compared to the intended trainee list to determine whether the right people are attending the session, and it also facilitates later follow-up evaluation. Pat keeps notes throughout the session, jotting down any redesign ideas, problems, or special circumstances that occur during the session. Lastly, trainees complete a brief feedback instrument that allows them to express their opinions about the quality of the session, the trainer, and the content; the form also asks for other ideas and reactions that trainees might wish to express and requests each respondent to complete a three-item rating scale assessing the general quality of the session (this last three-item scale is included for every session that Pat's department offers in the company).

Discussion of Scenario 1: The primary feature of the evaluation in this scenario is its simplicity. The session is not new, is well developed, and is not undergoing any major revision. The major purposes of the Stage III evaluation here are twofold: The first purpose is control, helping to assure that the session will be carried out according to its already established specifications. The checklist, the participant sign-in sheet, and the three-item rating scale on the feedback form are the evaluation procedures that serve this purpose. The second purpose is to capture any ideas for revision that may crop up; the notes that Pat takes, along with the trainee feedback forms, serve this purpose. Other less prominent purposes are also served. To foster a sense of accountability and a commitment to quality, the "customers" (the trainees) are encouraged to provide their opinions about the "service"—the training—they received, and thus the feedback form allows them to express any opinions they wish. In addition, the sign-in sheet and completed preparations checklist serve as a source of documentation for the session. Overall, the evaluation in this scenario is minimal, but it meets the very limited needs of this oft-repeated, brief, and well-developed form of training.

Scenario 2: The Wilberforce Company has spent the last few years developing an intensive three-day workshop for sales personnel to teach them how to sell the company's major new product line. The session has been thoroughly developed through extensive experimentation and pilot and field testing; an extensive set of materials and visual aids has been produced, and regional trainers have been trained to deliver the session to company branches throughout the world. Relatively elaborate Stage III evaluation procedures and instruments have also been produced for use in each regional session; further, evaluation data from each regional session will be duplicated and forwarded to the company's central HRD office. The Stage III evaluation procedures consist of (1) records of preparation expenses and attendees at each session; (2) trainee feedback forms that assess the ratings of key training activities (these are to be completed at the end of each of the three days); (3) a "midterm" quiz administered to trainees after the end of the second day of training (quiz data are aggregated to calculate a group score, and individual scores are given back to trainees so that they can work to remediate weaknesses before the end of the session); and (4) a feedback form several pages in length to be completed by the head trainer after the session, reporting documentation of the session and collecting ideas for revising the session's management and delivery system.

Discussion of Scenario 2: This scenario includes quite elaborate and systematic Stage III evaluation. Here, the major purpose is quality control to help assure that the company's large investment in this carefully designed session is protected.

The evaluation will provide feedback to the regional trainers to help them keep the session on track and data to the central training office to inform them about the consistency of the training's installation among the many branches. Branches experiencing significant problems or exhibiting sub par performance will be identified so that the central office may intervene. The further purpose of capitalizing on the experience of the regional trainers to aid in revision of the management and delivery system for this major training effort is served by the trainers' completion of postsession reports.

Scenario 3: In response to a persistent and growing need to reduce accidents, the Upschwartz Company is developing an experimental program that will teach supervisors to measure and chart safety-related behaviors among their employees and to provide positive reinforcement for employee adherence to the admittedly bothersome safety procedures. The session is new (materials are still in draft form) and is being tried out for the first time in a volunteer division. Stage III evaluation procedures include the following: First, trainees will meet in a group session at the end of the session and respond, in a discussion/ interview, to a series of questions about their opinions and reactions to the program. Second, two observers will monitor the program and keep extensive notes. One of the two will keep a log of activities, noting especially departures from and discrepancies with the original training plan; the other observer will record interactions with trainees and pay special attention to trainee reactions, difficulties, and so forth. Third, trainees will complete a detailed end-of-session rating form; data from this form will be quickly aggregated during a break and then used to stimulate and focus the discussion in the postsession group meeting.

Discussion of Scenario 3: As in the previous scenario, evaluation here is relatively elaborate and systematic. In this scenario, however, the session is in a very early developmental phase. Thus, the Stage III evaluation is aimed at gathering a maximum amount of detailed information to help in revision. The focus is partly on identifying discrepancies from the program plan; but, unlike the previous control-oriented scenario, the purpose here is to capitalize on discrepancies, using them as "opportunities" to identify and investigate needs for revision. In this scenario, the program's embryonic status is an open and obvious issue; departures from the design are fully expected and even desired, so that the experience of trying out the program can yield maximum learning benefit to the HRD staff.

Scenario 4: The Able Consulting Company has for several years been delivering a program to area industries on conflict management for first-line supervisors. Many trainers for the firm have commented on a phenomenon that occurs when groups are formed so as to be about evenly constituted by males and females. When the groups are equally balanced as to sex, the ability to recognize emerging conflicts is enhanced, and thus the remainder of the program runs more smoothly and mastery of final skill objectives is more widespread. The consulting firm's management is interested in proving the validity of this hunch so that if it is true and greater levels of mastery could be promised to clients, it might attempt to build male-female balance into the training selection and schedule portions of contracts with clients. And, of course, the program would be- · come more effective. Thus, the firm begins an experiment whereby, on a random basis, some programs are selected to intentionally achieve a balance between the sexes in the early program activity. Careful data are then collected (1) by an observing (not a participating) trainer to ensure that the activity is conducted exactly according to plan with no difference except in the balance of males and females, (2) through a performance observation at the end of the activity to assess trainees' ability to identify emerging conflict, and (3) by an end-of-session performance test (already a part of the Stage IV evaluation) to determine overall mastery of the program's learning goals. These data are collected in both the randomly selected "experimental" programs and the other programs being conducted as originally planned (with groups not evenly divided between males and females in the early activity).

Discussion of Scenario 4: The purpose of this Stage III evaluation is to test, in a formal and conclusive way, a pending revision to the program. The previously discovered hunch warranted more elaborate inquiry, and thus a minor research study was planned to yield some carefully controlled comparative data on which the consulting firm could base both a broad-scale revision to the training and further evaluation to assess the results of that revision. Stage III evaluation of the level of effort depicted in this scenario is aimed at investigating and confirming cause-effect relationships between specific HRD activities and their intended objectives so that the larger HRD program can be refined. Only relatively well-developed and "mature" programs are likely to benefit from Stage III evaluation of this type.

The four scenarios discussed in the previous paragraphs represent the varying levels of effort for Stage III evaluation, along with a few of its many possible purposes and uses. There are two points to be made here. First, Stage III evaluation can be implemented at varying levels of effort and to meet a variety of training development needs. Second, the particular means and ends of Stage III evaluation that might be pursued are entirely dependent on the needs and conditions (HRD development requirements, time demands, availability of resources, and so forth) present in any given instance. For example, I was once in charge of a large federal training project that incorporated a three-day regional workshop. The Stage III evaluation conducted the first time that the workshop was delivered was very different from the Stage III evaluation done on that same workshop several years later, after many, many sessions had been conducted. In the very early days, the prime concern was with participant reactions: Did they like it? Was it making sense? Would they come back from the first break? Evaluation in these early days was very intensive and focused mostly on logistic and participant reaction concerns. After data from such evaluation were used to fine tune the workshop, Stage III evaluation grew along with the workshop. In the later days, Stage III evaluation came to focus on research and development interests, on quality control, and on seeing whether occasional revisions were paying off in increased participant learning or efficiency of delivery. The point in this example is that Stage III evaluation should be responsive to the developmental needs of the HRD program; it should be planned to nurture the growth of the HRD design and process.

In any case, the overall aim of Stage III evaluation is to look at the actual installation and operation of an HRD program to determine whether it is heading in the right direction with the ultimate aim, of course, of making it head toward payoff with increasing certainty and effectiveness.

Deciding What to Evaluate

The first step in determining what aspects of HRD programs should be evaluated for any, or all, stages of evaluation is to establish and clarify the purpose for evaluation: What needs to be known? What needs to be decided? Why? Without a specific and clear understanding of purpose, evaluation cannot, and should not, be pursued. Stage III evaluation is no exception to this rule. But given an understanding of the general purpose for Stage III evaluation—to observe the operation of HRD to see how it is going—some general and useful guidelines for identifying critical implementation concerns can be identified.

Evaluation resources are, of course, limited, and thus it makes little sense to expend these resources on inquiries that are unlikely to yield worthwhile returns. Further, in any HRD program, there are varying degrees of certainty about different elements of the program design. A trainer might be quite certain, for example, that a particular exercise in a program is likely to proceed smoothly but feel very apprehensive about some other activity. In such an instance, assuming the trainer's perceptions are accurate, it makes sense to invest the limited Stage III evaluation resources in monitoring or assessing that part of the program where apprehension is greatest and/or certainty the lowest. Following are some systematic guidelines for determining where in the operation of a program to make observations and measurements to get the maximum yield from Stage III efforts. These guidelines will help identify those few "sore thumbs" in the program design where evaluation is most needed.

1. Areas that are functionally critical. The HRD design should be analyzed to identify the few operations that are critical points—the areas where, if a breakdown occurs, it is most likely to result in major damage to the program. For example, an activity might be meant to produce skills (outputs) that will be needed (inputs) in a significant number of other program functions. This sort of relationship is graphically depicted in Figure 4. Here, we see that activity 1.0 produces a result (an

Figure 4. A Critical Program Function.

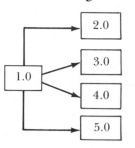

output) that serves as an input to several subsequent activities. Managers in a training workshop on performance appraisal skills, for example, might be expected to learn (in 1.0) the skill of identifying key employee performance deficiencies, which they will then learn to use for coaching (in 2.0), for annual appraisals (in 3.0), for development planning (in 4.0), and for succession planning (in 5.0). According to the analysis of the training design in this example, if something goes wrong in activity 1.0, four subsequent training activities are going to suffer. If, for example, the learning exercise planned for component 1.0 had confusing instructions, did not engage the trainees, or in some other way failed to operate as it was designed, the trainees would not "exit" the component with the ability to identify employee performance deficiencies. Thus, an obvious point for doing some Stage III evaluation is activity 1.0. The purposes would be to see if the activity is working as planned and, if not, to determine how it could be controlled and made to work, or to see how the subsequent activities might be redesigned so that they will work despite the failure of activity 1.0.

     2. *Areas of theoretical shakiness or concern.* Sometimes a training design contains activities that represent new, untried, or

unproven methods for HRD. These are activities that, from the point of view of learning theory or current knowledge of instructional design, have the shakiest foundations. The training design should be reviewed to decide whether it contains such theoretically questionable elements. Evaluation of these areas can then be considered. This guideline does not require a profound or elegant theory of learning as its basis. This guideline directs attention to any part of the design where one's knowledge of how HRD works leads to a concern that, in a particular instance in a given design, something might not work. A plan that called for hourly production workers to engage in a discussion of quality-control problems might prompt such a concern. In this example, there might be concern that the workers will not be used to such group approaches to HRD, will have difficulty verbalizing their thoughts, or will think that they cannot learn from each other. In other words, knowledge about learning and instruction indicates that this particular activity might have a serious design flaw and that the activity thus warrants observation during the implementation stage.

   3. Areas of control or management concern. Experience is a great teacher. Any HRD practitioner with some experience has learned that certain kinds of HRD programs run smoothly without any problems, that many activities pose only minor problems, and that some are consistently difficult to handle and fraught with problems. Such activities will sometimes have been weeded out of the program plan by Stage II evaluation. But usually any design will contain elements or activities that are tough to control or manage. For example, a plan that calls for participants to complete a homework task is supposed to work to reduce the variance in incoming participants' entering knowledge levels. Experience, however, says that this technique often introduces an unwanted variance into the program; some participants will do the assignment carefully, many will give it a cursory effort, some will not do it at all, one or two will forget to bring it with them, and so forth. If the subsequent HRD activity relies heavily on successful completion of that homework task, a red flag is raised for me. Getting all participants to actually complete such an assignment, or conducting the subsequent activity that relies on that assignment is very likely not to work at all or at least will present some problems. Here is a part of the design warranting a look during implementation. Thus, the control/management guideline suggests that an HRD design be reviewed to identify areas where experience indicates the likelihood of problems and failures; these areas then become prime candidates for Stage III evaluation attention.

4. *Areas of staff dissent, conflict, or uncertainty.* It is sometimes the case when more than one person is involved in the creation of designs that there are disagreements, value conflicts, or other uncertainties among the several parties over just how the HRD program ought to be conducted. When such disagreement is strong, it is often desirable to focus some evaluation attention on the disputed activity or element. Let us say, for example, that one faction has argued strongly that a self-instructional module be incorporated into a program in order to allow low-performing trainees to remediate their deficiencies prior to advancing in the program. Another faction argues just as vigorously that trainees will progress satisfactorily and that there is no need to waste time and effort on a remediation module. Assuming further that those opposed to the module win out over those who favor it, it would be a good idea to do some Stage III evaluation at the disputed point in the program to assess actual trainee progress. Evaluation at this point will help in making a decision about revising the design (should a module be developed?). And simply planning to carry out evaluation at this point in the program will help to appease the parties who "lost" the argument, thus preserving harmonious working relationships.

5. *Areas of particular research and development interest.* After an HRD design has been reviewed in light of the preceding guidelines, it is sometimes advisable to look over the design to see if there are any areas that require evaluation during implementation to further some research and development interest of the organization. When such opportunities of sufficient importance exist and there are adequate evaluation resources to indulge such interests, this kind of evaluation should be considered.

6. Special record-keeping and documentation concerns. Carrying out this guideline, though it is presented last on the list, often consumes a major portion of the Stage III evaluation resources. In almost any HRD program, there are particular documentation and record-keeping needs mandated by HRD department guidelines or by external evaluation requirements. It may be, for example, that evaluation of some HRD department operations in light of affirmative action and equal opportunity requirements is necessary. Thus, for any given program, it might be necessary to keep track of just who actually attends and completes a program, so that participation rates can eventually be compared against company goals and policies. In a federal training program that I once directed, the funding agency made it a requirement to monitor and document the nature and extent of trainee participation in the training design process. When Stage III evaluation concerns are mandated, the first order of business is typically to review the program design and identify these areas where evaluation to monitor, document, or keep records will be required.

The guidelines above are listed and discussed separately, because each should be considered in the preparation of a plan for Stage III evaluation. In practice, however, it is more likely that any given Stage III evaluation data collection procedure would respond to several of these guidelines at once. In other words, any particular activity or element in a design might be evaluated during implementation for a variety of reasons. The characteristics of persons actually attending a development program might be assessed, for example, because record-keeping requirements demand it (guideline 6); the right set of persons must attend the program or there will be severe consequences in later development activities (guideline 1); and a new and untried participant selection process is being used and there are fears that it might not work (guideline 3). All these concerns dictated some Stage III evaluation, and so it was decided to collect detailed preregistration data and compare the characteristics of actual registrants against a checklist of intended registrant characteristics.

Useful Stage III Techniques

This section describes, in alphabetical order, some espe-cially useful procedures for implementing Stage III evaluation. Each procedure is accompanied by one or more references to sources that will offer readers more information about it. While this listing is not exhaustive, I hope the alternatives it describes may suit readers' varied needs.

Interviewing. Interviewing can range from highly struc-tured procedures to quite "loose" and open-ended ones. At the highly structured end of the continuum, an interview is more like an orally administered survey questionnaire. More loosely structured interviews initiate conversation with several "probe" questions to stimulate thought and responses. Regardless of their degree of structure, interviews are an excellent means of gathering trainee reactions and opinions about the operation and design of training programs. Interviews are especially use-ful because they permit interpretation of gestures, expressions, and so forth, and they allow an interviewer to follow up and gain more detailed explanations of responses. Interviews can be conducted with single individuals or with groups of trainees (Henerson, Morris, and Fitz-Gibbon, 1978; Payne, 1951).

Key Participant Method. In this method, specially se-lected respondents provide information on the quality or other aspects of the HRD program. Key participants are usually chosen because of their expertise or special roles and are usually identi-fied either because of their formal roles or because they are identified as leaders by other participants. While their own be-liefs may contaminate the information they provide, they pro-vide helpful perspectives for judging a training effort. Getting information from just a few especially well-informed or astute respondents can be a very economical shortcut ("Key Partici-pant Method," 1980; Houston and Sudman, 1975).

Observations and Observer Ratings. The most widely used judgmental measure of performance is observer ratings. In this method, one person (perhaps a trainer) observes another and records verbal and/or nonverbal behaviors. Observations are especially useful in determining how participants react to and perform in training situations. Typically, a paper-and-pencil observational form is used, but audiotapes or videotapes have proven quite helpful in recording precise quantitative data—for example, the amount and frequency of speech by various group participants. A good procedure is to use a form that describes in considerable detail the behaviors to be observed so that the observer can check each behavior whenever it occurs. This form of scoring requires a minimum of effort on the part of the observer and can usually be developed so as to require the observer to make relatively few inferences.

In some cases, the observer is also asked to evaluate the behaviors on a rating scale. This requires more work and a higher level of inference on the part of the observer. The observer must not only record the behaviors but also evaluate them, and this is much more difficult to do objectively (Simon and Boyer, 1974; Weick, 1968).

Participant Follow-Up. Another common data collection method is the participant follow-up at a predetermined time after the program is completed. The follow-up evaluation almost always comes after an end-of-the-program evaluation. The follow-up normally involves the use of a feedback questionnaire, although variations include interviews and observations. Follow-up surveys can gather opinions about designs (Stage II), HRD operation (Stage III), or application and transfer of learning in the workplace (Stage V). Sometimes, the perspective that time can bring will yield more accurate and thoughtful data (Babbie, 1973; Phillips, 1983).

Trainee Rating and Reaction Forms. Perhaps the most popular evaluation method, trainee rating and reaction forms ask the trainees how they liked the training. Such forms may be administered at key points during or after the training. Typically, such forms ask for reactions about the quality of the trainers, design of the session, logistics and arrangements, and so forth. While this method has potential for gathering useful re-actions and is quite economical, its familiarity can prove a prob-lem; participants often give very glib and superficial attention to such forms or tend to be overly complimentary, not expressing reactions that they feel might upset the trainer or training staff. And when such forms are made long and detailed enough to get thorough data, they are not completed by respondents.

Nonetheless, trainee reactions are important. If trainees do not like a training program, chances are there is a problem that needs fixing. This method is especially good for discover-ing or confirming major problems (Babbie, 1973; Taylor, 1968).

Transactional Analysis. Transactional analysis could be a handy Stage III training technique, particularly in programs that involve some measure of attitudinal change. Transactional analy-sis focuses on the person and how he or she responds to stimuli from another person. Each exchange between two persons is called a transaction. Transactions occur whenever people com-municate, whether with words, tone of voice, or gestures.

A transaction consists of a stimulus from a given ego state (parent, child, adult) in one person and a response from the same or a different ego state in another. Through transactional analysis one becomes aware of which ego state the stimulus is coming from and to which ego state it is addressed. Transac-tional analysis involves the observation and recording of verbal behaviors by a trained observer and can thus be quite expensive. But when detailed transactional information is needed, this method works well (Berne, 1964; Bradford and Guberman, 1978).

5

Measuring How Well Learning Objectives Are Achieved

To produce change in skills, knowledge, or attitudes of participants is the immediate objective of HRD. The primary purpose of Stage IV evaluation is to determine the extent to which these changes have, in fact, occurred. A common definition of evaluation, particularly among educators, is that it consists of defining objectives, specifying those objectives measurably, and then assessing the extent to which learners have mastered those objectives. With a few minor additions and caveats, this definition accurately captures the spirit of Stage IV evaluation.

Any HRD program, whether a brief workshop or an extended professional development project, intends to leave participants with some new or expanded skills, knowledge, or attitudes. When the program is over, the measure of whether it has "worked" or not is the extent to which these intended skill, knowledge, or attitude changes have, in fact, been achieved. Tests given at the beginnings and ends of sessions (pretests and posttests) and participant self-rating scales are all common Stage IV procedures. Data resulting from these typical measures are most commonly used to make judgments about the impact of the HRD program but might additionally be used to give participants feedback, to certify their achievement, to modify the HRD program, and so forth. But regardless of whether such data measure skills, knowledge, or attitudes and regardless of how such data are to be used, the defining characteristic of Stage IV is that it evaluates the immediate results of HRD programs.

This chapter will further discuss the particular purposes and intents of Stage IV evaluation, present and discuss several uses for Stage IV evaluation data, suggest some guidelines and principles for deciding what levels of Stage IV evaluation may be appropriate, and then will close with an annotated listing of common and recommended procedures for carrying out Stage IV evaluation.

Purposes and Uses

The primary function of Stage IV evaluation is to assess the changes in skills, knowledge, or attitudes that HRD has, or has not, accomplished. The guiding question of this stage is, "Did the program accomplish its immediate outcomes?" From a program evaluation perspective, the general purpose served by Stage IV is to determine the extent to which HRD has worked to accomplish its intended outcomes so that HRD leaders can decide whether to do more, to recycle back to implementation or design questions, or to search for evidence that program-acquired skills, knowledge, and attitudes are actually being used or displayed on the job. If, for example, Stage IV evaluation data revealed that a skill-training session had failed to give trainees any significant new skills, it would not make sense to then follow up to see whether the (not learned) skills were being used. Further, in this example, a decision would have to be made as to whether the failure resulted from a design or an implementation error. It may be that the design was sound and could have imparted the skill objectives but that some lapse in implementation caused a failure. Or it is possible that implementation was sound but that the design itself was weak. Of course, the design error should have been remedied as a result of Stage II evaluation, and the implementation problems should have been fixed with careful Stage III evaluation, thus preventing a Stage IV failure from occurring at all. But, in the real world, such failures do happen, and they underscore the need for thoughtful Stage IV evaluation.

In most cases, however, Stage IV evaluation does not reveal a total breakdown in an HRD effort. Rather, the program is typically found to have accomplished some learning outcomes very well, some others not so well, and perhaps a few not at all. And this situation is further complicated when it is discovered, as it usually is, that trainees themselves vary in their individual achievement, so that a few learn quite well what the majority learn only marginally, and so forth. In any case, it is up to Stage IV evaluation to identify and discriminate among these varied accomplishments of HRD's objectives and to make good use of these results for the further development and operation of HRD. At this point, however, let us consider several more specific uses of and purposes for Stage IV evaluation:

1. *Accountability: gathering evidence that HRD has effects.* To demonstrate the efficacy of their programs, as well as to make revisions to them, HRD practitioners need to know what works and what does not. If, for example, a training program has promised to teach salespersons how to operate a new cash register, trainers will need to provide evidence to superiors within the HRD department and in the larger organization that the training program in fact imparted that skill. Such evidence might be used to make claims about the entire training program, or it might be used to make claims for only certain elements of the program. It might be, for example, that a portion of the program worked but that a unit on handling typical cash register malfunctions did not achieve its objectives. Thus, retraining in that component is needed, as is revision of the component.

2. *Looking for unintended results.* Stage IV evaluation might also concern itself with changes in skills, knowledge, or attitudes that resulted from a program but were not intended objectives in the first place. It is somewhat arrogant to assume that all the effects of HRD will be known in advance and that any HRD instance will achieve its intended objectives and only those objectives. Experience in education has shown, for example, that very often programs achieve many results besides their

intended ones and that sometimes these unintended results are not wanted.

I recall, from my early training experiences in the military, a session I conducted to alert new enlistees to the several operating errors one could make in working on a crucial piece of submarine detection equipment. These errors, if made, would result in problems severe enough to delay a ship's departure from port, often for several days. The intent of the training, of course, was to prevent such errors from occurring. Evaluation of the training (not conducted until many months later, as it happened) showed that trainees learned quite well about these potential errors and then went ahead and made them whenever shore romances or other attractions indicated the desirability of a few more days in port!

Again, it may be the purpose of a supervisory training program to teach trainees how to document employee behavior for performance appraisal, but in fact trainees may learn how to collect evidence for building cases for dismissing employees whom they have prejudged to be low performers. A thorough Stage IV evaluation should therefore seek to uncover any unintended, but nonetheless important, results of the HRD. Participants may learn some additional skills, knowledge, or attitudes that are desirable and others that are undesirable. Knowing about these can help HRD leaders revise existing programs to nurture the achievement of desirable results and extinguish undesirable results. In addition, knowledge of these unintended results can be used to plan for more effective transfer of learning into on-the-job results.

3. Determining trainee mastery of learning outcomes. Simply knowing which trainees achieved which learning results is a major Stage IV purpose. Rarely will everyone learn everything, or no one learn anything. Differential achievement is the norm. To determine trainee achievement, tests or other assessment devices need to be administered at the conclusion of training. Results of the devices can then be analyzed to determine who has mastered what objectives. Knowledge of trainee achievement can then serve several uses:

First, it can provide feedback to trainees. Feedback is a

crucial element in all learning. The level of achievement of trainees will be enhanced by providing them with feedback about their achievement. When this is done at regular intervals during programs, the programs will operate more effectively. Feedback can and often should be provided to trainees at the conclusion of programs so that they will know with some certainty just what they have achieved as a result of the HRD effort. Such data may help them in applying their new skills or knowledge and in deciding whether to pursue further learning, and it may have additional positive psychological results as well. Finally, helping trainees determine just what they have achieved from programs is both a matter of courtesy and an ethical obligation of the HRD division.

Second, knowledge of trainee achievement can provide feedback to trainers: When, during HRD operations, trainers know who has (so far) learned what, they can use these data to provide better guidance to trainees as to how to remediate or enhance learning. They will also be better equipped to modify remaining elements of the program, for individuals or groups, so that achievement of terminal objectives will be enhanced. Finally, trainers, like trainees, simply need feedback to meet the basic "how am I doing" psychological needs all humans have.

Finally, knowledge of trainee achievement aids in the certification process. In many cases, and particularly in skill-training programs, there is a need to provide trainees and their bosses with information about the nature and extent of trainees' new skills. Sometimes this assessment may represent formal, documented certification. Hospital employees, for example, may not be permitted to perform a certain medical procedure unless they are certified for that procedure as a result of formal and documented training. Or certification may be less formal. For instance, it may be advisable to inform trainees' supervisors in a simple but systematic way as to what new skills their employees have mastered. This is not only a courtesy but can serve to ensure that the training-acquired skills will be used and supported on the job.

4. *Planning for transfer of training.* The immediate skill,

knowledge, and attitude objectives of HRD are, of course, not an end in themselves. The purpose of HRD is to yield value to the organization, and this almost always means that HRD-acquired learning should be transferred to the job place. Specific and precise knowledge as to just what these learning results are will greatly help planning for transfer. If it is known, for example, that salespeople learned how to operate a new cash register but just barely mastered the skill of troubleshooting operating problems, then their supervisors might be instructed to provide extra support on the job when troubles occur. It is difficult, if not impossible, to plan for effective transfer of HRD if the learning results are not known.

5. *Planning of Stage V (follow-up) evaluation.* Just as knowledge about the immediate results of HRD is helpful for planning activities that will facilitate transfer of learning, the same knowledge is helpful for planning and focusing later evaluation of the application of learning. In the previous example, a skill-training session might have just barely met expectations for the intended exit level on a particular skill variable (the ability to troubleshoot a cash register). In this example, it would be advisable for Stage V evaluation to focus some attention on the question of how well and to what extent application of this skill is in fact taking place on the job. When Stage IV evaluation identifies particular strengths or weaknesses in the achievement of immediate learning outcomes, whether intended or unintended ones, these strengths or weaknesses become logical contenders for special Stage V evaluation attention. Evaluation of HRD's immediate outcomes provides a planning base for focusing Stage V evaluation in that it identifies projected problems or areas for concern.

6. *Marketing HRD.* A question that virtually everyone looking at a new HRD program asks is "What does it teach?" Stage IV evaluation collects data that can be used to provide accurate and credible responses to questions of this sort. Stage IV data about the achievement of immediate learning outcomes can be used in the aggregate to demonstrate the past (and therefore the likely future) results of HRD. Or such data might be partitioned to show results for particular subgroups or trainees.

For example, trainers might collect data to show the differential achievement of new versus experienced supervisors in a performance appraisal training program; these data then might be useful in helping managers decide which supervisors to send to this training program. Evidence as to HRD's results, particularly evidence in the form of reliable and valid measures of achievement, is extremely valuable in helping groups and individuals decide whether HRD is right for them.

Levels of Stage IV Effort

As with evaluation in other stages, there are varying levels of effort that can be invested in Stage IV evaluation, and the particular level of effort called for depends on the context and needs present in any particular HRD program. Several scenarios are listed below, each representing a different degree of investment in Stage IV evaluation. Following the scenarios is a discussion of their differences and highlights, and a brief list of guidelines for deciding just how much effort is called for in a given situation is presented.

Scenario 1: Richcare Hospital is training its radiologists how to operate a new and advanced piece of x-ray equipment. The equipment manufacturer's research has shown that operators must follow six steps in a precise sequence in order to avoid equipment malfunction and possible injury to patients. At the end of the training, operators are administered a simulation test that requires them to use the actual equipment and to apply the six steps with each of fifteen typical x-ray patient conditions (a dummy patient is used). A certified operator observes their performance and rates each trainee by means of a validated checklist. Trainees must score a perfect 100 percent with each of the fifteen patient types before they have completed the training. Scores for each trainee are entered into his or her personnel file under the signature of the certified operator, and a certification memo is sent to the qualifying trainee's supervisor. The training department keeps records on the percentage of trainees achieving the criterion score, and the training is modified regularly in hopes of achieving a higher percentage of trainee qualification in increasingly shorter periods of training time. Records of the proportion of trainees who qualify, as well as of the decreases in training time, are maintained and reported to the HRD department's supervisor, the vice-president for personnel. The dollar savings earned by training time decreases are also calculated and reported.

Scenario 2: The Dewdrop Corporation conducts occasional communication skill sessions for managers. Each session is about an hour in length and focuses on a particular skill or concern, such as "writing a clear and concise memo." At the close of these sessions, trainees rate their own level of skill and knowledge on each of the key objectives of the session. Trainees keep a copy of their ratings, and an anonymous copy of each rating is retained by the trainers. Individual trainees are encouraged to improve skills that they may not have fully achieved in the session, and they are also encouraged to refer to their self-rating after the session as they try out skills on the job. The HRD department collates all trainee self-ratings to get an idea of how well each session worked; these data are combined with trainee suggestions about and reactions to the session to make appropriate revisions and also to schedule future sessions on skills that trainees, as a group, felt were only minimally enhanced.

Scenario 3: The Upfield Company conducts training to provide knowledge of assaying and fermentation techniques to all its chemical operators. Prior to the general training session, a pretest covering all objectives is administered. General orientation training is conducted while the tests are being scored. Upon receiving scores, trainees are individually scheduled for particular sessions on the basis of their knowledge levels. Each more specific session in the program is also preceded by a pretest and followed by a posttest. Trainees score their own posttests, and correct responses are reviewed and discussed to resolve any confusion or errors. Trainees then remove their names from the posttest, calculate their "shift" score (the difference between their pretest and posttest scores), and hand all this in to the trainer. Trainees are provided individual self-training remediation materials for any objectives about which they remain confused or uncertain. The training department uses the (anonymous) pretest and posttest data to determine the overall effectiveness of the programs. These effectiveness data are then used in accountability reports, as well as to make revisions to programs. Records over time of changes in group pretest and posttest score shifts enable the department to track the effectiveness of revisions made to the programs; thus, a pattern of increasing shift scores indicates increasingly successful training.

Scenario 4: The Goodstuff Grocery chain trains all its cash register and check-out clerks in how to operate their Schwartz High-Speed self-reading registers. The grocery company has identified, through careful follow-up studies, the criterion level of operating ability that a new clerk needs in order to be successful on the job. The Schwartz registers are used in each of the chain's 400 stores, and even minor variations in trainee achievement of learning objectives, given the huge volume of business that the chain does, result in significant operating and retraining losses. Currently, the Goodstuff chain uses a training program provided by ABC consultants. A competitor of ABC, the XYZ firm, wants to sell Goodstuff its program, claiming that it is much quicker and cheaper and that it will produce as high a proportion of trainees at criterion level. Goodstuff sets up an experiment in which new clerks are randomly assigned to the old ABC or new XYZ training; an independent testing consultant knowledgeable in experimental methods conducts the study. Trainee test scores at the end of training (the same test was used in each of the two sessions) are calculated and compared. If the XYZ scores are the same as, or better than, the ABC scores, Goodstuff might decide to switch to the new program.

It is immediately apparent that there are major differences in context, in evaluation needs, and, as a result, in evaluation procedures among the four scenarios. In the first scenario, safety and performance needs required that trainees achieve a specified level of skill before being certified. For these reasons, careful, formal, and precise Stage IV data were required. The hospital could not afford, either ethically or financially, to allow anyone but a fully skilled operator to complete the training. The costs of a wrong decision—to certify a person who was in fact not skilled—would be great, and thus a significant investment in precise and accurate Stage IV evaluation is required. The second scenario is quite different. In this instance, given the relative importance of the program topic, a less formal test of achievement was called for. It was still important—as it always is—to provide trainees with feedback about their learning, but the potential consequences of a wrong decision were much less significant. If a person exited the training in scenario 2 without having fully achieved its objectives, this would not be a calamity. Further training would be available, and it would be unlikely that a failure to fully master the training would result in great personal or corporate harm. However, had the situation involved an insurance or legal firm and had precision in writing memorandums been crucial, Stage IV evaluation similar to that used in scenario 1 might have been needed.

Scenario 3 represented a more sizable, but still very manageable, investment in Stage IV evaluation. In this instance, trainee learning data played a key role in the design and operation of the training itself. Again, it was not crucial that everyone leave the training with a perfect achievement level (though this would, of course, be desirable and ought to be an eventual goal of all training). Trainees who did not meet all learning objectives had other remediation routes available (the self-instructional materials), and the consequences to the individual and the company of less than perfect training were not great. Nonetheless, Stage IV evaluation data were necessary to put the training design into operation, to select trainees for sessions, and to provide individualized remediation materials. In addition, Stage IV data were used to revise and account for training programs in a systematic way.

Scenario 4 (the grocery chain) represented a large investment in Stage IV evaluation. (The reader will note that this experiment was also a Stage II evaluation, that is, it involved a systematic approach to selecting the best design, relying heavily on Stage IV data.) In this case, the learning data would be used to make a major, expensive, and consequential decision. Further, the demands of the decision were such that data relating to causality—which session resulted in the greater achievement?—were needed; the grocery company needed some assurance that differences in scores (if any) were due to the training program and not to some quirk of the study. This required a careful and relatively expensive experimental approach to the Stage IV evaluation. The example is careful to point out, however, that the grocery company already knew—from previous Stage V and VI evaluation—that training of the sort offered by both programs was worthwhile and necessary. Stage IV experiments to find out which program achieves greater learning gains are worth very little unless HRD is needed in the first place! We hardly need to know which program better achieves a worthless objective.

More scenarios might have been provided, for there are many levels of effort and many variations in specific purposes that can be pursued in evaluation. But the four scenarios presented above should make the point that variable needs do exist and that different approaches are called for. Just how much, and what sort of, Stage IV evaluation is advisable in any given situation depends, of course, on that particular situation. But the following general guidelines may be helpful:

1. Always provide trainees feedback about learning. In virtually any HRD setting, trainees deserve to know to what extent they have learned and benefited from their training. Feedback is essential to learning. Further, it is a courtesy and a sign of respect for trainees to let them know how they have performed. This will not only help them organize and absorb what they have learned but will help them discover what they have not learned and to what they might devote future learning attention. Moreover, demonstrating this kind of respect and concern will breed a more favorable attitude toward future HRD and its providers. At the minimum, Stage IV evaluation should provide trainees reasonably accurate feedback about their own learning.

2. Methods should be chosen in light of needs for accuracy and precision and the potential consequences of error. Not all training requires precise, objective testing. Typically, trainees are good judges of what they have, and have not, learned. Thus, simply affording them the opportunity to reflect on, identify, and assess that learning will usually suffice. However, when certification is an issue and significant consequences rest on this certification (a raise or promotion, for example), it would be unwise and unfair to ask trainees to measure their own learning. In these cases, an independent, more objective method is needed. When the potential for serious harm or damage exists if an inaccurate assessment of learning were to occur, then increasingly more attention to precision and accuracy must be paid. The general guideline here is: "Be as right as you need to be. Don't waste money being more right than you need to be. But, if you need to err, be more right, rather than less right, than is necessary."

3. Plan to use learning data in making training revision decisions. The best reasons to revise training are based on whether it works or not. It is important to plan to collect, and then to use, data about whether trainees learn what they were supposed to learn. While Stage III data about how well training appears to be going are helpful and should be used for revision, the most convincing and defensible data to use in deciding to make, or not make, changes in training involve whether it works to accomplish trainee learning. For example, it may appear that trainees are confused and anxious in a session. To decide to change the training to remove this condition without any indication of whether worthwhile learning has occurred would be premature and inadvisable. It would be better to put some Stage IV data into the equation and then proceed with revision decisions. If the confusion and anxiety were real and did in fact impede learning, then it would, of course, be advisable to reduce them; but if worthwhile learning occurred and other data (trainee comments, for example) indicated that the apparent confusion and anxiety were really just signs of intense learning activity, then perhaps no revisions are needed.

4. Protect the individual's rights to privacy and confidentiality. Stage IV data can be very sensitive, for they often reflect on the relative competence and ability of individuals. In cases of certification, of course, it is necessary to inform others—supervisors, for example—whether trainees have achieved mastery. It would be inappropriate, however, for a supervisor to inspect training records to see which supervisees performed better than others in a recent HRD session and then base merit pay recommendations on such information. HRD practitioners who collect test data about individuals have a responsibility, ethical and often legal, to see that such data are used and safeguarded with the utmost concern for rights of privacy and confidentiality.

5. *Overcome traditional objections to testing with careful attention to testing design and professional responsibility.* It often happens that HRD leaders feel it is all right to test the achievement of some kinds of trainees, but not of others. They may feel, for example, that hourly employees in a machine operation skill workshop should be tested but that managers in a supervisory skills workshop should not be. For some reason, they think that managers would be demeaned, or otherwise offended, if they were asked to take a test. I would like to suggest that such testing "taboos" are hogwash! Yes, such misguided perceptions exist, but they should not dictate HRD behavior. In my mind, it is equally demeaning and offensive to require that managers spend considerable time in a workshop but then allow neither them nor the trainers to know whether the training worked. The guideline to follow is this: If the content the training imparts is important, then it is also important to know who has learned it. When testing is appropriately designed and administered and trainees are protected from embarrassment or other demeaning consequences of scoring or reporting, testing can and should be used as a Stage IV device—with *any* trainees. I fear that the testing taboo is often appealed to when HRD leaders would be hard pressed to specify just what it was people were supposed to learn from that supervisory skills workshop. If trainees understand that what they are learning is important and can be defined and measured, if they are assured that HRD leaders care whether they learn it or not and will use testing results to make training more effective, and if they are assured that their rights will be respected and that they will be given accurate feedback about their achievement, testing can and will be accepted.

6. *Clarify the kind of learning objective intended and*

measure it accordingly. There are three major learning objective categories: skills, knowledge, and attitudes. Further distinctions can be made among these. In this book, the following definitions of skill, knowledge, and attitude are used:

A skill may be defined as the ability to carry out some applied task. Examples of some typical skills commonly seen in training programs are "the ability to repair a washing machine control unit," "the ability to analyze a memorandum and determine its required reading level," or "the ability to use the company's performance appraisal system guidelines." The common and defining element in each of these examples is that trainees are expected to be able to do something as a result of training. If HRD is successful, then trainees should be able to demonstrate their ability to correctly carry out a given behavioral task at some defined level of competence.

Knowledge is defined as cognitive mastery of some principles, guidelines, rules, or other content. Knowledge differs from skill in that it is "invisible" until drawn out or applied in particular circumstances, and it does not include a behavioral component (though a test of knowledge always requires some sort of behavioral demonstration). Knowledge objectives require trainees to have internalized and retained in their minds some particular content so that they can recall it when needed and apply or otherwise use it appropriately. A training program might, for example, intend for trainees to learn safety rules or legal guidelines pertaining to their jobs. Knowledge objectives require further specification as to the level of learning intended —for instance, whether trainees should be able to merely recall the particular knowledge gained, be able to recite it when asked, or be able to use and apply it.

Attitudes are defined as values and beliefs held by persons. Attitudes are important to training in that they affect the probability of specific behavior. Attitudes are thus a predisposition to behave in a certain way. A positive attitude toward the importance of punctuality, for example, means that a person is likely to arrive on time. A positive attitude toward safety and the importance of protecting against risks to persons and property is likely to predispose a person to demonstrate proper safety behaviors. It is the behavioral dimension of attitudes that makes them important to trainers, for attitudes are closely related to performance. Attitudes have a knowledge dimension also, as it is unlikely that a person will have a positive attitude toward customer relations, for example, if that person is unaware of the guidelines and principles that impact on customer relations.

To a large extent, the distinctions among skills, knowledge, and attitudes are arbitrary and artificial. The ultimate goal of HRD is usually performance, and performance is the result of a person's knowledge, skills, and attitudes combined. Thus any HRD program is likely to include all three elements, and trainers will be continually involved in assessing, trying to change, and following up the impacts of the three elements. Nonetheless, it is useful for HRD practitioners to be able to identify the skill, knowledge, and attitude components of a given performance situation, for it is often the case that not all three elements are deficient and that only one may require a learning intervention. Further, HRD is often designed to impact only on a particular kind of knowledge. Thus, that knowledge element must be carefully defined and distinguished from the related skills, attitudes, and other knowledge elements that may be interwoven with the targeted objective.

Bloom's *Taxonomy of Educational Objectives* (1956) remains a useful guide to the various sorts of learning outcomes; Gagne and Briggs (1979) and Reigeluth (1983) are other sources especially helpful when preparing Stage IV (immediate outcomes) measures. With knowledge objectives, for example, one might identify a certain recall level of learning as desirable; thus, given a certain situation, trainees would be able to recall specific kinds of knowledge. Or an application level of knowledge might be desired, wherein trainees would be able to apply certain guidelines, principles, and so on. In any case, the important rule of Stage IV evaluation is to construct a measure appropriate to the particular level of learning objective being addressed. It would be inappropriate, for example, to use a recall test when application levels of knowledge were intended.

7. *When measuring skills, simulate on-job conditions as closely as possible.* In one of the HRD scenarios presented earlier, x-ray technicians were being trained to operate a new piece of equipment. A test of their skills was made using the actual equipment and a simulated patient. This example demonstrates adherence to guideline 7. It would have been inappropriate, for instance, to give them a paper-and-pencil test to assess this crucial skill. Likewise, travelers would be rightfully wary of being flown in a multiengine jetliner by pilots whose certification was based on a test flight in a single-engine light aircraft.

8. *Plan procedures to make maximum use of Stage IV data.* Stage IV data have a range of potential uses. A simple quiz on trainee learning can, for example, (1) be used to give feedback to individual trainees, (2) be used to give feedback to trainers to help them guide remediation plans for underachieving trainees, (3) be used by training managers to guide training design revisions, (4) be used by trainees' supervisors to assist with transfer-of-training applications, and (5) be used to help plan Stage V (follow-up) evaluation. The possible different uses should be projected so that Stage IV measures can be designed to meet them.

Useful Stage IV Procedures

This section describes, in alphabetical order, some common and especially useful procedures for implementing Stage IV evaluation. Each procedure is accompanied by one or more references to sources that will offer readers more information about it. This listing is not exhaustive, but it is meant to be relatively broad and it includes alternatives that I hope will apply to readers' varied needs.

Achievement Tests. The achievement test is an excellent technique for measuring what participants learned from a training effort. This procedure can be used to assess a variety of skills and application abilities. It involves the following general steps:

1. Identify the objectives of the HRD program.
2. Define each objective in terms of behavior and content. The objective should be clearly defined at the level of generality intended by the course planners.
3. Identify situations in which objectives are utilized. A test should sample these situations.
4. Devise ways to present situations that will closely represent on-job conditions and requirements.
5. Devise ways to obtain a record. This might be an answer sheet, a composition, an item, or a work product.
6. Decide on the terms to use in appraisal. Use terms or units that reflect the desirable characteristics of the participants' reactions in contrast to the undesirable or less desirable.
7. Devise means to get a representative sample. For example, from all possible required skills, knowledge, and attitudes from this training effort, a random or stratified sample of questions that measure these attributes should be used for testing achievement level (Gronlund, 1982; Tyler, 1983).

Interviewing. When a major expected Stage IV result is a matter of reactions and attitudes, interviewing—asking people about their attitude changes—is a potential Stage IV measure (Henerson, Morris, and Fitz-Gibbon, 1978; Payne, 1951; also see Chapter Two).

Knowledge Tests. Here, participants are administered a test after (or before and after) training is completed to yield a score derived from their response to test items. Test items are selected or constructed to effectively sample the domain of knowledge being assessed (for example, supervisory techniques). Test item formats may vary but typically are multiple-choice or short-answer (completion) items. Knowledge tests can be constructed to yield highly accurate and valid measures, and numerical scores allow extensive statistical analysis and reporting. Such tests are also useful as diagnostic devices and thus can help strengthen learning (Ebel, 1965; Gronlund, 1982; Tyler, 1983).

Performance Tests, Simulations, and Role Plays. Performance tests are intended to assess specific skills. At the end of a
session on how to troubleshoot a radio, for example, trainees
might be given a radio to repair and then observed to see whether they can do it correctly. Or the radio might be previously
rigged to have one or more particular problems. In this case,
more objective performance data would be available, as the test
could measure whether the actual problem was diagnosed and
how long it took to solve the problem. Performance tests can be
constructed for any number of manual or cognitive skills (Mager,
1984; Ribler, 1983; Yelon, 1982). In interactive skills, such as
countering customer objections in a sales setting, providing
coaching feedback in a performance review, or answering customer questions, role plays are especially helpful. When highly
rigorous measures and high levels of consistency from testee to
testee are not especially important, then trainees can role play
for one another if they are given explicit guidelines. When greater test precision is necessary and to be sure that performance is
tested equally among all trainees, the simulated performance
must be standardized. A simulated customer might appear on
videotape, for example, while trainees are asked to write down
how they would counter each objection that the customer
makes on the screen (Horn, 1977; Megarry, 1977).

Self-Assessment and Reports. Participants can usually
serve as very accurate and sensitive judges of their own achievement levels, and when there is little threat or coercion involved,
they can be expected to honestly report on their own achievement. Thus, self-assessment measures are a good Stage IV technique. Self-assessment scales are very open ended, asking participants to list things they think they have or have not learned or
to list attitudes they hold. Again, participants might be given a
predetermined list of learning objectives that they will then rate
according to their level of achievement. Sometimes, self-assess-
ments made before and after a learning session can be used to
determine whether a change in knowledge or skill levels has occurred. When awareness may affect a prerating self-score (participants might learn how much they *did not* know!), the pre-

test can be readministered after the session. However, when participants might not, prior to training, be aware of their own levels of knowledge (for instance, out of ignorance, they might think *before* training that they know a great deal, then learn from training that they actually know very little!), caution with the use of preassessments and postassessments is advised (Henerson, Morris, and Fitz-Gibbon, 1978; Shrauger and Osberg, 1981; Taylor, 1968).

6

Evaluating How Learning
Is Used on the Job
and Improves Performance

Stage V evaluation involves assessing the extent to which HRD-acquired skills, knowledge, and attitudes are being "transferred" to the job. Stage V evaluation begins when HRD is complete, or at least complete for some trainees, and when Stage IV evaluation has indicated that at least some portion of the intended immediate learning objectives was achieved. Preconditions for Stage V evaluation are that (1) some trainees have completed HRD and that (2) these trainees have learned something worth following up.

The domain of Stage V evaluation is typically, but not always, the workplace. The domain of Stage V evaluation is never the HRD program itself, for Stage V is concerned with what happens to the results of HRD, not with whether training has achieved its immediate learning objectives in the first place (this is the focus, as seen in the preceding chapter, of Stage IV evaluation). Another way of stating this is that Stage V looks at *actual* performance, not *ability* to perform. Thus, Stage V evaluation usually involves measuring how trainees use their training, when they use it, how much they use it, and so forth. Typical Stage V methods aim at recording behavior and involve such procedures as follow-up surveys, observation, and analysis of job records.

Human resource development in today's organizations is usually extensive and quite varied and typically involves a wide range of expected benefits in job behavior, personal habits, and morale and other organizational health factors, to name just a few. Thus, to define Stage V evaluation as measuring just on-the-job skill usage would not be enough. Programs are often aimed at a variety of changes and results, and so Stage V evaluation must be very carefully focused, in each instance, to be responsive to the particular "logic" and objectives found in that instance.

This chapter therefore begins with an analysis of the relationship between Stage V evaluation and HRD's logic. Following this, the several purposes and uses for Stage V evaluation are listed and discussed. The next section presents some useful questions to guide the design of Stage V evaluation. Then, as in other chapters, various levels of Stage V effort, and guidelines for deciding their appropriateness in particular settings, are presented. The chapter closes with a listing of common and useful Stage V evaluation procedures.

Stage V and the Logic of HRD

The most obvious and common example of Stage V evaluation is found in skill training. This kind of training responds to the fact that some employees need certain skills to perform their jobs correctly, and thus training is conducted to give them those skills. Trainees are then supposed to return to their jobs and correctly use the training-acquired skills in performing their jobs. Eventually, the company will benefit from the application of these skills in decreased scrap rates, higher-quality products, increased output, and so forth. It should be noted in this explanation that the benefit to the organization derives not from what was learned but from what actually gets used. This provides the basic reason for being of Stage V evaluation: Training is not done for the sake of learning alone but for the sake of providing value to the organization through improved job performance.

For most types of HRD, value to the organization results

from use of training-acquired skills, knowledge, and attitudes. In a training program that teaches repair persons to use a new time-saving troubleshooting procedure, for example, value to the organization will occur when repair persons correctly use the new procedure, thus realizing a time savings, which will in turn translate into greater profits or more time available to conduct more repairs. In this example, the "logic" of training projects a behavior change (using the new procedure) that results from learning how and when to use the new procedure (the learning, or Stage IV, objectives). Then, so goes the logic, a savings in time will occur, resulting finally in some benefits to the organization (more profit, more productivity). Stage V evaluation as applied in this example would focus on who was using the new procedure, how and when they were using it, and whether they were using it correctly. Stage V evaluation would also look at how much time the new procedure saved. Eventually, of course, Stage VI evaluation (as will be discussed in Chapter Seven) would pursue the question of how much time savings were adding up across uses, and how much value to the organization was in fact being achieved as a result.

But not all HRD follows the very clear and discrete logic of the skill-training scenario. As was noted in earlier chapters, HRD can follow different routes to achieve organizational benefit, and not all these routes involve transit through an on-job behavior step. Sometimes, HRD is expected to have impact in the workplace, but this impact will be evidenced in other than strictly job-related behaviors. For example, health and wellness programs are expected to help employees change their life-styles and health-related habits (eating and drinking habits, for example). The expectation is that the overall health of employees will improve and that the organization will see a reduction in sick leave, insurance payments, and so forth. Even in this example, of course, there is a behavioral route; HRD participants are expected to modify some important health-related behaviors in order for the program to eventually succeed.

In other sorts of programs, where advanced education benefits are available to employees, there may be no easily discernible changes in workplace behavior intended. When the logic of HRD's value to the organization is construed as a reward or employee benefit, job behavior changes may not be necessary for the organization to benefit. In such cases, the belief is that the very availability of the HRD program yields such benefits as higher morale, increased commitment, and even better employee retention rates.

All such benefits, however, are measurable and could be documented. Whether the results of HRD are to be traced through specific job-related behavior changes or through aggregate measures of employee retention, reduced turnover, decreased sick leave, and so forth, the point is that they often must be traced, measured, documented, and eventually related to the HRD efforts from which they did, or did not, derive. This last statement should not be construed to mean that practitioners must seek to discover proof that such indirect results in fact accrue from minimal HRD interventions. The pursuit of such proof is rarely, if ever, necessary in the first place, nor is it easily achievable. But HRD practitioners should be ready to pro duce *some* evidence, even if such evidence amounts only to subjective testimonials from participants. This kind of evidence is better than no evidence, and the very pursuit of evidence will usually turn up information helpful in making HRD more effective.

In some instances, Stage V evaluation might be used in a very "classical" manner to measure and document specific aspects of job behaviors. In other instances, Stage V may pay little if any attention to trainees' on-job performance, and evaluation efforts will quickly make the transition to Stage VI and begin to examine whether benefits are being realized for the organization. In still other instances, Stage V evaluation might assess whether HRD-acquired knowledge, skills, or attitudes have been retained and whether the potential for on-job use, and thus organizational benefit, remains intact. For example, a nuclear generation plant might train key personnel to deal with an extreme emergency. While the hope is that trainees will never have to use these skills, it is highly important that they possess them. Now, certainly, HRD cannot be judged a "failure" if Stage V evaluation turns up no evidence of usage! In this sort of case, Stage V evaluation might better be aimed at assessing trainees' ability to retain the skills that they might someday have to use. If the ability to deal with the possible emergency is in fact important (a Stage I argument), then organizational benefit can be argued from knowing (1) the extent of actual skill retention and (2) the cost of creating and maintaining this skill in the first place. A program can demonstrate, and even improve, its productivity merely by aiming at increasing retention and the capacity to behave as desired while maintaining or decreasing HRD costs. The benefit-to-the-organization argument, in this kind of example, can be made without the skill ever actually being used; or, put another way, Stage V evaluation would focus on observed capacity to behave rather than on actual behavior.

The point of all this discussion is that the logic of HRD provides the key to the sort of Stage V evaluation that should be done. Practitioners must carefully consider the incremental steps and causal assumptions that HRD must "transit" through on its way from immediate learning outcomes to eventual benefit to the organization. The job of Stage V evaluation is to assess and monitor these incremental changes, so that HRD can (1) intervene if necessary to actualize these planned changes and (2) take credit when and where credit is due for such incremental and eventual changes as occur. In many cases, this will entail measuring on-job behavior and skill application. In other cases, however, it may involve assessing changes in personal behaviors both on and off the job, or it may involve assessing endurance of changes in attitudes, predispositions to act in certain ways, retention of skills and knowledge, or capacity to behave in desired ways. In any case, Stage V has a consistent job: to determine whether, and to what extent, the expected incremental results of HRD are, in fact, taking place. These expected results —the "steps along the path" to organizational benefit—are derived from the specific logic of any HRD instance.

Purposes and Uses for Stage V Evaluation

As is true with the preceding stages of evaluation, there are several worthwhile purposes that Stage V evaluation can serve. Clarity about particular purposes to be served is crucial to being able to design a good evaluation, and so some typical, and not so typical, purposes and uses for Stage V evaluation will be listed and discussed here. For the sake of clarity, the purposes and uses discussed below refer, for the most part, to Stage V evaluation that focuses on on-job usage of training. In reviewing these purposes and uses, however, the reader should remember that not all HRD follows this same logic. The uses and purposes presented in the following will apply in virtually any instance, regardless of the particular logic of that HRD.

1. *Revising training.* A major benefit of evaluating HRD's transfer to the workplace is realized as the HRD itself is revised and improved on the basis of the results of Stage V inquiry. It might be discovered, for example, that a training program for repair persons has resulted in the use of repair skills but that trainees are experiencing difficulty in diagnosing repair needs. Further inquiry might suggest that the problem derives from trainees' lack of confidence in their own proficiency; providing more practice in future training sessions would thus be indicated.

Or to give a somewhat different and more complex example, suppose that Stage V evaluation of a safety-training program turned up the fact that trainees were not adhering, on their job, to a particular procedure that they had learned thoroughly (according to results of Stage IV evaluation) in the training program. Further inquiry indicates that Stage I evaluation made a faulty assumption about the extent to which these trainees' supervisors would nurture and support the use of this new procedure; trainees are not (as was planned) being supported by their supervisors in their attempts to use the procedure. In this example, the training program may need revision to now include some sort of training for the trainees' supervisors, in an attempt to get them to recognize the value of the new procedure and to learn how to support its use.

It is a rare program that sees transfer of training to the workplace in exactly the manner intended. More typically, some trainees will end up using some of the training in unexpected ways. Finding out about both the "hits" and the "misses" of transfer will invariably suggest how the program might be revised in the future to result in more complete, accurate, and worthwhile transfer.

2. Planning interventions to support increased transfer of training. As noted above, HRD rarely works out exactly as it was supposed to, and when Stage V evaluation indicates less than perfect transfer, modifications to future programs can be made. But what about trainees who are now on the job but are not using their training the way they are supposed to? For present "graduates" already back on the job, Stage V evaluation can be very useful in planning ways to get improved on-job performance. When, for example, evaluation of a managers' workshop on performance appraisal disclosed that a few trainees were having difficulty setting measurable performance standards for their employees, a company decided to use a "buddy" system for a while, teaming the managers having difficulty with some other managers who were performing just as hoped for. After a short time, further evaluation showed that everyone was now up to snuff.

Many options for intervening—retraining, training others, changing job aids, creating new aids and job guidelines, to name a few—are available to help trainees better use training-acquired results. None of these methods can be planned or effectively used, however, if it is not known whether they are needed or with whom they are needed. So, Stage V evaluation can be very productively used to find out where learning transfer is below expectations and can then be further used to monitor results after interventions to improve transfer have been tried.

3. Planning ahead for Stage VI evaluation. Eventually, most training practitioners will look to evaluation as a means of assessing, and making claims for, the value that HRD delivers to the organization. In some instances, the logic of the value argument will require a demonstration of changes in on-job behavior. Consider, for example, a training program that has trained salespersons to use a new selling technique that is supposed to produce more sales. Stage V evaluation should seek to document instances of correct usage of the new technique. These instances of use would then form the basis for further (Stage VI) inquiry into the impact on sales quantity that has resulted from using the new methods. The logic of the value argument in this example depends on two key phenomena: (1) there must be actual and correct use of the new procedure, and (2) its use must produce more sales. The Stage V evaluator should be constantly on the lookout for instances of training applications that can be effectively investigated for evidence of value and worth to the organization.

Sometimes, the training will not transfer exactly as planned to the workplace. But unexpected usages may nonetheless have potential Stage VI benefits. It may be, to return to the previous example of salespersons learning to use a new selling method, that only a very few of them have even tried the new method. And it may be that even these few have not been using the method correctly but have modified it to suit their own particular styles and needs. Assume, for this example, that two salespeople have modified the method in order to save themselves time in preparing for a sales contact but have not used the new technique at all in actually dealing with clients (the way the method was meant to be used). It would be very shortsighted for the Stage V evaluation to conclude that the training itself was a failure and cease all further inquiry! Rather, the potential value of the unexpected usage should be explored. Perhaps the modified usage really does save time, permitting the salespeople to make more contacts per week, and thus results in increased sales after all. If this were the case, training has achieved at least a partial Stage VI success. Further, these results would bear consideration in possible revisions to the training. Stage V evaluation should thus seek to determine *why* the users changed the technique, how many others are using it in different ways, and so forth. This information could then be cycled back into the HRD program design itself, resulting in revisions to the program that would yield more such on-the-job usage of training.

Stage V evaluation should therefore be designed and conducted with an eye to Stage VI evaluation. Value claims for HRD—the benefits it has produced for the organization—are usually impossible to support without specific, clear, and accurate evidence of how HRD is actually being used. Sometimes, Stage V evaluation will uncover unexpected applications of training that may have produced organizational benefits. These will represent possible "paths" to value that may, or may not, lead to fruitful results. But the paths must be explored, and Stage V evaluation must be ever watchful for clues to the paths.

4. Documenting and accounting for transfer of training. Most HRD is intended to result in changed behavior. Thus, on-job application of HRD is an expectation and represents a "claim" that training is held accountable for. One purpose for Stage V evaluation, then, is simply to document the nature and extent of transfer of training to the job. This documentation itself can meet a variety of purposes and has a variety of uses. Following are several common uses of documentation of transfer that designers of Stage V evaluation should keep in mind when evaluation is planned.

The first of these uses is creating a data base for further Stage VI inquiry. Sometimes (but sadly, not as often as should be the case), a needs analysis preceding HRD documents and assesses the pretraining job behavior levels of trainees. A needs analysis might, for example, record the nature and frequency of violations of safety procedures among power-plant technicians. After training, and assuming that the training was successful enough to produce some results, Stage V evaluation should aim at documenting the nature and frequency of violations of safety procedures now that trainees have returned to the workplace. Differences in the types and rates of violations can then be analyzed, using economic or other references (for example, severity of injury) to determine the value of the before-and-after behavior changes.

A second purpose of documentation is to produce evidence for marketing and public relations use. Potential consumers of HRD have an interest in, and a right to know about, the expected results of HRD as it impacts the workplace. Thus, Stage V evaluation of ongoing programs can create a data base that will allow certain claims to be made. Consider, for example, a workshop offered by an organization to help supervisors more effectively deal with conflicts arising from multirace relations. Stage V data might reveal that in the past the program has consistently produced certain kinds of changes in some types of settings (in a unit with lower educational levels, for instance), but not in other settings. Thus, even in instances where skill and knowledge transfer claims can be made for a program, it is important that potential users understand the particulars of what they can expect. In such cases, there is little substitute for clear and detailed job-usage data, as opposed to making claims for what trainees can be expected to learn. Both sellers and buyers of training should talk in terms of actual results rather than in terms of potential for results (learning only).

Lastly, documentation of transfer can produce a data base for ongoing research into HRD needs and results. The workplace, rather than the HRD classroom, represents the richest source of data from which existing programs can be assessed and from which future HRD needs can be derived. The immediate impacts of HRD must survive and, one hopes, thrive in the workplace. Without detailed and accurate knowledge of the ever changing milieu of the workplace, HRD planners are at a severe disadvantage. And once HRD is conducted, transfer to the workplace will be incomplete in most cases and will often require further intervention in order to achieve maximum results. Again, there is no substitute for data about, and derived directly from, the workplace.

Levels of Stage V Effort

As with the other stages of evaluation, the level of effort necessitated in any given instance of Stage V evaluation is a function of that particular instance's needs and peculiarities. Some HRD programs may require a heavy dose of Stage V effort, while others may require very little. Following are some brief scenarios of Stage V evaluation planning and use that vary dramatically in their level of effort.

Scenario 1: The Hiteck Corporation, a small electronics firm, provides (partial) tuition reimbursement to employees who wish to further their learning. The program is administered by the HRD division (a one-person operation), but it is provided mostly as an employee benefit program (at the urging of the personnel department) because it has proven vital to recruiting new employees. Administration of the program takes very little time, and while it appears to aid recruiting efforts, very few people have in fact made use of it. The HRD unit director keeps careful records of who uses the program and also conducts brief interviews with users when their program ends. At this interview, she asks employees who have gained further education to tell her in what ways (if any) they believe that they will be able to use what they have learned on the job, at home, or elsewhere in their lives. About a year later, she schedules a second interview to review and document any instances, planned or unplanned, in which the program participants feel that they have used and benefited from their education. During this session, the HRD director is careful to provide strong encouragement for even greater use, since reported instances seem to have value for both the individual and the company. Results of all interviews are filed by the HRD director. To date, such evaluation efforts have taken up about three hours of time per year.

Scenario 2: The Biltrite Machine Tool Company has initiated a new safety training program based on data collected over several years that indicated a poor and worsening safety record. The previous safety-training program provided bimonthly lectures to shop employees on such topics as the importance of safety rules, procedures to avoid danger, and so forth. Despite good attendance at the lectures and test data showing good knowledge of the content, there has been no increase in safety behaviors; in fact, there has been an increase in the accident rate. The new program represents a radical departure from the old. In the new program, floor supervisors are taught two skills: (1) how to observe and statistically chart instances of safety behaviors and the general accident rate in their areas and (2) how to recognize and give positive reinforcement to employees who are following safety rules. To assist with follow-up, the HRD director visits each area once a month, checks on the charts and graphs being posted in the shop areas, and discusses any emerging problems with the floor supervisor. The HRD director keeps careful records of how often the charts and graphs are updated, as well as of their accuracy and completeness, and he also has floor supervisors keep a log of when, how, how often, and to whom they have provided positive reinforcement.

On his visits, the HRD director casually observes adherence to safety rules and checks these observations against the logs being kept by the supervisors. Each month, the HRD director aggregates safety data from the charts of all areas and produces a monthly total report and chart that are given to the production manager and also posted in the employee cafeteria and locker room. It is hard to go anywhere in the Biltrite Company without seeing a safety behavior and accident rate chart! After the first six months of the new program (and without a single lecture on safety to a single employee!), Biltrite has reduced its accident and lost-time rates by more than 70 percent; and, according to the training director's aggregate chart, the decrease rate is improving monthly. An interesting phenomenon, evident from the logs maintained by supervisors and from accident reports, is that accidents and safety violations, when they do occur, involve *new* employees in almost every case. Based on these data, the HRD director has decided to reinstitute the safety lecture program as a self-contained slide/tape module for new employees only.

Scenario 3: The Kash Company has been conducting a series of management seminars on a variety of topics (conflict resolution and performance appraisal, for example) for all its junior managers. The programs are very popular, and senior managers typically try to get all their managers to attend at some point. But other than the regularity with which offered seminars are filled, there are really no data available as to whether, or how, the seminars affect management performance. The programs are also very expensive, particularly in terms of time spent in HRD (several weeks, total). And while there is no particular pressure to reduce HRD's budget, the company has been experiencing a decrease in sales, and budget cuts may come in the future.

The HRD director therefore decided to do some evaluation. Based on records of learning and trainer reports, seven recent "graduates" who performed especially well in the seminar were selected. These so-called success cases were then to be followed up several months after the program. The HRD director hired an industrial psychology graduate student to conduct sev-

eral in-depth interviews with each of the seven trainees to identify and describe instances in which HRD-acquired knowledge
has been used by him or her. The HRD director chose the "success cases" (people who learned the content the best) on the
assumption that if anyone was using the HRD, and if it was
making a difference for anyone, it would very likely be these
seven trainees. As it turned out, many instances of HRD application were discovered and defined. Interestingly enough, some
were planned, and others were a complete surprise to the trainers who never dreamed anyone would use their materials that
way. Some instances of usage seemed to promise real value to
the organization (in one case, a lawsuit was headed off through
conflict resolution), while others did not seem particularly valuable after all.

In one instance, a trainee had used training to plan and
conduct better meetings. Stage V data showed that (1) biweekly
meetings were 30 percent briefer when the new procedures were
used and that (2) the meetings were rated as "more effective"
by attendees. Later, by translating meeting time saved into sal-
aried time saved, Stage VI data would show that this *single* application saved enough money to pay for the *entire* HRD program!

The success case data were used in several ways. First, the
HRD director made up a survey form to poll all management
trainees to see which of the behaviors uncovered in the success
cases they were either using or not using; the survey was carefully designed to include both promising and unpromising applications. Follow-up results were also provided to all trainees and
their bosses in an effort to get even more application of training by stimulating peoples' imagination as to how they might
use the seminars. And, lastly, the results were used in the program itself to create more examples of, and suggestions for, how
HRD might be used on the job.

Scenario 4: The Everclean Company makes washing machines that it sells throughout the country, and then provides
maintenance and repair training to a nationwide network of
licensed dealers. As part of its customer service and quality-
assurance program, the company collects data from every dealer-

ship on the nature and frequency of repairs. These data are then centrally aggregated in the company's computer. As a simple measure of its maintenance training, the training division has the computer print out a summary of repair data for each region where it has recently provided (or not provided) repair training. The frequency and types of repairs and re-repairs are compared against when and where training has been provided. Based on these data, the HRD division is able to chart (and document) how much and how well its training is being used. The data printouts and summaries require approximately ten minutes of time per month from the training division secretary.

Scenario 5: Local Telephone's HRD division helped start a company wellness program. The program asks participants to complete a detailed survey questionnaire on their health-related habits and behaviors. Each six months, the HRD division selects a small randomly drawn sample of program participants (and nonparticipants) and readministers the questionnaire. Overall health habits and behaviors are compared between participants and nonparticipants, and a calculation of differences between participants' behaviors before and after training indicates whether habits have changed and, if so, whether the changes are enduring.

Scenario 6: Midstate Power conducts emergency procedure training for all its personnel. So far, in the eighteen-year history of the company, there has been no emergency that required use of the procedures. The HRD division each year selects a small sample of personnel and retests them on emergency knowledge and attitudes by means of a brief written test. Test scores are analyzed, and refresher training is provided for those dimensions that appear to be fading out over time. Test results in summary form are provided to supervisors, who brief their employees on which aspects of training are holding up and which are not. The government regulatory commission conducts simulated emergency drills at the plant every three years, and so far these have shown a thorough level of preparedness.

The preceding six scenarios represent differing levels of Stage V effort. In some scenarios, a great deal of effort was invested in assessing and using data on the implementation of

HRD-acquired attributes. In the Biltrite Company's safety-training program (scenario 2), for example, the supervisors were
trained to collect follow-up data, and they maintained graphs
and charts representing not only employee performance but
also their own performance after training. In this scenario, the
follow-up (Stage V) data played a key role in the "logic" of the
HRD. That is, the follow-up data were used as part of a carefully planned change effort. Given the key role these data were
to play and the extensive use planned for the follow-up data, a
considerable investment in Stage V evaluation was required.

The Kash Company's management seminars (scenario 3)
also represented a substantial investment in Stage V evaluation,
but the purposes and use for follow-up data were quite different. The Biltrite scenario used Stage V data as a part of the
training itself. In the Kash example, the Stage V data were used
primarily for evaluative purposes. Kash was making a large investment in management training but had virtually no data on
hand to demonstrate if, or how much, these efforts were paying off in changed job behavior. In this scenario, the magnitude
of the HRD effort called for a commensurately large investment
in finding out if, and how, the HRD was being transferred to the
workplace. Additionally, the Kash Company planned to get
considerable mileage from its Stage V evaluation. Not only was
the company collecting data to assess and perhaps defend and
justify its management training, but the Stage V data collected
from success cases would also make a substantial contribution
to improving the program itself.

The other scenarios represented considerably smaller
Stage V efforts. In these scenarios, the Stage V evaluations were
specially tailored to match the particular needs of the programs
to which they were applied. In the Everclean washing machine
scenario, Stage V evaluation data represented the results of repair training from the very end of the training's "path of logic."
In this instance, the data represented aggregate results of training in terms of the nature and extent of repairs actually made.
On the basis of these data, the HRD department will be able to
make very substantial and well-documented claims as to the
applicability and utility of its training. And little more work has

to be done in order to translate these results into bottom-line Stage VI benefits.

The Hiteck educational benefits example (scenario 1) represents a similarly minor Stage V investment. But in this example, the transfer of HRD, because of the nature of the HRD program, is not documented as changed job performance. Rather, the HRD department head collected perceptions about the worth and utility of programs from past participants. According to the "logic" of this HRD endeavor, a tuition-reimbursement program, participants would use and benefit from their education in very different, individualized ways. The purpose of the program was largely for recruiting and retention of employees. Thus, at Stage V, the major expected results would be that participants would find the program individually worthwhile. The HRD head also made efforts to encourage maximum possible use, both for individuals and the company, of the HRD received. In this respect, this scenario is similar to the safety-training example; in both cases, Stage V data are used as a means of extending and ensuring the utility of the HRD program.

Local Telephone's (scenario 5) follow-up of its health program participants also represents a relatively minor, though probably sufficient, investment in Stage V evaluation. In this scenario, the trainers based their follow-up on a pretest survey questionnaire administered as a regular part of the program. It was a relatively easy and inexpensive matter to select a sample of participants to survey again and to look for evidence of changes in personal behavior—the reason for the program's existence in the first place. Again, as in other scenarios, we see Stage V evaluation efforts being specifically tailored both to the needs for data and to the HRD program's structure and purpose.

The Midstate Power scenario represented the special case in which HRD is not expected, except in very extreme and unlikely circumstances, to result in changed on-job behavior. In this scenario, the logic of HRD calls mainly for retention of learning so that changed behavior is possible. Thus, the Stage V evaluation here was very similar to Stage IV evaluation: it assessed knowledge, but it assessed knowledge well after the conclusion of the HRD intervention itself. It should also be noted that in this scenario, as in others, the resultant Stage V data were used not only to gauge the success of the HRD but to further and extend transfer of learning. In this scenario, the Stage V results were used to plan refresher HRD when and where a need for it was indicated.

In summary, the scenarios represent some divergent and some common Stage V notions. In each scenario, a different level of investment in evaluation was evidenced. And differing methods for evaluation were used, depending on the particular needs of the programs and the particular structure of the programs themselves. In several of the scenarios (the health program, the safety-training program, and the washing machine repair program), the evaluation made use of data already collected as part of the program itself. Moreover, in most of the scenarios, the Stage V data were used for several purposes and were almost always used to make ongoing changes and improvements to the programs to help them pay off. The overarching principle to be gleaned from review of these scenarios is that in every case evaluation was done with utility in mind. The evaluation was designed to be used; and, most often, multiple uses for data were found.

The Seven Guiding Questions for Stage V Evaluation

The typical Stage V evaluation that focuses on on-job usage of training-acquired skills, knowledge, and attitudes should be guided by a common set of general questions. Sometimes, however, not all these questions will be applicable. So the reader should recognize that the particular HRD program being evaluated, its context, and the evaluation needs and intended uses must ultimately guide the evaluation. The guiding questions, each with a brief explanation, follow.

1. Who is using the training? It is often the case that not all HRD graduates will use their learning, nor will all use it the same way. Sometimes, HRD will transfer for some types of participants, but not for others. Or some types will use it more correctly or more often than others. Thus, a Stage V evaluation should seek to identify the specific characteristics of HRD's users and nonusers—for example, their roles, their ages, their previous training, their motivation and interest, and the myriad other characteristics that might, in the particular program being evaluated, differentiate among the successful and unsuccessful users.

2. What aspects of the HRD are being used? Just as not everyone will use HRD, so too not all the HRD content will be used. Typically, some parts of the program will be transferred to the workplace, and other parts of it will not. The follow-up evaluation should aim to find out just which parts of the HRD training are being used in the workplace and which are not.

3. How is the HRD being used? Trainees who do use HRD will typically use it in different ways. Some managers might, for example, use their conflict resolution training in memorandums and other written communications but avoid using it in face-to-face encounters. Or, as another example, drill press operators in a manufacturing plant might use a new stock-loading procedure at different rates or in slightly different sequences. Trainees in virtually any field have an uncanny knack for individualizing training to suit their own particular needs, interests, whims, and idiosyncrasies. Practitioners must be aware of these individualized revisions, for they can drastically alter the impact of HRD, sometimes positively, sometimes negatively. To assume that HRD will be used exactly as delivered and intended is naive and can cause HRD to fail to capitalize on the many creative and adaptive applications that almost inevitably will occur.

4. When, where, and how often is the HRD being used? This question is related closely to the preceding question. It is very likely that those persons who are using training use it under some conditions but not under others. Supervisors might, for example, use a new performance appraisal procedure with employees who are generally performing well but not with their "problem" employees. This phenomenon would have considerable significance for assessing the value of the procedure, as well as for possible revisions to the program (for example, the program might be revised to include practice with simulated "problem" employees). Stage V evaluation should pay particular attention to, and seek out, the particular characteristics of the workplace and setting in which HRD is being used and not used.

5. How else is HRD being used? Just as it must be assumed

that trainees will individualize HRD in application, so it must be expected that HRD will result in some unexpected applications. A good example of this phenomenon can be found in an example used earlier. I recounted from my U.S. Navy experience that sailors were known to use maintenance training to inflict damage to equipment instead of repairing it, thus gaining a "reward" of more days spent in desirable ports. Stage V evaluation must therefore look for unanticipated uses of HRD. Sometimes, as in the example given, these applications will be negative, thus calling for intervention to extinguish or alter them. In other cases, however, there will be positive instances of unanticipated application that can be nurtured and incorporated into future programs or extended to other graduates of HRD.

6. *How well is HRD being used?* The degree of correctness of HRD application will vary among trainees, settings, types of uses, and so forth. A major Stage V question, then, is to seek out the level of accuracy and correctness with which the HRD application is being made. Benefit to the organization, if HRD's initial "logic" was right, will depend on trainees using their learning correctly. Thus, where HRD is being used correctly, benefit should follow; where HRD is being used incorrectly, then intervention should be made to change behavior.

7. *How do trainees know whether they are using HRD correctly?* This final question is more subtle than the six that preceded it and has more implications for revising and nurturing HRD than it does for simply assessing or accounting for HRD's transfer. The most fruitful applications of HRD will occur when users of programs develop their own particular cues and systems to tell themselves how well they are using what they learned. A supervisor using a new performance appraisal system might, for example, begin to notice how his employees' verbal and nonverbal behavior changes as he tries out his new methods. Based on these cues, he might make subtle revisions and adjustments to his approach or might on occasion even abandon use of the new method. For another example, a drill press operator trying out a new stock-loading procedure might notice that, in order to drill holes cleanly, she has to shift her body position to gain a better angle of sight. Discovery of the particular techniques that

trainees use to give themselves feedback on their performance can be very valuable in extending HRD transfer to others who have not yet discovered these techniques. The best HRD will include methods that trainees can use to assess and modify their own on-job performance. Very often, of course, early versions of an HRD program will not include this feedback content. If Stage V evaluation seeks out this information, then HRD can be continually improved and refined.

Guidelines for Planning Stage V Evaluation

As was noted earlier in the chapter, there are numerous levels of effort and purpose that may characterize any given application of Stage V evaluation, and a particular application may concentrate different degrees of attention on the various Stage V evaluation questions outlined in the preceding section. As in the preceding stages of evaluation, the major determinants of just what gets evaluated in Stage V, and how it gets evaluated, are the particular needs and interests of the HRD situation being evaluated. With this said, we can turn to a presentation and discussion of some general guidelines that should be considered when planning and conducting a Stage V evaluation:

1. Use needs data in the planning and conducting of Stage V evaluation. All HRD aims at solving some problem or otherwise filling some organizational need. When the decision to conduct HRD has been correctly made in the first place, there will be some existing data that support or demonstrate the need that precipitated the HRD decision. If, for example, a company has decided to train its salespersons to use a new selling technique, there ought to be some data to support the contention that (1) the new method is worth learning and, if used, would do some good and that (2) salespersons are not already using the new method. These data are the needs data. Some of these data (for example, that the method could have positive consequences) will be used to pursue Stage VI evaluation. But the data about what methods salespeople were using prior to training, and how much what they were doing is like or unlike the new method, will be very useful in doing Stage V evaluation.

First, the needs data can be viewed as a base line to compare data about posttraining behaviors with data about pretraining behaviors. This comparison yields an estimate of how pervasive and potent the training has been. Second, the needs data, even if they are quite insubstantial and highly subjective, can form a solid starting point for deciding what sorts of Stage V data to collect. The needs data might show, for instance, that sales behaviors prior to training were especially ineffective for a certain product line and that concerns for lagging sales in this product line were the major factor precipitating the training. It might make sense, then, to begin the Stage V inquiry by looking at sales behaviors related to this product line.

Even if no formal needs data exist, the Stage V inquiry can still "return" to the needs stage. In these (not unlikely!) cases, HRD practitioners will have to reconstruct the needs data by asking decision makers why the HRD effort is being carried out, what sorts of problems it was meant to solve, and so forth. Responses to these inquiries can then be used to focus the Stage V evaluation.

Another "return" to the needs stage may be called for when there is an absence of formal needs data. After HRD, data about posttraining behaviors could be collected. These data could then be presented to people in the organization along with such questions as "Are these behaviors right?" "Are they any good?" "Are they different from the way things used to be?" Discussion of questions like these would help reconstruct the setting prior to HRD and would also serve to determine whether any worthwhile behaviors resulted from the program. It is possible, of course, that even when worthwhile behaviors can be associated with a program, these behaviors already existed or might have come about regardless of the HRD. Whether HRD has had any value is, of course, the Stage VI question and will be dealt with in the following chapter. Moreover, in the absence of any needs data at all, it will be exceedingly difficult to establish that HRD has served a worthwhile goal or need. Nonetheless, the Stage V evaluation should return to the needs data or, in the absence of data, to the needs situation by attempting to reconstruct it. Consideration of the particular circumstances and incidents that caused people to believe that HRD was needed in the first place will provide important direction to Stage V inquiry and help it to focus on important post-HRD behaviors.

    2. Involve participants and important others in the planning and operation of the evaluation. Stage V is a search for evidence that HRD has made a noticeable difference in the organization and its operation. Often such evidence is difficult to find, partially "disguised," spread widely throughout the organization, and hard to extract from people and events even when it does exist. For all these reasons, getting others involved in the search may help it succeed. Sometimes the only people who will be able to "see" the results of HRD will be those directly impacted by it. This may be especially true in the early period right after HRD has been conducted and the new behaviors are just beginning to "come out." Often, if these new behaviors are not noticed and nurtured, they will quickly wither and be crushed by the old way of doing things. Involving trainees, their bosses, and their subordinates in the Stage V evaluation will not only help identify new behaviors and changes, but it will help emerging changes grow, take hold, and spread to others.

    3. Aim at success. In the typical Stage V instance, it is more than likely that only a portion of the HRD will transfer to the workplace. While it is true that looking for, but *not* finding, evidence of HRD transfer provides useful information (knowing what did not work helps determine what did work), non-instances of transfer can scarcely be nurtured. For this reason, it is important that successful instances of transfer be discovered—and discovered early, lest they be extinguished before they have a chance to flourish. Using data collected from the HRD program itself, particularly Stage IV and Stage III data, will help focus the follow-up evaluation on areas and incidents in which HRD is most likely to have had an impact. Consider, for example, a training program in which managers have learned a variety of new methods and approaches for interacting with their employees. Stage IV data from this training might reveal that particular skills were especially well learned and positively received; these, then, become high-potential contenders for the earliest Stage V inquiry. The evaluation should focus on those skills whose transfer to the workplace seems most imminent.

This guideline should not be construed to mean that the Stage V evaluation should be "rigged" to look only for successful transfers and to ignore failures. Eventually, Stage V must produce a full accounting for the transfer of all the HRD, letting the chips fall where they may. But it should be remembered that a major purpose for evaluation is to make HRD pay off. Best serving this purpose often dictates that the Stage V evaluation effort be initially focused on areas and instances in which success can be found, nurtured, and built back into later iterations of the HRD.

4. *Make HRD self-correcting by training trainees to do their own Stage V evaluation.* When training includes teaching trainees how to assess and modify their own posttraining behavior, it not only eases the Stage V burden but helps make the training pay off. Consider, for example, a training program that has taught clerks in a store how to operate a new cash register. Now, the Stage V question is "Are they using the new machines and using them correctly?" To address this question, assume that we have trained an evaluator to observe clerks at work and to identify correct and incorrect uses. Assume further that having noticed many incorrect uses, this observer has begun to give the clerks feedback, with the result that their correct usage is increasing (a worthwhile result). Because the observation takes time and clerks are spread throughout many locations, it takes numerous observers to get the Stage V job done and, even though it is paying off in terms of higher correct usage rates, the costs of observation are prohibitive. Think how much more cost effective it would be to train the clerks to do their own observation and give themselves—perhaps through charts, graphs, and other job aids—their own feedback! Now, the Stage V task becomes one of aggregating, and perhaps occasionally verifying the accuracy of, the data already being collected. In this case, the Stage V evaluation task is much easier and less costly, and the benefits of the observation and revision of behavior are no longer limited to those few employees whom we can afford to observe.

5. *Avoid overcontrol when designing and conducting*

Stage V evaluations. Stage V data collection is very similar in format and function to the common managerial tactics involved in control—collecting data about employees' performance, then comparing actual performance to expectations in order to resolve discrepancies. Because of this similarity, the warning commonly made in management literature needs to be made for Stage V evaluation: Beware of overcontrol. If employees think that data collected about their performance may be used to their detriment, then the evaluation is in for serious problems. Employees may try to sabotage the system by failing to record or allow access to data, or they may record and report falsified data. Avoiding this potential for negative reaction requires careful sensitivity, planning, and tact. More specifically, involving others in the evaluation can do much to prevent these negative reactions. And clearly identifying and communicating the purposes for collecting the data (to assess HRD and to ensure its payoff) will also help.

6. *Use existing data wherever possible.* This guideline is associated closely with the preceding one. Because Stage V data can be construed as "control" data and may thus be biased or unreliable because of these perceptions, it is advisable to use already existing data. Such data are far more credible and are less likely to be tampered with or distorted to reflect a desired outcome than are data collected solely for an evaluative purpose. The typical organization already has on hand vast quantities of data that can be tapped for the evaluation. Sales reports, minutes of meetings, activity reports, government and regulatory agency reports, work schedules, production records, expense and other reimbursement claim forms, logs and diaries, repair and maintenance records are just a few examples of the many sources of data found in the typical organization that can be readily accessed for a Stage V evaluation.

A second major reason to use existing data is, of course, expense. Using existing data will cost less money than creating records and reports just for the HRD evaluation and will also place fewer burdens and demands on employees, who are probably already loaded to the hilt with reporting and record-keeping responsibilities.

7. *Beware of the "hard-to-evaluate" refrain!* I have often

encountered training managers who avoid Stage V evaluation—especially with so-called management-training programs—because they claim that such HRD cannot be evaluated. They claim, typically, that this kind of HRD training is quite general in nature and, unlike training provided to production workers, is not meant to produce specific skill changes and behaviors on the job. Yet these same managers will object vehemently when it is suggested that perhaps their management training is worthless and is not meant to produce anything of value. Of course, they proclaim, the HRD training has value, but it is very hard to say just what use will be made of it afterwards. This guideline says that such arguments most often are used (not necessarily intentionally) to mask bad HRD. To have value, a training effort must intend consequences. To claim that it has no consequences is to deny it any value and might lead to exchanges like the following:

Trainee: Say, this stuff looks pretty good. But, tell me, I'm having a little trouble seeing just how I might use this when I get back to my job. Can you give me an example of when and how I might use this new material?

Trainer: No, I'm sorry, I can't. This training is all pretty vague and general, and no one has ever really thought about how it might get used. Good question, though!

Any HRD worth its salt would, of course, allow the trainer to respond very differently to this good question, with one or more specific instances of when, how, where, with whom, and so on to use the HRD content. When it is said that management training is hard to evaluate, this usually means that the specific applications of the content will vary from manager to manager and from instance to instance. It is not that the HRD has no application value but that the application value is variable. Nor is it true that there will be no behavioral application of the HRD; rather, the behaviors applied will vary from instance to instance in degree and in the consequences that result from them. In addition, it may be difficult to trace secondary effects of the managers' use of new behaviors.

With management training, then, Stage V evaluation will have to dig a little deeper to identify specific sorts of results to look for. Moreover, Stage V evaluation may have to begin its search with fairly broad parameters, casting a general net until it begins to discover and identify, with increasing specificity, the particular results and uses of HRD in the workplace. Indeed, Stage V evaluation can make a major contribution by searching out specific applications of what trainees learned in management programs, and then cranking these back into the program design so that management trainers can begin to build increasingly more specific and relevant application and skill practice into their training.

Useful Stage V Procedures

This section describes, in alphabetical order, some common and especially useful procedures for implementing Stage V evaluation. Each procedure is accompanied by references to one or more sources that will offer readers more information about it. This listing is not exhaustive, but it is meant to be relatively broad; specifically, it includes alternatives that I hope will suit readers' varied circumstances.

Behaviorally Anchored Rating Scales. The Behaviorally Anchored Rating Scales usually measure the subject's job performance and are a useful mechanism for conducting a Stage V evaluation (Fogli, Hulin, and Blood, 1971; Sashkin, 1981).

Follow-Up: Participant. Another common data collection method is the participant follow-up at a predetermined time after program completion. The follow-up evaluation almost always parallels an end-of-the-program evaluation and normally involves the use of a feedback questionnaire, although variations include interviews and observations. Follow-up surveys can gather opinions and behavioral data from trainees, their bosses, or their supervisees. Care must be taken in constructing items to avoid "loading the deck" to discover only positive outcomes, and careful sampling must also be used to avoid bias (Babbie, 1973; Orlich, 1978; Phillips, 1983).

Interviewing. Interviews can also be used to discover usage of HRD. Interviews are especially pertinent when the specific behaviors and uses to look for are not known beforehand.

Observation. On-the-job observation is a very direct method of determining the nature and extent of HRD transfer. Unfortunately, observation can be quite expensive and time consuming, as it requires an on-site observer. Moreover, observation requires careful sampling, as it is possible that significant job behaviors have in fact changed but that these changes are not seen while the observer is present. For these reasons, direct observation is usually replaced by indirect observational evidence, such as a survey of performers, or an interview of supervisors. But sometimes direct observation of job performance or direct observation and recording of factors in the workplace (safety violations, for example) can be very useful. Observation methods typically require a carefully constructed observation instrument, so that observers know what to look for and can keep an accurate record of observation results. Observation is an especially good Stage V method when expected behavior changes would be frequently displayed, as in a very repetitive task, or when results of HRD use are especially obvious (Cartwright and Cartwright, 1974; Patton, 1980; see also Chapter Four).

Performance Appraisal. Performance appraisal data may provide a good basis from which to identify and record changes in on-job performance. This would assume, however, that performance appraisal data are specific, accurate, and up-to-date (from my experience with performance appraisal, an unlikely assumption!). In any case, performance appraisal reviews could at least indicate whether supervisors are more or less satisfied with performance, and such changes in performance as were found could be related to HRD interventions. And in instances where supervisors themselves were trained, the *quality* of performance appraisal data would itself indicate on-job changes. Thus, performance appraisal data could be systematically collected for samples of trainees and analyzed to indicate changes in job performance (Olson, 1981; Webb and Campbell, 1981).

The Success Case Method. The success case method has been developed to meet the need for evaluation of certain kinds of HRD efforts that are not amenable to traditional measurement-based evaluation. For instance, programs that have popular consumer appeal but unclear or hard-to-measure benefits or programs for which there is neither time nor money available for broad-scale assessment both lend themselves to evaluation that utilizes the success case method.

This method works as follows: Soon after a program has been conducted, a handful of success cases are identified; that is, individuals are selected who appear to have benefited especially from the HRD. (They are often selected simply on the basis of the intuitive judgment of the trainer or HRD director.) These few success cases are then followed up through an inquiry that asks "How have you used the HRD program? What benefits can be attributed to its use? What problems did you encounter in using the program? What were the negative consequences of the HRD and/or its use? What criteria did you use to decide if you were using the program correctly or incorrectly?"

Success cases may be studied through short interviews with a few trainees or through more elaborate approaches, such as case and records analysis and observation. While this method does not purport to produce a balanced assessment of the total results of HRD, it does attempt to answer the question "When HRD works, how well does it work?" Knowing the answer to this question in detail could provide practitioners with powerful information to use in demonstrating the worth of HRD, redesigning or modifying programs, or designing broad-scale questionnaires based on specific and recognizable consequences and uses of HRD programs (Brinkerhoff, 1983).

Unobtrusive Measures (Artifacts Analysis). Archeologists pick up and analyze artifacts to determine what people did in the distant past. Evaluators of HRD can work in much the same way. If, for example, trainees back on the job were supposed to make considerably more use of reference manuals, then the manuals should show signs of such use: frayed edges, bent pages, thumbprints, and so on. Telephone records, expense reports, minutes of meetings, access reports, usage records, and so on could all be analyzed to indicate performance patterns. One clever evaluator once discovered that managers were being more careful about rewriting and revising letters and memorandums by analyzing the contents of trash cans! The key to artifacts analysis is to ask "If X were being used, then what would I see?" Asking this question leads to creative evaluation approaches (Webb and Campbell, 1981).

7

Determining How Well the HRD Investment Has Paid Off

When HRD has worked, it should have delivered something of value to the organization. In the framework of the Six-Stage Model, HRD begins as a response to a need or opportunity in an organization. Stage VI brings HRD back full circle to the needs, problems, or opportunities it was originally intended to serve. The specific charge of Stage VI is to determine just what value has been returned to the organization by HRD and whether, considering the costs of HRD, that value is worth the expense.

Consider, for a simple example, a training program that was initiated at a grocery store to enable check-out clerks to operate a new cash register. The initial problem (need) was precipitated by the purchase of new registers; then, further Stage I inquiry determined that clerks would require new skills and knowledge to operate the new machines (of course, the projected costs of training should have been a factor in deciding whether to buy the new cash registers in the first place). Assume that the training evolved successfully through the stages of design, operation, immediate learning, and on-job transfer. Stage VI evaluation begins at the point that transfer of training to the workplace has been successfully achieved and documented. Now, it must be determined what value the new behavior (correct use of the cash registers) has created and how this value compares to the costs of the training. In this example, quicker and more accurate customer transactions, better inventory control, and decreased employee turnover as a result of eased working conditions might be among the major benefits of the training. Stage VI evaluation would assess and document these benefits, estimate or measure their value, and then compare them to the costs of the training. The worth of the training would thus be derived. (However, very few of these applications of training and their worth should come as surprises. The decision to do training in Stage I should have projected these uses and their potential worth.)

Because Stage VI probes into the original reasons for the HRD (the use of new cash registers and their impact on profitability, customer service, employee satisfaction, and so forth), it allows a decision to be made as to whether more, less, or a different kind of HRD is needed. That is, the organization can decide, on the basis of Stage VI evaluation, whether the original need has been sufficiently resolved or whether it deserves further intervention. In this respect, Stage VI evaluation repeats and recycles to the needs analysis stage.

It is important to recognize why Stage VI and Stage I are closely knit. Stage VI brings the problem-solving aspect of HRD full circle. Stage VI "returns" to the needs analysis stage, revisiting HRD's precipitating needs to determine whether they have been successfully resolved. Stage VI is the last stage in an existing cycle of HRD, but it is also the first stage in any future HRD efforts in the same area. Stage VI evaluation will help determine whether the HRD program was worth it in terms of the value that has resulted to the organization; it will also help determine whether any more intervention is needed if the initial problems and needs have not been fully resolved.

Stage VI evaluation above all assesses the value of training's payoffs. Sometimes, these values may be readily calculated in dollar terms. When training was initially intended to reduce operating costs, increase efficiency, make operations more profitable, or otherwise directly address the bottom line, then Stage VI evaluation can usually focus readily and directly on dollar-based results, and these benefits can be readily compared to the costs of HRD. If, for example, a training program for computer maintenance personnel resulted in more usable computer time for employees, the dollar benefits of such results could be fairly easily measured or estimated. If such benefits were worth $100,000 and training costs totaled $10,000, then a tenfold worth of training (or a training payoff, or return on investment of $90,000) is easily gauged.

But not all HRD is so easily converted to familiar accounting calculations. Sometimes, the results of HRD may be very difficult to translate into dollar benefits, or their conversion to dollar benefits may be misleading. A life-saving training program at a power plant may, for example, have been credited with the saving of one person's life. To measure the dollar savings in lost time, death compensation, and so forth of the saved life in comparison to the costs of the training program might yield a net "loss" to the training program. But in cases such as this, the value of the life saved is not properly calculable in such terms. Rather, the organization would make a subjective judgment that such training is worth its cost, regardless of the apparent net loss in bottom-line figures. Because much HRD does not readily lend itself to cash calculations, Stage VI evaluation often must include alternative, more subjective and judgmental means of estimating the value of HRD payoffs.

The first section of this chapter takes an overview of the four key questions that guide Stage VI evaluation, presenting also the essential concepts and definitions incorporated into this evaluation stage. The next section discusses varying levels of Stage VI effort and uses brief scenarios to demonstrate some of the major approaches to estimating the value of HRD payoffs. The third section presents and discusses guidelines for designing and conducting Stage VI evaluation. The chapter then closes with a listing of some typical and useful Stage VI information collection procedures.

Key Stage VI Evaluation Questions

The overarching focus of Stage VI is to determine whether HRD did, in fact, achieve the purposes it aimed for in the first place. Because HRD's purpose is always to render something of value to the organization, Stage VI involves value estimating, which is a complex task. And Stage VI evaluation is further complicated by the fact that HRD renders value to an organization by a relatively convoluted and uncertain chain of events, from creating new learning of skills, knowledge, or attitudes, through changes in behavior of employees, to eventual benefits. So, while the basic Stage VI question is, "Was it worth it?" the complexity of Stage VI evaluation can be partially resolved by dividing this basic question into four related questions:

- What benefits have resulted from HRD?
- What is the value of each benefit (in dollar or other terms)?
- How do these benefits compare to the costs of the HRD program?
- To what extent has the initial HRD need or problem been resolved?

   1. What benefits have resulted from training? This question leads directly from Stage V, which determined what behaviors and other workplace changes (products, information, and so on) resulted from HRD. Stage VI extends and documents each of these identified changes to their point of ultimate value to the organization, that is, to the point at which HRD results have value in and of themselves in light of the goals and culture of the organization. These final benefits of HRD are the last point on the chain of the logic of HRD. Table 9 below depicts examples from several typical HRD programs of likely chains of logic and typical points of ultimate benefit.

   Note that in Table 9 the "ultimate benefits" vary, depending on the sort of HRD exemplified. The several "chains of logic" (as depicted in the middle column) also vary and reflect the particular intentions of the particular kind of HRD represented. These intentions might be different, even in cases where the HRD programs are similar. A safety-training program might, in variance from the safety-training program shown in Table 9, aim at decreasing accident rates and thereby produce savings in downtime and injury compensation. Or, for another example, a manager's sensitivity program might intend to increase

Table 9. Some Examples of HRD "Chains of Logic" and Ultimate Benefits.

Learning Outcomes	Chain of Logic	Ultimate Benefit
Reactor operators learn safety skills	Safety regulations are adhered to; safety violations decrease	Company maintains federal license and receives fewer fines
Supervisors learn how to do better performance appraisal	Supervisors set better performance standards; performance is more accurately gauged; supervisors give better feedback; employee performance improves	Employees are more productive and produce more profits
Equipment operators learn better maintenance skills	Equipment is better maintained; downtime decreases	Production increases
Scientists and researchers learn how to become "intrapreneurs"	More new projects are begun and supported	Product line is increased and is more competitive
Managers learn how to be more sensitive to employee needs and concerns	Managers spend more time interacting with employees; managers elicit and listen to important employee concerns	Employees are more satisfied and content with employment conditions
Executives learn community leadership skills	More executives in community leadership and volunteer positions	Community agencies and projects receive more effective leadership

productivity or reduce employee turnover. Or a performance appraisal program might, unlike the one exemplified in Table 9, attempt to increase employee satisfaction as its major, ultimate benefit. The point here is that the ultimate benefits intended for HRD are particular to the program's context. Ultimate benefits will vary from setting to setting and are a function of the particular value structure and culture of the organization.

The examples of ultimate benefits shown in Table 9 also represent a sort of hierarchical taxonomy. The example of the safety-training program—a program that is needed if the plant is to retain its license and avoid fines by the regulatory commission—reflects a concern for survival: the organization needs this outcome in order to continue its operation. The performance appraisal and the maintenance-training programs each exemplify a concern with profits and productivity; the ultimate benefits in these two examples represent a desired increase in profitability. Training scientists and researchers in "intrapreneurship" and other creativity skills represented an attempt to expand the organization's product line, the ultimate benefit being corporate growth and expansion. Sometimes, HRD programs aim to achieve outcomes that impact on the quality of work life or otherwise improve the welfare of employees. The sensitivity training program for managers reflected such a concern for employee well-being. Lastly, giving executives training in community leadership skills represented an effort by the organization to impact on general social welfare. The taxonomy demonstrated in these examples is as follows:

- Survival of the organization (lowest level)
- Profits and profitability
- Growth and expansion
- Employee welfare
- Social welfare (highest level)

Distinctions among levels in the suggested taxonomy are not absolute, and any given HRD program might aim at benefits that subsume several levels. The employees who feel more content and satisfied as a result of improved performance appraisal may also be more productive, and thus we may have a combination of profitability and employee welfare. Or the company whose executives become active in community programs may achieve an enhanced image, leading eventually (through more favorable taxation arrangements, for example) to greater profitability. And, certainly, there is a very pragmatic viewpoint available that says that the concern with employee welfare, social welfare, and other such apparently philanthropic matters is really just the profit motive wolf in sheep's clothing.

Nonetheless, the taxonomy should be helpful in seeking to identify and document HRD's benefits. Any given HRD instance is likely to be aimed at only one, or perhaps two, of the outcome levels in the taxonomy. The safety-training program shown in Table 9, for example, is mainly concerned with corporate survival. It may yield further benefits as well (renewed licensing would, perhaps, make employees feel more secure). But these secondary benefits need not concern the Stage VI evaluator. The program's main intention was to prevent safety violations that would lead to a loss of licensing. If this training program achieves that payoff, then the program has accomplished an outcome of value, and this outcome is, according to the logic of the program, sufficiently valuable to justify the training. Of course, if primary benefits are not achieved or have low value, secondary benefits would have to be looked at.

It is up to Stage VI evaluation to define, identify, and describe the ultimate benefits expected from the HRD effort being evaluated. If HRD has followed the recommendations of the Six-Stage Model, these expected benefits will have been identified prior to the program's operation (that is, at Stage I). But, very often, practitioners will have to conduct Stage VI evaluations of existing programs for which no Stage I effort has been documented. In these cases, it is necessary to "back through" the Six-Stage Model, identifying what trainees have learned, how they are using that learning, and what is resulting that may have value to the organization. Reference to the hierarchical taxonomy shown earlier may help to identify potential areas of organizational benefit.

In any case, Stage VI evaluation will have to work toward

specifying, identifying, describing, and documenting those results of HRD that can be construed, in and of themselves, to be pay-offs—things of value to the organization. These "things of value" are the end points on the chain of events resulting from HRD.

Before leaving this first question, it is worth pointing out again the relativity of HRD's value. The value of HRD is not an absolute quantity. It varies from setting to setting and is a function of the setting itself. What one organization sees as valuable (a satisfied employee, for example), another might view as almost worthless. Thus, determining what the results of HRD have been will require some degree of value clarification, and it will also require close knowledge of the organization in which the HRD to be evaluated resides. While there is much talk of a need to be "objective" in evaluation, the forgoing discussion should impress upon the reader the ultimate *subjectivity* of evaluation, as it deals with value assessment and expression. This value orientation becomes of paramount importance in the next Stage VI evaluation question.

2. What is the value of each of the benefits of HRD? To be considered a benefit, a result of HRD must obviously have some value to the organization. Whereas the first key question dealt with identifying and describing benefits (and thus raised the value question), this second question aims to quantify, or otherwise estimate the magnitude of, the value of HRD payoffs.

Sometimes the benefits of HRD will lend themselves readily to conversion to dollar calculations. A 3 percent gain in productivity can, for example, be relatively easily translated into a specific gain in profitability. A 5 percent decrease in scrap rate can likewise be readily expressed as a certain cost saving. Typically, savings in time, effort, materials, and other inputs to the production process can be easily converted to dollar values, as can training results that have impacted on quantity or quality of production (outputs). Where this is the case, Stage VI evaluation can produce, after the costs of HRD have been calculated, cost-benefit comparisons and ratios in dollar terms.

But it is more often the case that only some of the benefits of HRD can be so readily converted and quantified. A performance appraisal training program might have reduced the time managers spend in assessing and recording performance, thus making possible a dollar-expressed time-saving benefit. But that same program might also be responsible for an increase in employee morale and job satisfaction. Estimating the value of these "softer" benefits may be more difficult (though not impossible). Moreover, in a culture that values such employee benefits highly, what would be the purpose of even trying to affix dollar values to them?

While it is probably possible to attach dollar values to virtually any event or result (chemists can, for example, calculate the "worth" of a human being by using the market rates for chemicals present in the human body), it may not be worth the effort involved. Costs for some HRD programs may be relatively inconsequential, and thus an elaborate and costly assessment of the value of their results would not be called for. In other cases, the results of HRD might be of such obvious and great importance that they are relatively "priceless." Programs that result in saved lives or in dramatic improvements in safety or the quality of work life, that meet licensing and regulatory requirements, or that provide due process and other basic human rights and safeguards are examples of such "priceless" programs. Decisions to mount HRD programs of these kinds are based on global and basic values in the first place, and the programs are not intended to result in profit increases or cost reductions.

This recognition that not all HRD benefits lend themselves to familiar dollar-accounting procedures does not mean, of course, that practitioners should pay no attention to the efficiency of such programs or should let their costs run amok. Rather, evaluation of these programs will focus on whether they are continuing to provide effective results (high learning rates and thorough transfer and durability of results), while maintaining or even reducing costs. The Stage VI model argument for the worth of programs like these will be based on demonstrating that they are producing their results with demonstrated efficiency in HRD inputs and activities.

For example, a safety-training program in a power plant might have amply demonstrated that it does, in fact, reduce the incidence of fines and the possibility of the company's losing its license. It might be shown, for instance, that in divisions where training has been conducted within the past six months, safety violations are significantly lower than in divisions that had not received recent training. If the reduction in safety violations is, in itself, extremely valuable, attempts to convert reduced violations to dollar gains are not necessary. If the training unit can demonstrate that the expense of training is minimal—say less than 10 percent of the average fine levied by the regulatory commission—then this is probably ample "proof" of the training's worth. Or assume further that the HRD unit is not content to rest on this "minor expense" laurel. Rather, it seeks to increase the training's efficiency through improved training materials or computer-aided instruction. Now it can demonstrate its ability to deliver the same value (reduced violations), while spending less on training than had previously been the case. Training has now been able to demonstrate increased productivity: the same benefit has been achieved at lower cost. This approach—measuring costs of HRD for fixed-value or nonquantified benefits—is called the cost-effectiveness calculation.

In any HRD instance, however, Stage VI evaluation requires that the value of payoffs (benefits) be assessed in some form. When it is practical and advisable to assess these benefits in dollar terms, Stage VI will incorporate procedures typically used in accounting and cost-benefit assessment. In some cases, only some of the benefits of training may be so accounted for. In other cases, Stage VI evaluation may gather judgments from the organization's leaders and decision makers in order to assess the value of HRD payoffs. These value judgments might be systematically and formally collected through such methods as Delphi techniques, nominal group techniques, panel reviews, or other value clarification and opinion-gathering methods. Alternatively, less formal and systematic approaches might be used, sometimes no more complex than asking the organization's leaders what they think or presenting them with a summary of documented benefits of HRD and asking, "Well, was it worth it?"

Assessment of the value of HRD benefits can be a complex process because it involves many different value perspectives and opinions. Production line employees may value a safety-training program highly because it makes them feel less liable to injury, gives them the sense of having mastered another area of expertise, and makes them feel respected by the company. Their supervisors, however, may not like the program because it interferes with short-term production rates in the months during which training is scheduled. By the same token, managers may value the program because it reduces operating costs in terms of lost time and injury leaves, and staff executives may like it because it reduces liability insurance premiums. Finally, the board of directors may be somewhat opposed to the program because it represents an increase in overhead costs and decreases the funds available for capital expansion. All these perspectives (and probably others) combine to make up the "value" of the program. It would be wrong to judge the program's total value on the basis of any one of these perspectives. Stage VI evaluation must seek out and document these various perspectives, so that whoever makes the decision as to the overall worth of an HRD program is playing with the advantage of the "full deck" of perspectives. While there is no pat method for weighting each of these perspectives and summing them up into a final judgment, it is nonetheless crucial that each perspective enter into the decision-making process. If a decision maker is unaware, for example, of the benefits of the program in terms of employee security and morale, a bad decision to end the program, based only on its negative impact on short-term production rates, might be made.

When the value of HRD results is evaluated for skill-training or other programs in which particular on-job behaviors are intended, being very *specific* about training results is crucial. Training value—value to the organization—can *only* result from specific, observable, discrete performance changes. Thus, the performance changes must be very carefully identified. A management-training program might, for example, have enabled three managers to conduct briefer staff meetings. The specific time savings from these shorter meetings (assuming meeting *results* are constant) can then be readily expressed as a dollar savings by factoring in staff salaries.

3. How does the value of the program's benefits compare

to HRD costs? Comparing the benefits of HRD to the costs will, of course, entail estimates of each of the costs and benefits. As was noted in the discussion of the preceding Stage VI question, attaching dollar costs to benefits may sometimes be done only partially and at other times may not be done at all. But some estimate, whether in dollar terms or not, must be made of the value of the benefits that HRD has produced. Likewise, some estimate of HRD's costs must always be made. In the case of the HRD side of the cost-benefit equation, program costs will most typically be calculated in dollar terms, but they may also be expressed in other quantitative terms that have direct cost consequences, such as amount of time spent, amount of tangible resources consumed, and so forth.

Whereas the benefits of HRD may be difficult to convert to dollar values or it may even be unnecessary to attempt to do so, the dollar costs of HRD can always be accounted for. It is a relatively simple matter, though perhaps tedious, to identify and calculate the costs incurred in developing, delivering, and supporting HRD programs. Or at least this is true of the direct costs of programs, such as the trainer's time, rental of space, use of supplies, participants' travel, and so forth. Other, more indirect costs will be more difficult to account for. The salaries or wages paid to trainees while they are attending a program on company time should be added to the program's costs, for example. And assuming that trainees are productive in their jobs, then the loss of productivity resulting from their involvement in HRD might need to be accounted for as well. Salespeople attending training, for example, are being paid for their time but are not earning sales for the company during the training period. Then, of course, there are all the overhead expenses of training, such as maintaining the training unit, providing the services (personnel and accounting, for example) the unit requires, and so forth.

Programs entail opportunity costs as well. Dollars spent on HRD are not available for purchasing capital equipment, increasing fringe benefits, or bolstering corporate and individual performance in other ways. If Stage I analysis was correctly and thoroughly conducted, then such opportunity costs were considered in the first place as a part of the decision to do HRD.

But it is often the case that no Stage I data exist. It will then be necessary to make estimates of the opportunity costs of HRD—identifying other potential interventions and their costs. It may be, for example, that an operator skills-training program for cashiers has produced lower error rates and thus has positively impacted profitability. But if a simple job aid (a printed set of instructions affixed to each cash register, for instance) could have produced the same results as training, but at a small fraction of the cost, then training may not have been a cost-effective solution to the performance problem. Thus, it is possible that HRD can yield a "profit"—the payoffs of HRD may have more value than the program costs, as in the example of the cashier training—but that there will be cheaper alternatives that yield equal or greater benefits. Stage VI evaluation will have to identify such potential alternatives and estimate their costs and benefits in comparison with those realized from HRD.

Many excellent references and guides to cost accounting in HRD exist (see especially Cascio, 1982, and Spencer, 1986), and the reader desiring more guidance in these techniques is directed to them. In addition, the typical organizational setting (a corporation, for example) contains an accounting unit with expertise in accounting principles and procedures. This book will make no further effort to detail how to account for HRD costs. But, as noted a few paragraphs earlier, HRD programs and settings call for different degrees of specificity and thoroughness in cost accounting, and likewise may entail different attention to differing cost aspects. A training program that keeps salespersons in training and thus out of their territories for long periods of time, for example, would have to pay significant attention to the costs of lost sales opportunities. In contrast, a sales program that engaged persons in training only during slack periods could practically ignore that consideration. Some HRD programs might involve relatively large development and production expenses or might use expensive equipment. A flight-skill training program for pilots, for example, might have relatively low costs for trainer and trainee time but incur huge expenses for rental or purchase and maintenance of a sophisticated flight simulator.

Once HRD costs and benefits have been estimated, their

comparison is a relatively simple matter. When HRD costs and benefits have been expressed as dollar values and these dollar expressions seem reasonably accurate, then the worth of training can be expressed as a familiar cost-benefit ratio. If, for example, a program cost $10,000 and produced benefits valued at $100,000, then the HRD program made a tenfold return on the money invested in it. But note again that such an estimate of the worth of HRD requires a high degree of faith in the accuracy and completeness of the estimates of cost and benefit. It is often not the case that cost, and especially benefit, estimates will be deserving of this faith. Nor will it always be the case that it will be worth it for evaluation of HRD to spend the time and effort required to produce completely trustworthy estimates.

Sometimes, if not often, the comparison task is likely to be a matter of "comparing apples to oranges." Consider, for example, this comparison of two hypothetical safety-training programs conducted in a company that does $1 million of business a year. Each of the programs has been reliably shown to have saved at least three employees' lives last year. Program A cost $1,500; Program B cost $500,000. No estimate of the dollar value of the human lives saved is available. Nor is it necessary. One can say, quite readily, that Program A was very obviously "worth it"; $1,500 is not much to spend to save one life, much less three. Program B, we would also have to conclude, was probably worth it, for lives are of inestimable value. But there will be a "but" appended. Isn't this a pretty expensive training program? Why is it so expensive? Couldn't the same results be achieved for less money? Now, for further discussion's sake, assume that the industry average for similar safety-training programs is $3,000. Given this information, Program A seems to be a bargain, for it has produced valuable benefits (lives saved) for only half the going rate. Program B, in contrast, produced equally valuable benefits but appears to be wasteful and inefficient, costing many times the industry average! Surely, a likely decision here would be to look at the training very closely and identify how it might be made more efficient but with no reduction in effectiveness. Of course, even assuming that it were possible, the company would hardly want to roll back the clock and delete the $500,000 program, given the three lives saved. But worthwhile as the program was, the $500,000 spent on it turned out to be overly expensive and wasteful.

In this example, a comparison of "apples to oranges" was in fact made, and made quite easily. The training costs were expressed in dollars ("apples"), but the benefits were expressed as the number of lives saved ("oranges"). The value of the benefits is readily recognizable and estimable because of the culture and shared values of the setting. Were this same example set in some hypothetical context where lives were not valued at all, then the conclusions would have been quite different. The point is that most HRD benefits will be amenable to such valuing. Trainers will have to seek out value positions, clarify them, and perhaps even stimulate dialogue on values among those who make decisions about HRD programs and whether to continue their support. A number of the Stage VI procedures listed at the close of this chapter involve techniques for raising, identifying, and prioritizing value positions and claims.

4. *To what extent has the initial HRD need or problem been resolved?* This fourth and final key question might be considered by some to be the *first* question to ask. Here it is listed last, because it brings Stage VI evaluation back full circle to needs analysis, or Stage I. An HRD program is initiated to meet some need in an organization. That need might involve a performance deficit, a professed desire for training by some employees, or some other opportunity to achieve organizational growth and development. In any case, HRD was to deliver something of value to the organization. But even when the HRD program has run its intended course, it is not really complete until the question "Has HRD done its job?" has been asked.

Several responses to the question might be discovered. It may be that HRD has had a partial impact on the initial problem or opportunity but that more training is needed in order to finish the job, or the need may have been completely met. Again, the need may have somehow changed, so that the initial goals HRD set out to address have to be modified, because organizational conditions, needs, and opportunities have changed since HRD was initiated.

This fourth and final Stage VI guiding question should result in a decision about the future of the HRD program being evaluated. That is, if HRD has done, or not done, the job it was meant to accomplish, then HRD ought to be continued, or terminated, as the case may be. The purpose of this final Stage VI question is to avoid "run-on" HRD. Too often in organizations a good and worthwhile program will be initiated but then will be continued well beyond the point where it was needed. Proper attention to Stage VI evaluation can help avoid the waste and lost opportunity of "run-on" training. The decisions that can be made during this final phase of Stage VI are:

First, the program can simply be terminated. If the need or problem is fully resolved and HRD is no longer needed, then the program should be terminated. Or it may be that the need still exists but that the HRD program is unable to address it.

Second, the program can be continued. If the HRD is worthwhile and cost effective but the need remains and has been only partially addressed, then the HRD program should probably be continued. There are two variations here:

1. Continue but curtail the HRD if the need still exists but has been sharply reduced.
2. Continue and extend the HRD if the need has grown and expanded (this decision might typically be made after a successful pilot program).

Third, the program can be revised and then continued. It may be that HRD was not worthwhile, that the need still exists, and that there is reason to believe that the program could be successfully revised to make it both effective (able to address the need) and worthwhile, that is, cost effective. In this case, revisions should be made prior to continuing the HRD program.

Notice the recurrence of the term *need* in each of the potential Stage VI decisions listed above. Decisions about continuing, terminating, curtailing, expanding, or revising HRD require, quite literally, a "return" to the needs analysis stage. When original needs data are available, they should be dredged up and compared to similar data about conditions as they exist after the HRD effort has taken place. For example, consider a supermarket training program for cash register operators that was initiated because customers were complaining about long waits and observation data showed that operators were making numerous mistakes requiring considerable and time-consuming backtracking. These initial needs data were further supplemented by estimates of the costs of lost business and lost goodwill. After the training, Stage V data were collected that showed reductions in errors and concomitant reductions in customer waiting time for trained cashiers. The worth of the training in this example is established by comparing the training costs against the projected costs of lost business and reduced goodwill as estimated in the needs analysis.

However, let us further assume that, in the course of collecting posttraining data about error rates and customer delays it is discovered that (1) business has expanded because of a new housing development nearby and (2) the many newly hired check-out clerks are experiencing error and complaining customer rates similar to those present before training was initiated. While the training has been worthwhile in reducing the initial need, collection of posttraining (Stage V and Stage VI) data indicates the emergence of an expanded need. It seems therefore that the supermarket should continue, and even expand, its training program. Notice in this brief example how original needs data were referred to and how data similar to the original needs data were necessary to determine whether to continue or terminate the training. Stage VI "returned" to the needs analysis stage.

Levels of Stage VI Effort

As in all other stages of evaluation, varying levels of Stage VI effort are called for depending on the particular magnitude of a program, the importance of its needs, and a myriad of other contextual factors. Again, as in previous chapters, I will present and then discuss several scenarios to demonstrate different levels of effort and to identify some of the factors that determined the appropriateness of the level of effort pursued.

Scenario 1: The Fabufax Manufacturing Company had recently hired a large number of new drill press operators. Through careful performance audits, customer rejects and contract defaults were eventually traced back to an unacceptably high scrap rate and faulty quality measurement procedures among the new operators. A skill-training program for the operators was begun when it was further discovered that selection procedures had failed to identify their unfamiliarity with the equipment they were using. In addition, their supervisors received training in maintaining accurate statistical quality-control graphs. Follow-up audits two, six, and eighteen weeks after the training resulted in considerable revisions to the training, chiefly in the form of on-site "refresher" minisessions for operators and supervisors. A second round of audits revealed that the program had finally taken hold; the scrap rate was down, quality was up, and quality assessment accuracy in the operators' division was at a near-perfect level. Further, reviews of contracts and surveys of reactions of contractees who received manufactured parts revealed that improvements in quality had favorably affected profitability; the training had proven worthwhile, despite the considerable costs incurred by adding minisessions on the job site. A final review of the needs analysis data was conducted by the HRD and personnel directors, who also looked at projections of hiring needs and personnel retention data. On the basis of these reviews, it was decided to terminate the training, as no new hiring was projected. Further, it was decided to keep a close watch on scrap and quality rates and to provide regular feedback to operators and supervisors, so that conditions did not slip back to pretraining levels.

Scenario 2: The Old Saw Company experienced an especially good year and had some HRD budget left over. It was decided to spend some of the surplus (about $5,000) to send a few executives to a professional development experience of their choice. One chose an outdoor recreation program, another a listening skills workshop, and the third a seminar on office automation. A few months after the sessions, the HRD director scheduled a thirty-minute interview with each executive. The interview sought to document the perceived value of the HRD, as well as any benefits to the organization that the executive could identify as having resulted from the experience. Both the outdoor recreation attendee and the listening skills attendee felt very positive about their experiences and, while they could not point to specific changes that they had made in their jobs, they both claimed to feel much more positive about their work. The executive who attended the office automation seminar returned in a highly energetic state, convinced that there was a widespread need and opportunity for automation at Old Saw. She had had several discussions with the chief executive officer and was coordinating a study of several company functions. As a result, the HRD director decided (1) to ask the chief executive officer to make an annual executive development grant available and (2) to cooperate with the office automation study to identify any potential additional HRD needs.

Scenario 3: For a number of years, the Comfy Office Furniture Company had been in a declining market, and profits were likewise in a slow, but steady, decline. A better economy promised new markets, however; and as a result the HRD director had been closely involved in companywide productivity studies. A decision was made to capitalize on the coming strong market by instituting a team-production approach. In this approach, development of each product—an office information center, for example—would be overseen and coordinated by a team that would control production from customer need, to design, to prototype, to final production. As a part of this new organization, the HRD director suggested, and was commissioned to undertake, team-building and project management training. A survey of employees and a review of the pertinent literature had shown that these skills were crucial to a product-team approach.

A pilot program was begun with the first three product teams. After one year, a review of profit records and customer satisfaction survey data showed that the new team concept resulted in both greater profits and a higher-quality product. Reports of team leaders, analyses of team records and reports, and a survey of team members showed correct and effective use of the training content. A review of this training usage data was conducted during a forty-five-minute meeting of a review panel that consisted of two trained team leaders, two new (untrained) team leaders, the personnel director, and the vice-president for production. The panel also reviewed data showing that the training costs were less than 3 percent of total production costs. Given the apparent contribution of training to this successful innovation, the panel recommended that the training be continued and extended to all product teams.

Scenario 4: The Lookgood Clothing chain conducted a two-hour session on conflict resolution and management for all its supervisors. The program had been initiated in response to an annual survey of supervisors and employees that indicated a significant increase in reports of friction between employees and their bosses. Follow-up "focus group" interviews with a small group of employees indicated that the problem was real and seemed to stem from some changes recently made in shift hours and from expansion and reorganization of each store into "boutiques." A quick check of productivity and sales data confirmed the success of the reorganization, and, in fact, almost all employees liked the new structure. But conflicts had emerged as a part of adjustment to the changes, and supervisors were apparently failing to guide employees through the transition. A large number of supervisors attended the two-hour session, and feedback and skill-test data showed that it had taught new skills. Three months after the training, a brief survey was sent out to a sample of "graduates" who were asked (1) to report on which of the techniques they were using and (2) to give their estimate of the proportion of conflicts they were now successfully resolving. Survey data showed a high level of use of the new skills and a high estimate of successful resolution of conflicts. A later comparison of annual survey data confirmed these estimates. Given the relatively low cost of the training, the HRD director and his assistant deemed it a success and decided it was no longer needed. But they also decided to readminister the annual survey to a random sample in three months' time to determine how lasting the results were.

Scenario 5: For a number of years, the Sweetpea Corporation, a large sales and marketing conglomerate, had conducted a one-week session for mid-level managers entitled "Systematic

Management." The session was offered several times a year and was always fully attended. Informal contacts with higher-level managers—the bosses who sent their junior managers to the session—indicated no complaints about the program. End-of-course feedback forms (the only evaluation of the session conducted) showed that participants were pleased with the session and enjoyed it as much as any other kind of training they had attended. Further, the session had been around for so long that no one in the HRD unit could really remember when it was started or even just why. A new HRD unit director, as part of a review of all HRD programs, decided to undertake a Stage V and Stage VI evaluation of this program—an apparent winner but expensive to conduct. From training records, a small group of "success cases" (managers who were especially enthusiastic about their training and who seemed to learn a lot from it) were selected for a follow-up study. Interviews were conducted with each selected trainee in order to identify (1) how they had used the training and (2) what differences in their job behavior and what benefits to the corporation had resulted from those uses. A comparison group of managers who had been selected to attend the training but for various reasons did not were likewise interviewed. Results of the interview showed considerable differences between trained and nontrained managers in the use of two particular skills: writing memorandums and conducting meetings. But these two skills comprised only a small fraction (a portion of the first and third days of the session) of the total session; dig as they might in interviews, the HRD staff could find no further evidence that the training had been used.

Further study of selected memorandums produced by trained managers compared to other managers' memorandums validated the conclusion that the training had improved writing skills. Likewise, follow-up investigation of meeting behavior among trained managers showed that their subordinates spent 20 percent less time in meetings than the subordinates of untrained managers. Moreover, these subordinates reported (in a survey) great satisfaction with meetings, and a review showed no difference in the quality of decisions reached during these meetings compared to decisions reached by untrained managers in their much longer meetings. Conversion of this time savings into dollars yielded an estimate of $50,000 savings per year for the company. Unfortunately, the entire training session that produced these two benefits (better memorandums and shorter meetings) cost well over $500,000 when all expenses were added up. The program, despite its popularity, was apparently far from being cost effective. The HRD unit recommended that it be drastically revised and set out to create a less expensive session that would impact directly on writing skills and the ability to plan and lead meetings.

Each of these five scenarios involved an inquiry into needs data; that is, in each case the determining factor in whether HRD was "successful" was its impact on some important organizational problem or need. In those scenarios in which needs data had already been collected, they were referred to again, and some effort to collect similar but post-HRD data was made. In scenario 4, for instance, the annual employee survey data were referred to as a means of gauging the impact of the training on the original need. In scenario 5, there were no original needs data (in fact, no one could remember why the HRD program had been started in the first place!). Nonetheless, an investigation into whether the training was, in fact, addressing any significant needs was conducted. In this scenario, however, the needs analysis was done after the training. Those trainees who were most likely to have used the training were followed up, and an inquiry into how they were using the training, and what needs that use was addressing, was made. Further, the value of the impact—the worthwhileness of the needs being addressed—was estimated. Thus, all scenarios were similar in that needs data were addressed, and an estimate of the cost-benefit ratio or cost effectiveness of the HRD was made.

But the scenarios differed in methods used and in the amount of effort expended to collect and analyze Stage VI data. Scenarios 1 and 4 represented relatively minor HRD investments, and thus a relatively minor amount of effort went into their evaluation. Further, in scenario 2 (the executive development grants), the HRD was not only inexpensive, it was popular, and a superficial inquiry into its impact showed that it apparently produced worthwhile results. Thus, a more elaborate study of its contribution to the organization was not warranted. The management training session in scenario 5 was likewise popular, but there were doubts about its contributions (since no one knew why it was needed), and it was a very expensive and visible program. In this scenario, the more elaborate and costly evaluation was probably warranted; the potential savings were enormous, given the magnitude of the HRD program.

The decision to evaluate, and how much evaluation to invest in, is influenced by a multitude of factors. But as the scenarios demonstrate, a major consideration is the potential payoff of the evaluation. If decisions involving large resource allocations are pending, then it would be worthwhile to devote considerable resources to evaluation. In scenario 3, for instance, a decision as to whether to extend HRD to all furniture company employees was to be made—a potentially costly and therefore important decision. Thus, considerable effort was expended in a Stage VI evaluation to help determine the exact worth of the pilot program. But large expenses in evaluation need not be occasioned only by commensurately large potential resource investments. When HRD has a very direct bearing on the bottom line or is very closely linked to customer impact, maintenance of the corporate image, or other values that the organization is highly committed to, then relatively large investments in evaluation may be called for. In scenario 1, for instance, the manufacturing company was evaluating HRD that had resulted quite directly in customer satisfaction with company products. Because the program in this scenario was so closely tied to a major value of the organization, considerable evaluation effort was justified. But when HRD is of little consequence or makes only a minor or indirect contribution to major organizational needs, then relatively less investment in evaluation might be called for.

But that raises a further question, namely, why an organization would want to spend any of its precious resources on HRD of little potential consequence or value. Most organizations, of course, would not want to squander their resources in this manner. So, the issue becomes one of the *relative* potential value of HRD and its relative impact on the bottom line or other major values of the organization. The greater the expenses of HRD and the greater its potential effects on important organizational goals and needs, then, typically, the more effort it is worth spending in evaluation of it. The scenarios also demonstrate the dramatic impact of context on evaluation. Evaluation responds to political concerns, the economic environment, the particular needs and goals of the organization and the HRD unit, and the interests and needs of individuals. All these factors, and more, go into the decision to evaluate and also into the decision as to how, and how much, to evaluate.

Guidelines for Planning and Conducting Stage VI Evaluation

Stage VI evaluation requires some special and particular considerations. Guidelines bearing particularly on Stage VI evaluation are listed and discussed in the following paragraphs.

1. Consider a Broad Range of Training Impact Variables. The results of HRD vary according to the types of programs conducted and include a wide diversity of impacts, each having potentially significant value to an organization. A partial, but by no means exhaustive, listing follows (readers desiring more information on this subject are referred to Phillips, 1983; Laird, 1978; Donaldson and Scannell, 1978). Some potential HRD impacts include increased outputs, cost savings, time savings, improved quality, customer satisfaction, reductions in scrap rates, reduced product liability, reduced job dangers, increases in health and wellness, reduced injury and sickness benefits, reduced grievances, reduced downtime in equipment, greater stock turnover, reduced employee turnover, reduced training time, reduced absenteeism, reduced customer complaints, improved customer relations, and so forth.

But HRD programs have a range of less direct payoffs that also bear consideration. Even when achievement of direct benefits is not evident, HRD programs, and even just their availability, may generate employee goodwill and strengthen morale because HRD is seen as tangible evidence that the organization cares about its employees.

Moreover, the HRD function produces other sorts of results and opportunities of value to an organization. Various HRD sessions and programs may provide research opportunities, both formal and informal. As a management-training program is conducted over a period of time, the trainees learn about management, the HRD unit learns more about how to train managers, and the organization gains a deeper and broader pool of abilities on which to draw in the future. Additional sorts of benefits may accrue. Human resource development units may publish materials and professional articles or conduct formal research. Programs represent investment opportunities where an organization may "bank" and protect excess profits. Programs afford professional growth to trainees and trainers alike.

Lists of potential HRD impacts could stretch for many pages. The point is that there are many impacts. Evaluators of HRD should not limit themselves too narrowly to the direct, explicit goals that a particular HRD program has aimed for.

2. Look for Specific HRD Applications. Organizational benefits derive from complex and interactive factors, including but certainly not limited to those factors on which HRD might impact. And HRD will typically have a diverse range of impacts. For these reasons, it is crucial to search for and clarify specific and concrete results of HRD. This guideline was included in Stage V also, for value will derive only from specific applications of HRD. Also, the documentation and presentation of specific evidence of HRD impacts will be far more credible to decision makers than will vague and general claims of impact. A claim, for example, citing "sixteen specific instances of HRD payoff" is more credible and persuasive than "many payoffs were noted."

3. Involve Others and Use Multiple Perspectives When Assessing Training's Value. This guideline is closely related to the first one. One factor contributing to multiple payoffs of HRD is the fact that different people and groups in an organization hold different expectations for HRD and thus represent different value perspectives. The broad involvement of these several "stakeholders" will help ensure that HRD gets a fair and complete hearing, and broad involvement also helps build trust, commitment, and understanding of the training function throughout the organization.

4. Consider a Wide Range of Cost Factors When Assessing Training's Costs. Just as training has a broad range of potential value, so it has a broad range of costs. It would be unfair and unwise to ignore the many and varied costs of training when making estimates of training's worth. Again, an exhaustive listing of possible costs will not be included here, but several categories and types of costs have already been noted. (The reader may want to refer to Spencer, 1986, which deals with the subject of training costs in detail.) Some cost factors to bear in mind are (1) direct costs, including training materials and facilities, trainer salaries and benefits, and trainee wages and travel expenses; (2) overhead costs, such as clerical and technical support, utilities, data-processing equipment, and furniture rentals; (3) indirect costs, such as lost trainee productivity during training, disruptions to schedules and costs of hiring substitutes when trainees are absent, lost supervision and management time when supervisory personnel attend training, time spent in selection of trainees, and readjustment time after prolonged absence of trainees from their jobs; and (4) opportunity costs of training, including the opportunities lost or delayed by investing funds in training versus some other activity or product, such as employee benefits, new equipment, new facilities, and so forth.

5. Refer to Specific Data from Preceding Evaluation Stages. Stage VI evaluation cannot be done, and should not be attempted, without reference to preceding evaluation. Stage V evaluation, for example, should have produced documentation of specific changes in the workplace attributable to HRD. Stage VI evaluation should built on each of these discovered results and, as appropriate, ask stakeholders to attach value estimates to the results. The value of HRD is not abstract or general; it is concrete and specific and derives directly from changes in employee behaviors and perceptions and from other observable results, such as decreased scrap and defects, increased production, time savings, and so forth.

Stage II and Stage III data—information about the design and implementation of HRD—provide the basis upon which costs of training can be estimated. The program design will provide guidance and clues about the kinds of direct, indirect, overhead, and opportunity costs to be considered. Stage III data should include sufficient documentation as to how HRD actually took place so that operating costs can be calculated.

Finally, Stage I data (information about precipitating needs, problems, and conditions in the organization that call for HRD) will provide a referent for establishing value. And the needs and context data should provide guidance and clues about who are the major stakeholders and referent groups to be included in a comprehensive assessment of the worth of HRD.

Useful Stage VI Procedures

This section describes some common and especially useful procedures for implementing Stage VI evaluation. Each procedure is accompanied by one or more references to sources that will offer readers more information about it. This listing is not exhaustive, but it is meant to be broad enough in the alternatives it includes to apply to readers' varied circumstances.

Case Study. Case studies have the potential to generate rich subjective data that can aid in the assessment of the organizational impact of a training effort (Armstrong, Denton, and Savage, 1978; Borg and Gall, 1983; Schatzman and Strauss, 1973; Stake, 1973).

Customer Surveys. This method entails surveying an organization's customers to detect the value of HRD programs. There are three principal approaches to surveying: personal interviews, telephone interviews, and written questionnaire surveys. Personal interviews are expensive but enable the researcher to better control the respondents selected, to make sure that all questions are asked in proper order, and to maximize the two-way flow of communication. The telephone survey is a useful method for conducting informal interviews or studies that require factual answers to a limited number of questions. The written questionnaire (also called the mail questionnaire by virtue of its method of delivery to respondents) can be a most economical and effective method of conducting surveys. This mail survey method avoids the expense and difficulties associated with an interviewer-conducted survey, it can secure hard-to-reach respondents, it has no geographical limitations, and it can often secure the kinds of personal information that are virtually unobtainable through other survey methods. Its principal drawback lies in the failure of many persons to respond, which limits both the completeness of the survey and the representativeness of the sample. Moreover, questionnaires often are not answered carefully and completely and delays in response may hold up the final results of a survey. When the level of response is low, the cost per completed return can be quite high (Babbie, 1973; Orlich, 1978; Myers and Mead, 1969).

Cost-Benefit Analysis. There are six basic steps involved in doing a cost-benefit analysis:

1.   Identify the decision makers and their values. This usually consists of indicating which people are to be included in the analysis and how different values are to be weighted relative to one another.
2.   Identify alternatives. This requires understanding clearly what the decision choices are. When the alternative to program A is program B, use benefit-cost ratios that compare the two programs directly rather than ratios that compare each program to the null alternative of no program.
3.   Identify costs. Costs include all direct and indirect expenses, and there may be opportunity costs as well.
4.   Identify benefits that individuals, groups, or organizational elements will enjoy as a result of the program.

5. If possible, translate the potential worth to beneficiaries and the possible costs in terms of some comparable data, such as dollars saved, absences reduced, productivity gains, and so on.
6. Aggregate and interpret the valued effects. The various valued effects of a program can be combined in a calculation of net benefits or of a cost-benefit ratio (Kearsley, 1982; Cascio, 1982; Spencer, 1986; Thompson, 1980).

Performance Records Analysis. Records to use in measuring performance are available in every organization. They enable management to determine performance in terms of output, quality, costs, and time. In most organizations there are also records suitable for measuring the improvement resulting from an HRD program. If not, additional record-keeping systems will have to be developed for analysis and measurement. The costs involved here, of course, have to be weighed against the expected return for the entire program. Some examples of performance records are records of absenteeism, accident costs, complaints, overtime, dollar savings on equipment, grievances, production schedules, total output, and turnover.

For the purpose of an HRD evaluation that uses existing records, the following steps are recommended:

1. Identify and select appropriate records related to the proposed objectives of the program.
2. Determine if a sampling plan is necessary. When a large number of participants are involved in a program, a sampling of records may be adequate to supply the information needed.
3. Convert current records to usable ones. For instance, the average number of new sales orders per month may be presented regularly in the performance measures for the sales department, and the same may be true of the sales costs per salesperson. However, in the evaluation of an HRD program, the average cost per new sale is needed. The two existing performance records are combined to get the data necessary for comparison.

4. Develop a collection plan. This plan will define when the data are to be collected, who will collect them, and where they will be collected (Phillips, 1983; Webb and Campbell, 1981).

Productivity Measurement. Here, measures of "output" are compared to measures of "input" to create a ratio. For example, the number of successful tasks completed is divided by the total task costs. Keeping track of this ratio over a period of time allows a unit to gauge changes in productivity as outputs and inputs vary. Productivity measures actually incorporate other kinds of measurement; for example, "successful tasks" would have to be defined and measured by a performance test or other measure. Similarly, the denominator (in this example, total task costs) requires separate measurement. Productivity measures can be "total" as in the above example, or they can be a matter of "partial" costs—for example, the number of accurate forms completed over the hours of secretarial time required to carry out this task. Productivity measures are especially useful in that they quantify organizational results in a meaningful way and can help "keep score" of productivity improvement efforts aimed at by HRD (Adam, Klershawer, and Ruch, 1981; Landy, Zedeck, and Cleveland, 1983).

Performance Audit. The performance audit is both a technique for assessing human performance and a set of procedures for systematically determining the value of possible improvements (Gilbert, 1978; Mager and Pipe, 1984; Rummler, 1976).

Return on Investment Analysis. The term *return on investment* (ROI) usually refers to pretax earnings measured against controllable assets, which can be expressed as:

$$\text{ROI} = \frac{\text{pretax earnings}}{\text{average investment}}$$

It measures the anticipated profitability of an investment and is used as a standard measure of the performance of divisions or profit centers within a business. For HRD program evaluation, the return may be expressed thus:

$$ROI = \frac{\text{net program benefits or savings}}{\text{program costs (or program investments)}}$$

The investment portion of the formula represents capital expenditures such as a training facility or equipment plus initial development or production costs. The ROI may be calculated prior to an HRD program to estimate its potential cost effectiveness or after a program has been conducted to measure the results achieved. ROI calculations are appropriate when the program benefits can be clearly documented and substantiated even if they are subjective. The nature of the program can also have a bearing on whether or not it makes sense to calculate a return on investment.

Other methods for evaluating investments include the payback period and the present value or discounted cash flow methods. With the payback method, the total investment is divided by the annual savings to arrive at a time period (years and months) when the program will be expected to "pay back" the original investment. Thus, if the initial program costs are $100,000 with a three-year useful life and the annual net savings from the program are expected to be $40,000, then

$$\text{payback period} = \frac{\text{total investment}}{\text{annual savings}} = \frac{100,000}{40,000} = 2.5 \text{ years}$$

The present value method of ROI analysis hinges on the basic reality that money has a time value. In other words, a given sum of money is more valuable now than later, since money generates interest from its use. The concept and techniques of present value analysis allow us to quantify the benefit of money we expect to receive in the future compared with the value of money today. Whenever a return is calculated, it must be compared with a predetermined standard to be meaningful. A 30 percent ROI is unsatisfactory when a 40 percent ROI is expected (Phillips, 1983; Cascio, 1982; Spencer, 1986; Sweeney, 1979).

8

Making Evaluations Useful to Organizational Decisions

The preceding chapters have discussed evaluation of HRD in considerably more detail than it would probably ever be applied in any one particular program or setting. A brand-new training program, still in a very early stage of development, for example, should concentrate primarily on Stage I and Stage II evaluation efforts. Not only would it make little sense to expect impacts and organizational results from HRD that has barely had a chance to get off the ground, but premature impact evaluation pressures can stifle the necessary and natural development of programs as they evolve through their various stages. Again, a program that has been in operation for a long time and is no longer undergoing regular revision or other "tinkering" would benefit most from Stage V and Stage VI evaluation emphases and would not be suited to evaluation approaches meant for emerging and new programs.

Typically, then, no single HRD program evaluation addresses all six stages of the model, and those stages of the model that are most applicable receive differing degrees of attention, depending on a number of factors. Deciding just what aspects of an HRD program to evaluate, what stages of the model to emphasize, what particular purposes the evaluation should meet, and whose information needs to serve with the evaluation is the thrust of this chapter.

Whereas the preceding six chapters of the book have

dealt with individual stages of the Six-Stage Model, the remaining two chapters will deal with the model as a whole and provide guidelines, examples, and discussion to help readers design useful evaluation of HRD programs. This chapter first presents five basic steps to be considered when designing and conducting an evaluation. The remainder of the chapter addresses the first two of these five steps: focusing the evaluation and translating that focus into a set of evaluation questions that will guide data collection. The final three steps (collecting data, reporting results, and managing the evaluation) form the content of the final chapter.

Steps in the Evaluation Design Process

Any evaluation of HRD programs entails five critical decision steps, each of which represents a decision to be made before a complete evaluation design can be constructed:

1. *Evaluation focus:* What is the purpose of the evaluation? Who is it for? Why should any evaluation be conducted? What stages (of the Six-Stage Model) should be pursued? What aspects of the training program should be evaluated?
2. *Evaluation questions:* What particular questions will the evaluation seek to answer?
3. *Data collection and analysis:* What data and information need to be collected and how should the data and information be analyzed?
4. *Reporting:* Who will get what information from the evaluation? Why will they get it? When? In what format?
5. *Management of the evaluation:* What management tasks will the evaluation entail? Who will do what, when, where, and so on? What will the costs be? What resources will be needed?

As will be discussed in more detail later in this chapter, there is often recycling among these steps. For example, information discovered when data are collected and analyzed may engender more evaluation questions, which will in turn require more data collection. And the steps are often repeated in an iterative fashion, as evaluation proceeds from general inquiry to increasingly more specific investigations. Nonetheless, virtually any evaluation must pay careful attention to each of the five decision steps. Steps 1 and 2 (evaluation focus and evaluation questions) are especially important, for these two steps create the objectives for the evaluation. All data to be collected, all reports to be written, and all evaluation tasks to be managed (the final three steps) are the *means* by which an evaluation will serve its purpose: to address the evaluation questions that derive from the evaluation's focus.

Evaluation Focus

Focusing the evaluation is similar to focusing a camera; many variables have to be considered. What is the picture for? Who will be looking at the picture? What is it supposed to portray? Given all that, where should the camera be pointed, and just what should be "snapped?"

There are many things about an HRD program that could be evaluated. Evaluation could address trainee reactions, the importance of needs, the causes of performance problems, the appropriateness of HRD materials, the skills of training leaders, the quality of program facilities, the adequacy of trainer preparation, what trainees learned, who is using what was learned, who is benefiting from HRD, and how much value HRD is delivering for its cost. But an evaluation can probably afford to look at just one or only a few of these many aspects of HRD.

Evaluations serve different audiences. One evaluation might be intended for the benefit of HRD staff, while another might be meant to serve HRD consumers. Sometimes an evaluation might serve a wide range of audiences, including trainees, trainers, HRD managers, trainees' supervisors, the organization's leaders, and even the general public. In contrast, other evaluations serve only one audience.

Evaluation of HRD can serve many purposes. One evaluation might seek to compare two competing program alternatives to see which works best, while another evaluation might be aimed at identifying what needs to be revised in a program. Yet another evaluation could be pursued to determine if a program has met the performance needs of its trainees.

Just how an evaluation is designed—what data it will collect, when it will be conducted, to whom it will report, who will run it, and the kinds of conclusions it will make—will all depend on its focus. The focus for an evaluation is composed of the preceding three elements: (1) the purposes it is meant to serve, (2) the audiences whose information needs it aims to meet, and (3) the major aspects (costs or trainee learning, for example) of the HRD program or function that it will investigate.

All three of these focus elements must cohere. They must be properly identified and suitably interrelated for the evaluation to work. It would be a dysfunctional evaluation, for example, that had as its purpose to help trainers revise their teaching performance but did not include trainers as an evaluation audience. A primary concern during the focusing step is to make sure that the three elements (audience, purposes, and program aspect to be assessed) do, in fact, hang together in a sensible and balanced way. Until the evaluation focus is clear, is judged to be logically sound, and is agreed to by the major audiences for the evaluation, then evaluation planning should not proceed to planning for data collection, reporting, and managing evaluation tasks. In other words, it would make little sense to plan the operation of an evaluation that was not aimed at workable and useful goals.

Evaluation Purposes. Table 10 lists some of the more typical purposes that an HRD evaluation might serve. They are listed according to stages of the Six-Stage Model:

Table 10. Some Typical Evaluation Purposes.

Stage I	• Assess existing needs
	• Validate needs
	• Rank and prioritize needs
	• Determine magnitude and importance of needs
	• Determine whether needs are HRD problems

(continued on next page)

Table 10. Some Typical Evaluation Purposes, Cont'd.

- Determine the potential value in meeting needs
- Identify perceived needs and "wants"
- Determine which groups and/or individuals embody needs
- Assess performance, skill, knowledge, or attitude levels
- Assess and clarify causes of problems
- Assess opportunities for training results
- Assess new goals and directions for training
- Account for training needs

Stage II
- Determine strengths and weaknesses of a given HRD design
- Select a "winning" design
- Compare competing alternative HRD designs
- Identify needs for revision in designs or materials
- Identify opportunities to make an HRD design more efficient
- Rank order a set of HRD designs
- Identify perceptions of key groups about an HRD design
- Account for HRD design adequacy

Stage III
- Identify strengths and weaknesses of the HRD operation
- Gain more control or consistency in the HRD operation
- Identify participant reactions and perceptions
- Identify and head off emerging problems in the HRD operation
- Identify HRD staff development needs
- Identify HRD material and logistic problems
- Control quality of delivery of repeated or concurrent HRD program operations
- Monitor and document HRD operation and expenditure of resources
- Monitor achievement of interim operating milestones and objectives

Table 10. Some Typical Evaluation Purposes, Cont'd.

	• Account for HRD operation and resource expenditures
Stage IV	• Determine learning levels of participants
	• Compare pre-post gains
	• Select, certify, or accredit successful trainees
	• Rank order trainees by achievement levels
	• Give feedback to trainees about learning
	• Determine group achievement levels
	• Create a data base regarding achievement
	• Account for learning and immediate HRD results
Stage V	• Identify successful applications of HRD content
	• Locate problems in applying HRD content
	• Create an applications data base
	• Provide feedback to HRD "graduates"
	• Support supervisor efforts to reinforce training applications
	• Decide which parts of HRD are or are not being used
	• Link HRD results to HRD programs
	• Account for HRD applications
Stage VI	• Estimate value of HRD applications
	• Compare value of different applications in same or different HRD programs
	• Determine cost-benefit results of HRD
	• Decide whether more or less HRD is needed
	• Account for HRD costs and results

Even a casual review of Table 10 reveals a large number of potential evaluation purposes. Since no evaluation could address more than a very few of these many potential purposes, a crucial part of focusing an evaluation involves identifying and clarifying purposes. Sometimes the focusing step will include limiting the purposes of an evaluation, so that it will not be stretched too thin and, by attempting to serve too many purposes, will serve none of them well.

A useful way to identify and clarify an evaluation's purpose is to consider the stage of development that the HRD program is currently in or is about to enter. In Chapter One it was explained that all training proceeds through identifiable and predictable implementation stages (that is, the six stages of the Six-Stage Model). As Table 10 demonstrates, evaluation purposes can be readily grouped by, and are linked to, the evaluation stages. Thus, considering what stage an HRD program is involved in will greatly help in identifying and clarifying the evaluation purposes that can be most usefully served.

Consider, for example, a new supervisory training program that a company has recently adopted. Assume that there is already considerable evidence that the program is needed (supervisors are not skilled in carrying out certain important tasks) and assume also that there is evidence that the program in fact teaches the skills it was intended to. Finally, assume that the program has been initiated as a pilot program and that HRD management wants to decide whether it should eventually be extended companywide. Given this scenario and the stage of development of the program, a considerable investment in Stage V and Stage VI evaluation is probably called for. The decision about extending the training should be based on the value this program has in resolving supervisory problems, and thus it is important to know just how, and how much, the training is being used on the job. And since the program is new and presumably developing, the evaluation should also focus on how well the training-learned skills are being applied, so that remediation, support, and revision of the program can be facilitated to get the maximum possible benefit, in terms of on-job usage, out of this HRD program. Thus, the evaluation purposes will be primarily related to Stage V and will be further defined to help HRD managers (the evaluative audience) make (1) decisions about revising the program and supporting use of the training and (2) decisions about whether the HRD program shows enough promise to be kept at all.

Or we can look at a somewhat different example. Assume that a sizable HRD unit in a large company has been offering a supervisory skill-training program for a long time. In fact, the program has been around so long that no one can remember (or seems to care) whether a needs analysis was ever conducted, or even why the program was started in the first place. In any case, the program is there, and seems to be popular, if not successful. Trainee feedback (and attendance) evidences a well-run, entertaining, and solid training program. There is no evidence, however, that trainees learn anything valuable, or that what is learned gets used or ever makes a difference in the company. Despite intuitive reactions (managers would not send their supervisors to the program if it were not useful and so forth) and in the face of decreasing company profits, the HRD unit is under pressure to audit its operations to look for potential cost savings. This program, given its magnitude and prominence, is a likely contender for such an audit, and so the unit decides to conduct an evaluation of it. The primary purpose of the evaluation is to determine whether this particular program has any redeeming value. Should it be continued? Could it be trimmed without any significant loss to the organization? In this instance, as in the previous example, the evaluation would likely focus on Stage V at first and then move quickly on to Stage VI. The Stage V evaluation would be intended to discover any promising uses of the training content in the supervisors' jobs. Then the value of these uses would be estimated and compared to the costs of the program. Possible outcomes of such an evaluation might be to cut the program, to trim it back, to modify it to get more value from it, or to otherwise revise it to make it pay off. In any case, the purposes and setting of this example demonstrate an evaluation whose focus would be on the later evaluation stages.

When a program is in a very early developmental stage, however, the later impact stages (Stage V and Stage VI) would not be an appropriate focus. Let us say that a company, in an effort to reduce HRD costs, is in the process of converting a major portion of its orientation program from classroom training to an interactive videodisc format, which individual trainees would use on the job during slack time. Assume that the program content has been tested over many years of operation and that a feasibility study has indicated that the shift to a self-instructional format would work and would save money. As the first few modules are developed, considerable investment in Stage II and Stage III evaluation would be warranted. In this example, groups of past trainees and their supervisors might be convened to review and critique "storyboard" mock-ups of the modules before the expensive process of converting them to videodisc is begun. Later, when the modules are tried out, trainers might observe the first few trainees, then interview them as they complete a module. This would be a way of discovering trouble spots, confusing directions, and so forth that might require modifications in the content and format of the modules. New HRD workshops, new manuals, or other new HRD interventions would likewise benefit from early and thorough Stage II and III evaluation to help refine and revise the HRD to give it the maximum possible chance to pay off.

The point here is that HRD programs should be analyzed to determine their stage of development and to identify the growth and development needs that evaluation can best serve. Caution must be exercised not to force premature impact evaluation (Stage V and Stage VI) when a program could benefit from more attention to its development. While all HRD must eventually prove itself in terms of appropriate payoffs for costs expended, the pressure for accountability should not be allowed to stifle the necessary growth and development process. Good HRD is not born overnight—it grows slowly and needs the thoughtful and patient nurturing that the early stages of evaluation can give.

Evaluation Audience. Another key consideration in focusing an evaluation is to identify and clarify the audiences for whom the evaluation is being conducted. Evaluation is not done for its own sake but is meant to meet some individual's or some group's information needs. Instructors, for example, may need information to help them improve their training skills; HRD designers may need information to revise a program; managers may need information on how HRD works in the job place so that they can decide whether to send their employees to a program; and executives may need information on HRD's cost effectiveness to make planning and budget decisions. In any HRD context, there are many potential audiences, and all have their own particular information needs and interests. No single evaluation focus and no single evaluation method can meet these multiple needs, interests, and evaluation purposes. Thus, it is imperative that HRD leaders carefully consider just which audiences and which purposes an evaluation is meant to serve. The worksheet in Table 11 is helpful for determining and clarifying evaluation audiences and purposes. In Table 11, the worksheet has been completed for a hypothetical supervisory skill-training program.

Table 11. Audience/Purpose Worksheet.

Audience	Purpose	Object of Inquiry
Instructors	Feedback on skills	Presentations during training
Training design staff	Revise program	Training delivery and results
Participants	Feedback on learning	Participant learning
Training manager	Decide whether to continue program; account to top management	Cost effectiveness; learning results; trainee reactions

Notice that Table 11 shows several audiences and that each audience represents a different interest and perspective. Trainees would want and need feedback on how well they have mastered workshop objectives but would probably have little interest in cost effectiveness, while the latter would be of major interest to the training manager. To work well, an evaluation must meet the information needs of its several audiences, and thus clarification of just who these audiences are and why they are interested in the evaluation is a crucial step in the evaluation design process.

What Aspects of HRD to Investigate. Notice also that Table 11 depicts the "object of inquiry" related to each audience and purpose. This represents the particular element or aspect of the HRD program that must be investigated to meet the evaluation purpose and audience needs. No evaluation should attempt to evaluate everything about HRD programs. Rather, it should evaluate those aspects of the program that will yield the information required to meet audience needs and purposes. Deciding just what aspects of the training program to evaluate is the final decision in the evaluation-focusing step. What will get evaluated is, of course, determined by why the evaluation is to be done in the first place. An aspect of a program should not be evaluated simply because it is easily measured or especially obvious. Rather, purpose should dictate what gets evaluated. If, for example, a major evaluation purpose is to find out what parts of the training went well and what parts need revision, participant reactions and learning should be assessed. But if the purpose of the evaluation is to decide whether a training program is worth keeping, results to the organization and cost-benefit determinations should be assessed. Cost-benefit data, however, would be of little immediate use in making revisions to learning activities in a workshop, and trainee reaction and learning data would not be of much use to an executive making a decision as to whether to keep or eliminate a training program.

Determining what programs and what program elements and aspects will be subject to evaluative scrutiny is an extremely important part of the focusing step. This part of focusing clarifies the scope and boundaries for the evaluation. Without such scope and boundary decisions, no one can be sure what the evaluation might and might not be looking at. This sort of uncertainty can be very detrimental to an evaluation, as I learned from my involvement in the evaluation of a supervisor training program some time ago. The evaluation was intended for the HRD manager and her boss (a vice-president), and its purpose was to assess supervisors' on-job use of training in order to make revisions to the training and to determine whether follow-up training was needed.

As one might expect in a Stage V effort, this evaluation

gathered a great deal of supervisor performance data. As the data were reviewed, the HRD manager's boss became increasingly interested in what appeared to be a major supervisor deficit in conducting performance appraisals. From the vice-president's perspective, it looked as if unit managers (the supervisors' immediate bosses) were not regularly reviewing their subordinates' performance in the area of performance appraisal and were not setting appropriate long-range objectives. The vice-president met with the HRD manager and redirected the evaluation to include a closer look at performance appraisal behaviors and, more specifically, to investigate the extent to which unit managers were giving sufficient direction to supervisors. By the time I returned to this evaluation effort, it had taken on this new slant, and unit managers had come to feel betrayed; they were now taking heat for something that was completely unrelated to the training program whose evaluation they had initially agreed to support. In other words, the focus of the evaluation had changed: it had a new purpose and a new audience and was assessing an entirely different aspect of the organization, one not directly related to the HRD program.

The evaluation focus serves as a sort of "contract" for the evaluation, specifying what the evaluation is going to look at, for what purposes, and for whom. Because evaluations are meant to lead to decisions that may well affect resource allocations, it is critical that the "contract" be clear and specific, and it is likewise critical that the contract implied in the evaluation focus not be breached without the knowledge and consent of all affected audiences. Thus, it is important to secure agreement of all pertinent audiences to the evaluation focus. Securing such agreement may require considerable negotiation and often will require modification of purposes, revision to scope and boundary, and even addition of new audiences, a step that will entail further negotiation. Agreement, quite obviously, requires involvement, and so it is to this topic that we turn next.

As was noted, involvement of all audiences is necessary in establishing the evaluation's focus. Beyond this, however, is a need to build ownership and commitment. An evaluation design that has misinterpreted an audience's interest or has ignored a key audience is likely to do more damage than good. Moreover, an evaluation may be ignored or discounted if HRD practitioners are not careful to involve audiences in the evaluation design process by thoughtfully eliciting their interests and taking every step possible to be sure that the evaluation finds out what the audiences want to know and tells them what they want to know when they need it. Particularly when evaluation is a messenger of bad news—when it discovers that HRD has not worked or has not met some expectation for it—then prior involvement of audiences will be crucial. It is a characteristic of human nature to want to ignore bad news or to bend facts to make them look the way we want them to be. Thus, if the first involvement an audience has in the evaluation is when it gets a report on its failure, there is more likely to be rejection than usage of the evaluation data. However, if an audience has been thoroughly involved in clarifying expectations and reviewing criteria and evaluation measures, then when bad news comes, as it sometimes does, it will be far more difficult to ignore, and it is much more likely that the evaluation data will be used.

Once evaluation audiences, what is to be evaluated, and the purposes of the evaluation have been identified and agreed to, focusing is complete. The next step in the evaluation design process is to make the focus concrete and specific, delineating the particular questions that the evaluation will address.

Evaluation Questions

Evaluation questions represent the specific and operational focus of the evaluation. These are the questions that the evaluation will seek to "answer." Listed below are a few typical evaluation questions that might be part of an evaluation of a supervisory skill-training workshop:

- Did the right people actually attend the workshop?
- How helpful were the supplementary notes packages?
- To what extent did trainees master knowledge objectives?
- Who is using productivity measurement procedures in conducting performance appraisals and how accurately are they being used?

- Are workshop benefits worth the costs involved?
- Did attendees complete the homework assignment?
- What problems did trainees encounter on the job in using conflict resolution strategy B?
- Why didn't anyone use the value clarification procedures taught in the session?
- What additional needs for supervisory training should be addressed?

There are several points that should be noted about these evaluation questions. First, many, many more questions could have been listed. For any given HRD instance, there are dozens, perhaps hundreds, of possible evaluation questions that might be asked. But of all the many potential questions, only a relative handful should be addressed, and they should, of course, derive directly from the purpose(s) for the evaluation. If a purpose of the evaluation was to assess the adequacy of the publicity and participant selection process so that it could be revised if necessary, then the question "Did the right people actually attend the workshop?" is crucial, whereas the question "Did attendees complete the homework assignment?" would be useless. Evaluation questions derive directly from evaluation purposes and can be seen as further defining, or "operationalizing," the purpose or purposes of the evaluation.

Notice that evaluation questions may be quite narrow and specific or broader and more general. The question "Are workshop benefits worth the costs involved?" is quite general and would eventually have to be made much more specific before data could be generated to respond to it. But "Did attendees complete the homework assignment?" is quite narrow and specific, and a data collection procedure could be constructed without much more specificity and definition than already exist in the question. The function of an evaluation question is to bring sufficient specificity and clarification to an evaluation purpose so that suitable data collection procedures can be designed. Evaluation questions get "answered" with data; the trick is to decide just what data to collect in order to address the question. To determine whether trainees completed the homework assignment, a simple checklist for the trainer who collects the homework might be used, or participants might be asked to respond to an item on a questionnaire. Of course, for either of these data collection procedures to be accurate, just what was meant by "homework assignment" and "complete" would have to be clarified. But even given this need for further specificity and definition, the question "Did attendees complete the homework assignment?" is much more narrow and specific than the question "Are workshop benefits worth the costs involved?" In any case, when evaluation questions are general and broad, further definition and specificity will be needed before data collection can take place.

Lastly, it should be noted that the evaluation questions listed are representative of different evaluation stages. Questions such as "Did attendees complete their homework assignment?" and "Did the right people actually attend the workshop?" are responsive to Stage III interests (how well the HRD effort is going). "To what extent did trainees master knowledge objectives?" represents a Stage IV focus, and so forth. That evaluation questions represent different evaluation stages should come as no surprise, for evaluation questions further specify evaluation purposes, and evaluation purposes are arrived at, in part, through considering what stage of development the HRD program to be evaluated is currently in.

Evaluation questions will not be "cast in stone," nor will all evaluation questions be decided on before any data collection begins. In fact, sometimes the major purpose of pursuing an evaluation question is to make it possible to ask more, better, and more specific evaluation questions. Consider, for example, a Stage VI evaluation that is aimed primarily at deciding whether to keep, curtail, eliminate, or expand a long-standing management training program. What this evaluation will need to discover are what, if any, benefits have resulted from the training and whether these benefits were worth the cost of the program. Benefits would result, of course, if past trainees actually used the training on their jobs. Thus, an "early" evaluation question might be, "Who is using the training?" As this question is pursued, perhaps by sending a follow-up questionnaire to former trainees, specific users of the training will be identified. Data from these users will help define a more specific set of evaluation questions. It might be discovered, for example, that relatively junior managers are using the training primarily in scheduling, planning, and conducting staff meetings.

Later evaluation questions deriving from preliminary inquiry might be, "How effective are meetings conducted by training graduates who are using the training?" and "To what extent are training users conducting briefer and less frequent meetings?" These questions could be addressed by interviewing meeting attendees and analyzing records and minutes of meetings. Assuming that meetings conducted by trainees who were using what they had learned were in fact effective and consumed less time, the evaluation question "How much are meeting time savings worth?" could then be addressed and responded to. Finally, the more specific evaluation question "Are meeting time savings worth the costs of training?" could be asked and addressed by comparing training cost data to the data on the worth of the time savings realized by those trainees who used the training to conduct briefer and less frequent meetings. Notice how, in this brief example, the preliminary, broader, and more general evaluation question was iteratively redefined and made more specific by asking a question, collecting some data, asking more questions, collecting more data, and so on until the precipitating evaluation question "Was the training worth it?" has been addressed.

Evaluation questions are defined by considering evaluation purposes and restating these purposes as one or more questions. Sufficient evaluation questions have been defined when one can say, "If these questions were answered, then the purposes for the evaluation would be achieved." Because evaluation questions further define and operationalize evaluation purposes, it is very important that the evaluation audiences be closely involved in identifying, reviewing, and revising these questions. In addition, evaluation questions should be periodically revisited to determine whether they remain important and are needed to address particular evaluation purposes and audience information needs. Table 12 provides a worksheet on which several evaluation questions have been defined for each purpose listed in the workshop example shown in the table.

Another way of thinking about evaluation questions—a

Table 12. Sample Evaluation Questions for Different
Evaluation Purposes from Table 11.

Evaluation Purpose	Evaluation Questions
Provide feedback to instructors	• What are trainee perceptions of instructors' skills? • When and why did trainees get confused or have problems? • What and how much did trainees learn?
Revise program	• What problems occurred? Why? • What and how much did trainees learn? • To what extent did the training adhere to its plan? • What about the training did trainees like and what did they dislike?
Give trainees feedback on achievement	• What and how much did trainees learn?
Decide whether to continue the program and account to top management	• How do graduates perceive the quality and value of the program? • How do graduates' bosses perceive the value of the program? • Who has used the training and how? • What value has derived from its use? • How do estimates of its use value compare to training costs? • How do needs for this program compare in importance to other organizational needs?

way that helps prepare for the next evaluation planning step—
is to consider that these questions are what the data collected
by the evaluation will "answer." When the evaluation data are
in, these data will be used to arrive at answers and responses

to the evaluation questions. For example, the third evaluation question under the first purpose in Table 12 is "What and how much did participants learn?" Some data that might be collected in response to this question could be knowledge tests or participant self-reports on knowledge acquired from the training. Analysis of these test or self-report data would yield a response to the question "What and how much did participants learn?"

There is, obviously, a relationship between evaluation data and evaluation questions. If the question had been different—if, for example, it had been "Did participants gain significantly in knowledge?"—then different data would be needed—in this example, pre-post data would be needed to determine whether a gain in knowledge had taken place. Or if the question had asked, "Did participants learn more from workshop A than from workshop B?" then comparative data would be needed. Two points should be evident from this discussion. First, evaluation questions must be precise and specific. They need to reflect exactly what is to be learned or determined from the evaluation effort. If it is a matter of knowing whether one workshop was more effective than another, then the evaluation should reflect a comparative intent, and the question "Did participants learn?" would be imprecise, misleading, and inadequate.

Second, it should be obvious that evaluation questions determine the kind of data to be collected. That is, data are going to be collected to respond to evaluation questions. The evaluation will not simply collect random data or data that are easy to come by; but rather it will collect data needed to respond to the evaluation questions. In this sense, evaluation questions serve as the direct "objectives" of the evaluation effort. These questions are what the data will be collected for; the evaluation data are meant to respond to these questions.

This relationship of evaluation questions to data collection planning does not preclude a responsive approach to evaluation. Data collection can, and often does, lead to more questions. As was noted earlier, an evaluation will typically begin with some relatively general evaluation questions; then, as preliminary data are collected, more specific and more narrowly focused questions will be raised, leading to more data collection, and so on. In a Stage V evaluation discussed earlier, a preliminary evaluation question was, "How are trainees using their productivity measurement training?" When it was discovered that some trainees were using the training content in conducting performance appraisals, several more specific evaluation questions were raised, such as "To what extent are trainees using correctly formated productivity measures in setting individual performance objectives for first-line supervisors?" This second, far more specific and narrow evaluation question could not have been raised earlier in the evaluation as it simply had not occurred to anyone.

We can summarize the evaluation question planning step by saying that evaluation questions are identified and defined in response to evaluation purposes. The evaluation questions are identified through interaction with the audiences for the evaluation and must be sufficient in number, scope, and specificity to fully address each of the purposes of the evaluation. Finally, evaluation questions must precede data collection planning efforts, even though successive evaluation questions are likely to be raised as evaluation data are collected, analyzed, and considered.

Recycling to the Focus Step

The next chapter addresses the planning decisions that involve the "how" of the evaluation: what data will be collected and how it will be analyzed, how and to whom the evaluation will report, and how the whole effort will be managed. All these topics are discussed in the next chapter because, as has been noted, they should not be decided until the evaluation's focus is clearly established. But none of this should be construed to mean that the five evaluation decision steps, from focusing to managing the evaluation, should be followed in a strictly linear manner.

Evaluation design and focus issues regularly crop up throughout an evaluation effort. Typically, the focus step is, and should be, returned to several times throughout the course of an evaluation. Evaluation discovers new questions about the HRD programs and functions that it addresses.

Thinking about, designing, conducting, and using the results of an evaluation is an iterative, looping process, not a linear one. Design issues and concerns emerge not only before but also during an evaluative inquiry. A trainer might be in the midst of gathering follow-up data from a training program when a particular but unexpected use of the training content is discovered. This newly discovered use may require that the evaluation be redesigned to permit further exploration, the design of new data collection procedures, and even the addition of new audiences for the evaluation to report to.

Not very long ago, I was involved in evaluating a productivity measurement training program in a large, complex organization. The evaluation was focused especially on workplace use (Stage V) of the training and was in particular looking at whether and how much mid-level managers were developing and using productivity measures in their units. During an interview with one manager, I discovered that she had been using the productivity measurement approach in conducting performance appraisals with her employees; brief checks with other managers indicated at least some other instances of similar applications, though this use of the productivity training had never been mentioned in the training program. At this point, a special questionnaire was developed, with the aid of the personnel division, to determine how widespread this innovative use of the training was and whether there was a perceived need to extend the productivity approach to performance appraisals. In sum, the evaluation was well under way when an unexpected finding made it necessary to recycle it back to the evaluation design stage. This introduced a new evaluation audience (the personnel division), raised new questions, and required a new instrument, new analysis methods, extended reporting, and, of course, new evaluation activities to decide how to manage the new evaluation activities.

Again, it is often the case that some part of the evaluation does not work as planned, and thus redesign becomes necessary. In another instance from my experience, a series of interviews was to be conducted with regional managers in a large sales company. After the first few interview attempts, it became obvious that the interview method would not work. Interviewers had great difficulty in making interview appointments that would "stick"—cancellations and rescheduling were the rule. And when appointments were kept, telephone interruptions and the unavailability of needed data made the interviews nearly worthless. As a result, the evaluation was redesigned to incorporate group interviews during regional sales meetings, followed up with a survey questionnaire to gather additional evidence of the impact of training. While a more careful initial design might have ruled out the first interview plan, this need to redesign an evaluation because of unexpected factors and problems is more often the rule than the exception.

Typically, evaluation studies begin with a few, relatively simple inquiries, then grow more complex as data about HRD are collected and new directions for inquiry are discovered. Experience with the evaluation helps to refocus and redesign the evaluation as time goes by. Good evaluation works much the way a detective in a crime novel operates—discovering information and "clues," forming hunches, searching for new clues, forming new hunches, and so on until the "mystery" of the impact and operation of HRD is solved.

In summary, the five evaluation design decision steps, from focusing the evaluation to planning for its management, get cycled and recycled a number of times. Regardless of this, each step must always be dealt with, and dealt with in the order presented. That is, if a new evaluation question emerges, it must be determined whether this new question involves new audiences or extends the scope and boundaries of what the evaluation is investigating and whether new purposes are involved or old purposes should be modified. These crucial focus aspects should be settled before planning new data collection, reporting, and evaluation management tasks. To not reconsider the evaluation focus is to run the risk of subverting the evaluation's effectiveness and acceptance and the risk that the evaluation will become unfair, unethical, or even illegal.

9

Managing
the Evaluation Process
and Reporting Results

This final chapter addresses the most technical aspect of the entire evaluation planning process: deciding just what data the evaluation should collect, how those data should be analyzed, how, when, and to whom the evaluation should report its findings, and how all the evaluation tasks should be managed. The chapter begins with a discussion of the elements of and guidelines for planning data collection and analysis. The next section discusses reporting, a crucial planning step. Following this, the chapter addresses the topic of planning for management of the many evaluation tasks. It closes with some brief thoughts about making practical use of the Six-Stage Model.

While the discussion in this chapter will make reference to such technical concepts and methods as reliability, validity, research design, and statistical inference, two points should be borne in mind. First, the emphasis in this chapter is on the overall planning and conceptualizing of the evaluation's operation, and thus the discussion will be relatively nontechnical. Second, the major and most important part of evaluation planning—using the Six-Stage Model to conceptualize a worthwhile evaluation effort that will help make HRD pay off—is a conceptual, not a technical, activity. Data collection and analysis can benefit greatly from assistance by persons with special research expertise, such as skilled test developers and survey researchers. But it is important to remember that these technical experts should be called on only at the point when their expertise is actually needed; that is, after the evaluation information needs have been fully thought through and focused, and important evaluation questions have been identified. Evaluations of HRD programs are most likely to be truly useful when they have been built on a strong conceptual base and are not narrowly constrained by premature consideration of measurement and other technical questions.

Strategies for Data Collection and Analysis

This step begins with a review of the evaluation focus and the evaluation question. While the final task in data collection planning is to link a data collection method to each evaluation question, it is usually helpful to first articulate the overall data collection strategy. This forms the guiding conceptual base of the data collection and helps determine how many data are to be collected, the level of precision and certainty needed, and the scope of sampling and analysis techniques.

The data collection strategy should consider the purpose(s) for the evaluation and the general thrust of the evaluation questions. For example, in an evaluation to decide which of two supervisory training workshops is the most cost effective, the data collection strategy must provide for the collection of data that will make possible a comparison of the two alternatives. This strategy, then, might include giving the same performance test to samples of "graduates" from each of the two programs, comparing their test scores statistically, and using a common checklist for comparing costs of the two programs. If, for another example, an evaluation sought causal conclusions, such as deciding how much a certain session was contributing to machine operators' job performance, then the evaluation strategy could be based on experimental techniques (such as pre-post testing), including control and/or comparison groups. Or, to consider still another example, assume that an evaluation was being conducted to provide trainers in a lengthy and demanding management seminar with data on which they could base daily decisions about revising the training plan. This data collection strategy would have to provide for brief data collection procedures that would allow a quick return of results to trainers so that they could use the results to change the next day's plans. In this example, an experimental design strategy would be inappropriate, as causal inferences would not be required, nor would comparison groups be needed.

The data collection strategy will also derive from, and be responsive to, the information needs that motivated the evaluation in the first place. If the evaluation is to provide highly precise information and there is little margin for error (the consequences of a bad decision based on the evaluation could be disastrous), then the data collection effort must be intensive and thorough, probably incorporating data from large and carefully selected samples. If the needs are less monumental, however, perhaps data collection can be based on smaller samples and concentrate on collecting more convenient and less rigorous data.

There are a variety and range of data collection strategies that might be pursued. Some are based on experimental design approaches aimed at enabling causal inferences; these strategies require control and comparison groups and usually collect data about both groups who did and groups who did not receive HRD services. Some strategies make inferences from the groups measured to other, larger groups; for example, they try to determine if a workshop given to one group of employees would work for other employees. With a strategy such as this, careful and thorough sampling procedures are usually required, and data collection must make use of sophisticated inferential statistical methods. Where there is not a need for broad inference and the evaluative purpose is more descriptive, then smaller, less random, or more convenient samples can be used for data collection. Other strategies entail careful specification and measurement of objectives, while still others are more qualitative and naturalistic, focusing perhaps on anecdotal and subjective data collection.

There is a wealth of evaluation literature (for instance,

Brinkerhoff, Brethower, Hluchyj, and Nowakowski, 1983; Phillips, 1983; Stufflebeam and Shinkfield, 1985) that describes differing approaches to evaluative data collection. The point here is not to give an exhaustive catalogue of these different approaches but to stress to HRD evaluators that data collection should consider, and proceed from, a coherent strategy. Further, the choice of strategy should be responsive to and appropriate for the evaluation purposes and questions in each particular instance.

Linking Data Collection Procedures to Evaluation Questions

Each of the evaluation questions in the evaluation design must have a data collection procedure linked to it; that is, there must be data from which to infer "answers" to the questions. For example, if an evaluation question asks, "How effective were trainer delivery skills?" one or more collection procedures will be needed to gather data to respond to this question. Participant opinions about the trainer's skills could be gathered by using a survey questionnaire or by interviewing some or all participants. Another procedure to gauge the trainer's delivery skills would be to hire an expert observer to watch the trainer during the session and then complete a rating of the trainer's skills. Or, if an evaluation question asked "How much did participants learn?" participants could be given a test or asked to fill out self-ratings.

Notice that in two of the examples above there was more than one data source that could have been used to address each evaluation question. For any evaluation question, in fact, there is almost always more than one potential data collection and analysis procedure that might be used. A major aspect of this step, then, is deciding which procedure to use for each evaluation question. This decision process involves (1) generating alternative choices and (2) critiquing alternatives by means of some acceptable criteria.

Identifying potential data collection and analysis procedures is best accomplished by thinking first about indicators.

Indicators are "measurables" that reveal something about an evaluation question. Indicators "indicate" answers and responses to evaluation questions. For example, one indicator of trainer skill is trainee reactions. Another indicator of trainer skill is an expert's impression of that trainer. One indicator of trainee knowledge is a test score, another is a self-impression. Indicators of supervisors' use of a particular performance appraisal method might be completed performance appraisal documents, the impressions and opinions of the supervisors' subordinates, the impressions of the supervisors' bosses, or even the impressions of the supervisors themselves. Indicators are things that can be measured and that yield worthwhile information about an evaluation question.

Identifying and considering indicators will lead directly to identifying suitable data collection and analysis procedures. For example, let us look at the several potential indicators and related data collection procedures shown below for the hypothetical evaluation question "How well are supervisors conducting performance appraisals?"

Potential Indicator	Associated Data Collection Procedure
Supervisors' self-opinion	Administer a self-report survey
Bosses' impressions	Survey the bosses
Completed performance appraisal forms	Analyze a sample of appraisals
Subordinates' impressions	Survey the subordinates

Notice that each indicator directly suggests a data collection procedure. Given this, it seems legitimate to ask, Why bother with indicators? Why not just think up a data collection procedure for each evaluation question? The response to this concerns the validity of the data that are to be collected. Indicators are "what" will be measured, and it is the "what" that is measured that determines validity. For example, self-opinions could be misrepresented in order to make supervisors look good, especially if respondents felt that some reward or punishment was riding on the outcome. Bosses might be unfamiliar with how their subordinates (the supervisors) actually conduct performance appraisals, and performance appraisal forms might not represent the complete process. The trick in good data collection is to identify indicators that will be both honest and accurate measures. Careful consideration of potential indicators —the "what" of the measurement process—produces the kinds of data collection procedures that are most likely to collect valid data.

Once indicators have been considered and identified, the remainder of the data collection and analysis procedure can be planned. This will entail thinking through the details of data collection, including:

1. *What instruments or recording forms will be needed?* Instruments must be readily available or easily constructed and should be designed to collect data quickly, accurately, and with as little distortion and disruption as possible.
2. *What sample of objects or respondents is needed?* Often, it is not necessary or desirable to collect data about each object (each performance appraisal record, for example) or from each and every respondent, and in such cases sampling may be both possible and desirable. But in other instances—for example, when testing knowledge gained from training in order to certify trainees—it is necessary to measure all respondents. When possible, sampling should be used, for it saves time, money, and effort.
3. *When should data be collected?* The timing of data collection can be crucial. When designing a trainee follow-up survey, for example, it may be very important to wait long enough for training to be applied but not so long that a washout of training effects occurs. Likewise, waiting until the very end of a training session to administer a training reaction form can introduce bias, for the people who have remained may be only those who were very favorably impressed by the program. Timing of data collection is important for reducing bias, coming up with good data, and getting data when they are needed and likely to be used by decision makers.

4. *How will instruments be administered and returned?* A
    method for distributing instruments, along with a system
    for their collection and return, is obviously important but
    often overlooked. Distributing a questionnaire rather than
    simply having it available for pick-up could have a dra-
    matic effect on response rate, for example.
5. *What analysis steps and procedures will be used?* How data
    are analyzed will depend largely on what sorts of data are
    collected. It is likely, for example, that interview data will
    be analyzed by means of qualitative methods, such as read-
    ing and summarizing or classifying and cataloguing re-
    sponses. In contrast, survey data will more likely be ana-
    lyzed by means of descriptive statistics. But analysis will
    also be determined by what it is that needs to be known.
    If only a rough "guesstimate" is necessary to respond ade-
    quately to an evaluation question, then sophisticated and
    lengthy analysis procedures would be wasteful. The point is
    to plan and account for the specific analysis procedures
    that are likely to be the most productive and economical.
6. *How will data be stored, handled, and safeguarded?* While
    this seems an obvious consideration, it is one that is very
    often overlooked. Data must be readily accessible for analy-
    sis and reanalysis as needed. But they must also be safe-
    guarded so that they will not be compromised or become
    available to the wrong persons.

Decisions about each of the considerations listed above
are necessary to arrive at a complete data collection and analysis
plan. Again, while these decisions require considerable thought
and attention, it should be stressed that the data collection and
analysis plan is never really complete. Data collection and analysis planning, due to the recycling, iterative, and "looping" nature of the evaluation inquiry process, do not end until the evaluation is over.

Table 13 presents some further considerations to bear in
mind when designing data collection procedures. Each of these
considerations represents important measurement and research
criteria (for further information, see Borg and Gall, 1983;

Campbell and Stanley, 1966; Cook and Campbell, 1979; Joint Committee, 1981; Sudman, 1976). And since each is to some extent dependent on the others, trade-offs and compromises among them may be necessary. Achieving greater reliability, for example, often entails collecting more data, which costs more money, which begins to trade off against the cost consideration.

Table 13. Some Important Data Collection
Design Considerations.

Reactivity	You do not want *how* you measure something to change too drastically what you are after. A typical "laundry-list" questionnaire used to survey training preferences can, for example, shape and reprioritize a respondent's reaction; a simple interview question such as "Tell me what you'd like" might get a very different response.
Bias	Self-selected samples are often biased. A follow-up questionnaire to trainees might elicit returns from extreme groups only. Or a posttest administered only to those trainees who stayed until the very end of training might yield biased scores, since this sample of trainees might be more diligent, more motivated, and so on. Make sure that the sample of what you will measure is most likely to represent what you are after.
Reliability	Consider how to get the most accurate information. When, for example, multiple observers, interviewers, or raters are used, *train* them to promote and check for consistency. Be sure that *when* or *where* you collect data is not adversely affecting your data. Take time to make instruments readable, clear, and error free.

Table 13. Some Important Data Collection
Design Considerations, Cont'd.

Validity	The procedure should collect the data you are after and not something else. Be sure that there is good reason to think that the data collected are in fact responsive to the evaluation question. A self-rating on knowledge acquired may, for example, be more related to the entertainment value of the program than to what participants actually learned. Performance appraisal data might be more related to personalities and how well employees get along with bosses than to actual job performance. Again, be sure that what you measure reflects what you want to know about.
Interruption potential	The more a procedure disrupts the daily flow of HRD life, the more likely it is to be unreliable—or even sabotaged. An analysis of the contents of a trash can may tell you something about whether trainees valued your materials and is less disruptive than a questionnaire asking them to tell you if they valued them.
Pilot testing	Try techniques out before using them. Interviewers might try out a telephone interview with a few role-played participants. Or test a questionnaire on two groups of role-played trainees—one who loved the session and another who hated it. The questionnaire group scores should be different.
Need for training information collectors	Trained information collectors usually collect better (more reliable) information than untrained ones. Also, interviewers, product

(continued on next page)

Table 13. Some Important Data Collection
Design Considerations, Cont'd.

	raters, observers, and so on will do a better job if they know what to look for and how to tell if it is there.
Availability	Use data already available (records, reports, and so on). For example, a pre-post look at performance appraisal reports on trainees could indicate whether training is making an on-the-job difference. Available data are usually more credible and more objective than data collected specifically for the evaluation.
Protocol needs	Following traditional protocol is always a good idea. If you are not likely to be able to get needed clearance or permission, look for alternative information sources.

Reporting Evaluation Information

The fourth major evaluation planning step is reporting—the communications function of evaluation. A major notion to bear in mind when thinking about reporting in evaluation is that evaluation is for people! None of the content of this book will make the slightest bit of difference in making HRD pay off if people do not use it. The Six-Stage Model, as well as the evaluation efforts that accompany its use, requires the collection and reporting of information to people who can use it to make training make a difference. Thus, the reporting function requires major attention and consideration.

Reporting applies not only to the results of evaluation but also to information about the evaluation itself. Of course, it is evaluation results that people eventually want, and it is the results that will make a difference. But if people are ignorant of an evaluation's purposes or have been misinformed about its

procedures and application, they may prove to be highly un-
cooperative. So, reporting about the evaluation—its plans, its
operation, its progress and revisions—is likewise important.

The evaluation report function includes several elements:
(1) purposes, (2) audiences, (3) content, (4) format, and (5)
schedules. All these elements must be compatible and work in
harmony for the reporting function to be a success. It does little
good, for example, to give an audience some information (content) that it does not care about or cannot use. Or, in the same
vein, an audience might care about the content and need it, but
because the evaluation report format is too complex or uses
alien language and terms, they are unable to understand and use
the content. And, sadly, it is often the case that the right people get the right content in the right format but too late to be
of any use.

Six-Stage Model users will therefore want to consider the
report function, carefully planning a report schedule and carefully considering the purposes, audiences, content, and format
of the report. The following paragraphs provide more detail
about each of these functions.

Report Purposes. Each and every report should have a
purpose, and purpose should dictate the content and timing of
the report. In addition, a report purpose will always entail one
or more evaluation audiences. Some typical report purposes are

- to demonstrate accountability; that is, to show that objectives were met, criteria adhered to, expectations met, and so
  forth.
- to document what happens during a program, providing information for later reference about HRD operation, planning, expenses, activities, and so forth.
- to educate or promote understanding and awareness of key
  operations, issues, problems, successes, and so on.
- to facilitate, inform, or stimulate decision making.
- to gain support of training audiences and consumers for key
  issues, problems, effects, or uses relating to HRD.
- to market HRD in the organization; that is, to educate man-

agement and others as to the strengths, weaknesses, issues, problems, and potential and realized worth of the HRD operation.

Report purposes should be clearly identified and clarified for each evaluation audience and for each potential report event.

Report Audiences. As noted earlier, there are a variety of evaluation audiences and thus a variety of report audiences. Usually, it is wiser to consider a broad array of potential audiences. Reporting evaluation results to the managers of trainees, for example, can go a long way toward facilitating transfer of learning to the workplace. Evaluation report summaries provided to general employee audiences can stimulate interest in the HRD operation and help make employees more educated consumers of training operations. The evaluation reporting function should be seen as an HRD education and marketing function, and this will open up consideration of a wider range of audiences. Evaluation audiences include anyone with an interest or stake in the HRD function; for example:

- Those who finance and support HRD
- Regulators, licensors, or others who certify, authorize, or regulate HRD
- Advisory boards or other oversight groups
- Consumers of HRD, both trainees and their bosses or employees
- The HRD unit staff and consultants
- Professional groups and organizations
- Libraries and other clearinghouse units
- The general public
- Other units in the organization with a stake in the HRD being evaluated

Report Content. Report content is what the report is about and should be determined by the purpose for the report. Thus, there is no standard prescription for the content of an evaluation report. Rather, report content is a relative matter, depending on what the report is supposed to be about and what the audience needs to know in order for the report purposes to be met.

It is generally a good idea to differentiate reports—to send different brief reports to different audiences to meet different purposes—rather than to prepare large, all-inclusive reports. Typically, evaluation report audiences are busy and, like most everyone else, are already deluged with more information than they can handle. A lengthy and detailed evaluation report will become lost in this other "noise." Thus, recalling that the general purpose of evaluation is to inform action and decision making, we can formulate the rule for an evaluation report as: Keep it simple and keep it brief.

Content will be determined in part by the nature of the report, and there are several typical kinds of evaluation reports. Most readers are already familiar with the "final" evaluation report. This is the report after the fact, the report that summarizes the HRD effort and all the evaluation of the HRD effort. Progress reports describe the interim achievements of either the HRD or its evaluation. The general purpose of progress reports is to keep evaluation audiences informed, help them steer and control HRD, and help them prepare to use the concluding information from the evaluation. Interim or preliminary reports are more formal and typically are scheduled for specific times (at the end of a pilot workshop or at the end of the first quarter of HRD, for example). Sometimes, the content of interim reports is considered to be in draft form and thus is to be reviewed and reacted to by evaluation audiences before the preparation of a concluding report.

While report content may vary, the following generic format can generally be used:

I.   Executive summary—a one-page precis of the entire report, including a summary of all report sections in the briefest and most concise manner possible
II. Introduction
     A.   Purpose of the report
     B.   Audiences intended

      C.   Overview of content and structure
      D.   Key definitions (the training program addressed, for example)
      E.   Limitations and caveats
III.   Report body—to include methods, evaluation questions, data summaries, and so on
IV.   Conclusions and recommendations—to include action advised, recommended, or suggested (at times, this might better be the *first* section in the report)

Finally, report content should be carefully constructed to fit the needs, interests, and development level of the audiences for which reports are intended. The language used in the report should suit audience reading and educational levels. Examples and illustrations should be used, and these should be compatible with audience interests and experience.

Report Formats. The report format refers to the structure of the report and to the medium or means by which the report is communicated. Reports may be written, oral, or delivered through such media as film, videotape, panel presentation, public hearing, or role play. Or some combination of these media might be used. Take, for example, a large corporation that has been trying out a new supervisory training program on a pilot basis for the past year. Assume that the evaluation results are highly positive and that a preliminary report has indicated that a decision to replace the company's old training program with this new one is likely. The concluding report in this scenario might include a variety and combination of formats. A memorandum report summary would go to all managers and executives; a brief, simple, and concise report would be published in the company's weekly newspaper; a summary report of about eight to ten pages would be available to all managers who lead units containing a large number of supervisors (potential trainees); the HRD unit manager would notify all managers of her availability to visit managers and discuss the report; a public hearing would be scheduled to which all interested employees at any level could come to hear the report discussed by a panel of trainees, the evaluator, the HRD manager, and the vice-president for personnel and to ask questions about the new training program or its evaluation; finally, a complete technical report would be available in the training unit.

It is important to consider a variety of formats, paying special attention to making the evaluation information visible and interesting so that it does not become lost in the "background noise" of the organization. Nothing is more likely to be ignored than the typical boring, lengthy, and overly technical and academic evaluation report. It is very important also to consider an interactive report format. Research (Alkin, Daillak, and White, 1979) on the utility of evaluation findings has demonstrated that results are far more likely to be used when evaluation audiences have an opportunity to ask questions and discuss the results. Human resource development leaders should be available to respond to questions and discuss the implications of a report with key audiences. And this availability should not be passive; rather, report formats that proactively seek and engender interaction and discussion should be used.

Report Scheduling. The major emphasis in report scheduling is to be sure that audiences get reports when they need them. Evaluation results cannot be used in decision making if the report arrives after a decision has been made. But reports should also not be provided to audiences so far in advance of decision points that they will be ignored or forgotten. Timing is crucial.

The primary guide to determining report schedules is the purpose of the report. Thus, for example, if the purpose of the report is to help a steering committee decide on how to revise a training program, the report should be provided far enough in advance of the committee meeting that members will have time for reading it, but not so far in advance that they will put the report to one side and perhaps forget about it in the face of competing demands on their time. And the report schedule should provide committee members with the opportunity to raise questions or seek explanations and further information if they so wish.

Report schedules should consider other factors as well as the primary factor of audience need. These include

- major events in the life cycle of the HRD program, such as start-up, completion of a needs analysis, and end of a pilot program.
- audience events, such as meetings, decision points, elections, and budget reviews.
- events in the evaluation, such as completion of the evaluation design or collection of preliminary data.
- commonly accepted time intervals—quarters, fiscal years, and so forth.
- opportunities and events as they occur—for example, the discovery of a major problem or an unanticipated finding of major import.

In any case, a report schedule should be prepared, showing who is to get which reports, when, and how often. The report schedule can be assessed to determine if it is comprehensive and appropriate, and the schedule can be used to plan and monitor the report function.

Managing the Evaluation

An evaluation is like any other project within an organization or within the HRD unit that requires project management. And, like other projects, unless careful attention is paid to planning, organizing, directing, and controlling the evaluation, it will not be carried out successfully. Projects that are neglected have a nasty habit of "falling through the cracks." But evaluation efforts also have their own particular characteristics that require special management attention. Some of the more common management functions will be addressed first, then the unique characteristics will be discussed.

Managing an evaluation project is a matter of four major functions: planning, organizing, directing, and controlling.

Planning the evaluation has already been discussed in considerable detail in the preceding pages. Planning consists of identifying the evaluation's goals and objectives (its outputs), the tasks and activities needed to meet these goals and objectives (processes), and the resources (inputs) needed to carry out all the evaluation tasks and activities.

Organizing consists of assigning people (or units and groups) to each of the evaluation tasks. Organizing consists also of deciding how communication among these several people will take place and who is responsible to whom for task achievement and reporting. The evaluation must be organized to make optimal use of the company's resources and must be organized to ensure that responsibility and authority for task achievement are clear and reasonable.

Directing consists of two major elements: (1) providing task direction by telling people what it is they are supposed to do and (2) motivating and providing feedback (as in performance appraisal) to staff as they carry out their directed responsibilities. Directions to evaluation staff must be clear and specific, and there must be some systematic means of checking with staff to be sure that responsibilities are, in fact, clear and understood. Feedback on performance must be provided to evaluation staff members so that they can continually be kept informed about what they are supposed to do and how well they are doing it.

Controlling means taking steps to ensure that the evaluation goes the way it is supposed to go and achieves its objectives. Controlling consists of checking up on the evaluation, monitoring its activities, and redirecting it as necessary to be sure it achieves what it set out to achieve. In many respects, controlling an evaluation is like evaluating the evaluation.

As with any project, planning is the cornerstone for management success. The plan itself can be assessed for feasibility and adequacy to ensure, before implementation begins, that a sound plan is in place. The plan also provides the basis for clear and precise direction of the evaluation. If the plan is incomplete, unclear, and vague, then it is very likely that evaluation staff will be equally unclear and vague as to what they are supposed to do. Finally, the plan serves as the basis for control. The act of control is, in essence, a matter of checking for discrepancies between what is actually happening and what is supposed to be happening.

Needless to say, it is very helpful to have a high degree of group involvement when plans are created. Group involvement provides a check against unrealistic and unreliable plans and has the further benefit of building consensus and commitment. It is also advisable to use planning formats and media that are graphic and visible. Organization charts, matrix budget forms, and Gantt charts that graphically show schedules and task responsibilities are project management aids that have proven themselves in other project settings and work equally well for managing evaluation projects.

It must be emphasized, however, that evaluation efforts have some unique project management aspects and problems. Evaluation of HRD is typically organized as an "add-on" responsibility to other responsibilities in the organization. It is a rare evaluation that is so well financed and important that it has its own full-time staff. It is becoming increasingly popular, however, when large HRD evaluations are under way, to hire out the evaluation function to an external consultant or consulting agency. Whether the evaluation will be carried out in house or by an external agency, some sort of "contracting" is advised. Because evaluation responsibilities are often new and unique, because evaluation tasks will result in resource allocation decisions, and because they are often added on to people's existing responsibilities, it is important that just what is expected be clearly and specifically defined. When such responsibilities are assigned to internal staff, "contracts" may take the form of memos or letters. When evaluation is assigned to an external person or agency, a formal contract (though still, perhaps, only a memo or letter) is a necessity.

Another critical consideration to make when organizing the evaluation, especially when identifying the chief evaluator, is to avoid conflict of interest and potential bias, real or perceived. The evaluator or evaluation staff should not have or be perceived to have a particular axe to grind. Charges of conflict of interest, loading the evaluation deck, and so forth can seriously undermine the credibility of the evaluation.

Evaluation efforts require that management give special attention to safeguarding data and protecting people's rights and interests. An evaluation that gets out of control is not only unlikely to succeed but might cause irreparable harm to individuals and to the HRD unit. Assume, for example, that an evaluation of a management training program planned to collect end-of-session achievement scores from participants for the purpose of assessing the potency of the session. To gain cooperation from participants and to ensure accurate scores, participants were promised that scores would be used only in group-data form and would be destroyed after the session. If, subsequently, these test scores were accidentally released or otherwise found their way into the hands of these managers' bosses, serious problems could ensue. At the very least, the credibility and future operation of the HRD unit would suffer; at worst, careers could be jeopardized and lawsuits could result.

Evaluation efforts often entail technical elements and sometimes will require use of internal and external technical consultants. Moreover, the tasks being undertaken in the evaluation will at times be beyond the technical proficiency and knowledge of the evaluation coordinator. Managing technical tasks for which the manager has no particular expertise creates special demands for open, frequent, accurate, and trustworthy communication.

It must always be remembered that evaluation is a highly political activity; that is, it will inevitably be part of the ongoing struggle in an organization to gain power and influence in the decision-making process. And evaluation, especially when it is successful, results in decisions affecting resource allocations. For example, an evaluation that concludes that a particular training effort is not effective or worthwhile is very likely to affect the allocation of HRD resources and the assignment of HRD staff and may even result in staff and budget cuts. Whenever evaluation is undertaken or contemplated, staff members begin to consider whose ox is likely to be gored and to take measures to protect their own territory. Managers of evaluation efforts should pay special attention to political issues and conflicts. Often, this may suggest the formation of special steering and advisory committees to ensure broad representation in the evaluation and to provide for checks and balances in the evaluation endeavor.

In sum, managing an evaluation effort is similar to managing any project within the HRD unit and requires careful planning and management attention. But evaluation efforts bring their own special considerations as well, and evaluation managers will want to pay special attention to them. In units where evaluation is a relatively new venture, formation of an evaluation steering committee, along with regular evaluation staff meetings and special debriefings, will be helpful. A special effort should also be made to develop the unit's capacity for conducting evaluations.

It may have occurred to the reader that the evaluation of an HRD effort can be thought of in terms of its logic, just as (much earlier) in this book HRD as a whole was seen to have its logic. Thus, the Six-Stage Model can be applied to the evaluation of an HRD effort, just as it can be applied to HRD itself. In fact, to turn the model around and back on itself yields a useful and powerful way of viewing the design and management of the evaluation function. Briefly, here is how the Six-Stage Model can be used to raise meaningful questions about the evaluation of HRD and can help produce a more successful evaluation effort:

Table 14. Key Questions for Assessing an Evaluation Design.

Stage I	Is there a need for evaluation? Is evaluation likely to serve some useful and worthwhile purposes? Are alternatives to evaluation available?
Stage II	How adequate is the evaluation design? Are there alternative designs that should be looked at or used? Is the design feasible? sound? economical? likely to work? Will the design meet the intended purposes?
Stage III	How is the evaluation going? Is it working as planned? What problems are cropping up? Are interim evaluation objectives being achieved? Is the evaluation on schedule?

Table 14. Key Questions for Assessing an Evaluation Design, Cont'd.

Stage IV	To what extent has the evaluation achieved its immediate objectives? Did it produce the data it was supposed to? Are good "answers" to the evaluation questions available?
Stage V	Who is using the evaluation results? Are the expected usages for the evaluation occurring? What more needs to be done to get evaluation results used?
Stage VI	To what extent did the evaluation accomplish its goals? Did it achieve its purposes? What evaluation needs remain? Was the evaluation worth the expense?

This look at the Six-Stage Model as it might be applied to the evaluation of HRD brings us full circle. The model was proposed as a way to make HRD pay off and to demonstrate the impacts and worth of HRD. But as briefly outlined above, the model can also be used to make evaluation of HRD work. Evaluation, HRD programs, and even other sorts of programs are alike in that they are rational and systematic efforts to use resources to produce worthwhile results. The Six-Stage Model is meant to make programs more effective. It should make evaluation efforts as well as HRD programs more likely to pay off.

Some Closing Thoughts

The Six-Stage Model is an ideal. In a real world of limited resources and tight deadlines, the Six-Stage Model sets a direction and a goal for excellence. Perhaps, someday in the not-too-distant future, HRD functions will regularly be expected to account for themselves thoroughly at all six stages of the model. When this day arrives, HRD will have truly matured and will either survive on its demonstrated merits or go the way of the dinosaurs. In either case, it is to be hoped that what eventually happens to HRD results from rational decisions based on accurate and valid information. If HRD, or some HRD programs, prove to be really worthwhile and can justify their existence in terms of true benefits, they deserve to survive and even flourish. If they do not so prove, then we will all be better served by their extinction.

The tragedy will come if HRD truly deserves to thrive but is unable to convincingly justify its existence in a competitive corporate environment. If the message of the Six-Stage Model is not heeded, this scenario is a likelihood. In the face of this, the closing advice here is to begin putting the model into practice. It is true that the model represents an ideal, and probably no HRD effort could ever support all the evaluation that this book has prescribed. But this is no reason to ignore evaluation.

The prescription is to begin evaluation, guided by the Six-Stage Model. As evaluation is initiated and begins to pay off in better and more defensible programs, then more evaluation will become supportable and worthwhile. And, as more evaluation is done, HRD will become more effective and efficient. This is inevitable.

The task will not be easy. Good evaluation, like good HRD, requires time, effort, and thought. The task will also require an educational effort. It is often claimed, and rightfully so, that others in an organization do not want the kinds of evaluation information that this book prescribes. There are numerous people who do not know what HRD is all about and have not thought about or seen its logic. But it is often these very people who evaluate HRD and make decisions about it. An enduring fact of life is that evaluation is *always* done. Human resource development programs will be evaluated by someone, whether HRD leaders guide and conceptualize the evaluation or not. The HRD profession's job is to be sure everyone knows about HRD and is well informed about what it is and what it can (and cannot) do before it is evaluated by anyone.

So, the final prescription is: Use the Six-Stage Model, no matter how partially or briefly. Use it to evaluate HRD. Use it to guide the development and operation of HRD. And use it to educate the consumers and authorizers of HRD.

References

Adam, E., Klershawer, J., and Ruch, W. *Productivity and Quality.* Englewood Cliffs, N.J.: Prentice-Hall, 1981.

Alkin, M., Daillak, R., and White, P. *Using Evaluations: Does Evaluation Make a Difference?* Newbury Park, Calif.: Sage, 1979.

Argyris, C., Putnam, R., and Smith, D. M. *Action Science: Concepts, Methods, and Skills for Research and Intervention.* San Francisco: Jossey-Bass, 1985.

Armstrong, D., Denton, J., and Savage, T., Jr. *Instructional Skills Handbook.* Englewood Cliffs, N.J.: Prentice-Hall, 1978.

Babbie, E. R. *Survey Research Methods.* Belmont, Calif.: Wadsworth, 1973.

Berne, E. *Games People Play.* New York: Grove Press, 1964.

Bloom, B. (ed.). *Taxonomy of Educational Objectives.* Vol. 1: *Cognitive Domain.* New York: McKay, 1956.

Borg, W. R., and Gall, M. D. *Educational Research: An Introduction.* (4th ed.) New York: Longman, 1983.

Bradford, J. A., and Guberman, R. *Transactional Awareness.* Reading, Mass.: Addison-Wesley, 1978.

Bray, D. W. "The Assessment Center Method." In R. L. Craig (ed.), *Training and Development Handbook.* (2nd ed.) New York: McGraw-Hill, 1976.

Brinkerhoff, R. O. "The Success-Case Method: A High-Yield, Low-Cost Evaluation Technique." *Training and Development Journal,* 1983, *37* (8), 58–59.

Brinkerhoff, R. O., Brethower, D. M., Hluchyj, T., and Nowakowski, J. R. *Program Evaluation: A Practitioner's Guide for Trainers and Educators.* Boston: Kluwer-Nijhoff, 1983.

Campbell, D. T., and Stanley, J. C. *Experimental and Quasi-Experimental Designs for Research.* Skokie, Ill.: Rand McNally, 1966.

Cartwright, C. A., and Cartwright, G. P. *Developing Observation Skills.* New York: McGraw-Hill, 1974.

Cascio, W. F. *Costing Human Resources: The Financial Impact of Behavior in Organizations.* Boston: Kent, 1982.

Cook, T. D., and Campbell, D. T. *Quasi-Experimentation: Design and Analysis Issues for Field Settings.* Skokie, Ill.: Rand McNally, 1979.

Delbecq, A. L., Van de Ven, A. H., and Gustafson, D. H. *Group Techniques for Program Planning: A Guide for Nominal and Delphi Processes.* Glenview, Ill.: Scott-Foresman, 1975.

Donaldson, L., and Scannell, E. E. *Human Resource Development: The New Trainer's Guide.* Reading, Mass.: Addison-Wesley, 1978.

Doyle, M., and Straus, D. *How to Make Meetings Work.* New York: Berkley, 1976.

Ebel, R. L. *Measuring Educational Achievement.* Englewood Cliffs, N.J.: Prentice-Hall, 1965.

Esseff, P. J. *Instructional Development Learning System.* Columbia, Md.: Educational Systems for the Future, 1982.

Finkle, R. B. "Managerial Assessment Centers." In M. D. Dunnette (ed.), *Handbook of Industrial and Organizational Psychology.* Skokie, Ill.: Rand McNally, 1976.

Flanagan, J. C. "The Critical Incident Technique." *Psychological Bulletin,* 1954, *51,* 327–358.

Fogli, L., Hulin, C. L., and Blood, M. R. "Development of First-Level Behavioral Job Criteria." *Journal of Applied Psychology,* 1971, *55,* 3–8.

Gagne, R. M., and Briggs, L. J. *Principles of Instructional Design.* (2nd ed.) New York: Holt, Rinehart & Winston, 1979.

Ghiselli, E. E. *The Validity of Occupational Aptitude Tests.* New York: Wiley, 1966.

Gilbert, T. F. *Human Competence: Engineering Worthy Performance.* New York: McGraw-Hill, 1978.

Gronlund, N. E. *Constructing Achievement Tests.* (3rd ed.) Englewood Cliffs, N.J.: Prentice-Hall, 1982.

Guba, E. G., and Lincoln, Y. S. *Effective Evaluation: Improving the Usefulness of Evaluation Results Through Responsive and Naturalistic Approaches.* San Francisco: Jossey-Bass, 1981.

Hamblin, A. C. *Evaluation and Control of Training.* New York: McGraw-Hill, 1974.

Harless, J. "Front-End Analysis by Trainers." In *The Best of TRAINING: Interviews and Profiles.* Minneapolis: Lakewood, 1981.

Harrison, E. L., Pietri, P. H., and Moore, C. C. "How to Use Nominal Group Technique to Assess Training Needs." *Training/HRD,* 1983, *20* (3), 30, 32, 34.

Helmer, O. *Analysis of the Future: The Delphi Technique.* Santa Monica, Calif.: Rand, 1967.

Henerson, M. E., Morris, L. L., and Fitz-Gibbon, C. T. *How to Measure Attitudes.* Newbury Park, Calif.: Sage, 1978.

Horn, R. E. (ed.). *The Guide to Simulations/Games for Education and Training.* Cranford, N.J.: Didactic Systems, 1977.

Houston, M. J., and Sudman, S. "A Methodological Assessment of the Use of Key Informants." *Social Science Research,* 1975, *4,* 151–164.

Hunter, M. *Mastery Teaching.* El Segundo, Calif.: TIP Publications, 1982.

Isaac, S., and Michael, W. B. (eds.). *Handbook in Research and Evaluation.* (2nd ed.) San Diego: EDITS Publishers, 1981.

Jewish Employment and Referral Service. *Work Samples.* (Contract 82-4067-46) Washington, D.C.: Manpower, 1966.

Joint Committee. *Standards for Evaluation of Educational Programs, Projects, and Materials.* New York: McGraw-Hill, 1981.

Kearsley, G. *Costs, Benefits, and Productivity in Training Systems.* Reading, Mass.: Addison-Wesley, 1982.

"Key Participant Method." *Discrepancy Digest,* 1980, *4* (6), 5. Kalamazoo: Department of Educational Leadership, Western Michigan University.

Kirkpatrick, D. L. "Evaluation of Training." In R. L. Craig and L. R. Bittell (eds.), *Training and Development Handbook.* New York: McGraw-Hill, 1976.

Knowles, M. S. "Adult Learning: Theory and Practice." In L. Nadler (ed.), *The Handbook of Human Resource Development*. New York: Wiley, 1984.

Laird, D. *Approaches to Training and Development*. Reading, Mass.: Addison-Wesley, 1978.

Landy, F., Zedeck, S., and Cleveland, J. (eds.). *Performance Measurement and Theory*. Hillsdale, N.J.: Erlbaum, 1983.

Lenz, E. *The Art of Teaching Adults*. New York: Holt, Rinehart & Winston, 1982.

McKeachie, W. J. *Teaching Tips: A Guidebook for the Beginning College Teacher*. Lexington, Mass.: Heath, 1978.

Mager, R. F. *Measuring Instructional Results*. (2nd ed.) Belmont, Calif.: Lake, 1984.

Mager, R. F., and Pipe, P. *Analyzing Performance Problems*. (2nd ed.) Belmont, Calif.: Lake, 1984.

Megarry, J. (ed.). *Aspects of Simulation and Gaming*. 4 vols. London: Kagan Page, 1977.

Meigs-Burkhart, T. *Employee Training in America: A Comparative Assessment of Training and Development*. Princeton, N.J.: Opinion Research Corp., 1986.

Myers, J. H., and Mead, R. R. *The Management of Marketing Research*. Scranton, Pa.: International Textbook, 1969.

Nadler, L. *Corporate Human Resources Development*. New York: Van Nostrand Reinhold, 1980.

Olson, R. *Performance Appraisal: A Guide to Greater Productivity*. New York: Wiley, 1981.

Orlich, D. C. *Designing Sensible Surveys*. Pleasantville, N.Y.: Redgrave, 1978.

Patton, M. Q. *Qualitative Evaluation Methods*. Newbury Park, Calif.: Sage, 1980.

Payne, S. L. *The Art of Asking Questions*. Princeton, N.J.: Princeton University Press, 1951.

Phillips, J. J. *Handbook of Training Evaluation and Measurement Methods*. Houston, Tex.: Gulf, 1983.

Provus, M. M. *Discrepancy Evaluation: For Educational Program Improvement and Assessment*. Berkeley, Calif.: McCutchan, 1971.

Reigeluth, C. M. (ed.). *Instructional Design Theories and Mod-*

els: An Overview of Their Current Status. Hillsdale, N.J.: Erlbaum, 1983.

Reinhard, D. L. "Methodology Development for Input Evaluation Using Advocate and Design Teams." Unpublished doctoral dissertation, College of Education, Ohio State University, 1972.

Ribler, R. I. *Training Development Guide.* Reston, Va.: Reston, 1983.

Rummler, G. A. "The Performance Audit." In R. L. Craig (ed.), *Training and Development Handbook.* (2nd ed.) New York: McGraw-Hill, 1976.

Sashkin, M. *Assessing Performance Appraisal.* San Diego, Calif.: University Associates, 1981.

Schatzman, L., and Strauss, A. L. *Field Research.* Englewood Cliffs, N.J.: Prentice-Hall, 1973.

Schindler-Rainmann, E., and Lippitt, R. *Taking Your Meeting out of the Doldrums.* San Diego, Calif.: University Associates, 1975.

Shrauger, J. S., and Osberg, J. M. "The Relative Accuracy of Self-Prediction and Judgments by Others in Psychological Assessment." *Psychological Bulletin,* 1981, *90,* 322–351.

Shumsky, A. *The Action Research Way of Learning.* New York: Columbia University Press, 1958.

Simon, A., and Boyer, E. G. (eds.). *Mirrors for Behavior: An Anthology of Observation Instruments.* Wynecote, Pa.: Communication Materials Center, 1974.

Spencer, L. M. *Calculating Human Resource Costs and Benefits.* New York: Wiley, 1986.

Stake, R. E. "The Countenance of Educational Evaluation." In B. R. Worthen and J. S. Sanders (eds.), *Educational Evaluation: Theory into Practice.* Worthington, Ohio: Jones, 1973.

Stufflebeam, D. L., and Shinkfield, A. J. *Systematic Evaluation.* Boston: Kluwer-Nijhoff, 1985.

Stufflebeam, D. L., and others. *Educational Evaluation and Decision Making.* Itasca, Ill.: Peacock, 1971.

Sudman, S. *Applied Sampling.* New York: Academic Press, 1976.

Sudman, S., and Bradburn, N. M. *Asking Questions: A Practical*

Guide to Questionnaire Design. San Francisco: Jossey-Bass, 1982.

Sweeney, A. *ROI Basics for Nonfinancial Executives.* New York: AMACOM, 1979.

Taylor, J. B. "Rating Scales as Measures of Clinical Judgment: A Method for Increasing Scale Reliability and Sensitivity." *Educational and Psychological Measurement,* 1968, *28,* 747–766.

Thompson, M. *Benefit-Cost Analysis for Program Evaluation.* Newbury Park, Calif.: Sage, 1980.

Thornton, G. C., and Byham, W. C. *Assessment Centers and Managerial Performance.* New York: Academic Press, 1982.

Tyler, R. "Rationale for Program Evaluation." In G. Madaus and D. L. Stufflebeam (eds.), *Evaluation Models.* Boston: Kluwer-Nijhoff, 1983.

Webb, E. J., and Campbell, D. T. *Nonreactive Measures in the Social Sciences.* (2nd ed.) Boston: Houghton Mifflin, 1981.

Weick, K. "Methods of Organizational Research." In V. Vroom (ed.), *Methods of Organizational Research.* Pittsburgh: University of Pittsburgh Press, 1968.

Wexley, K., and Latham, G. *Developing and Training Human Resources in Organizations.* Glenview, Ill.: Scott, Foresman, 1981.

Yelon, S. L. "How to Lecture." Unpublished lecture notes and audiotape, Michigan State University, 1982.

Index

A

"Able Consulting Company," and implementation, 103-104

Accountability: and achieving objectives, 115; to customers, 77-78; and evaluation, 6, 35-36

Achievement tests, for measuring objectives, 128-129

Action research studies, for needs analysis, 60

Adam, E., 190

Adult learning, and program design, 88-89

Advocate teams, for program design, 90-91

Alkin, M., 227

Applications, of organizational benefits, 185. *See also* Stage V

Argyris, C., 60

Armstrong, D., 187

Artifacts analysis, for transfer of training, 159-160

Assessment centers, for needs analysis, 60-61

Attitude surveys, for needs analysis, 61-62

Attitudes, concept of, 126-127. *See also* Skills, knowledge, or attitudes

Audience: for evaluation, 200-201, 203-204; for reports, 224, 226, 227

Audience/purpose worksheet, 201

Audit, performance, 68-69, 190

B

Babbie, E. R., 62, 91, 111, 112, 157, 188

Behaviorally Anchored Rating Scales (BARS): for needs analysis, 62; for transfer of training, 157

Benefits. *See* Organizational benefits

Berne, E., 112

"Biltrite Machine Toole Company," and transfer of training, 142-143, 146

Blood, M. R., 62, 157

Bloom, B., 127

"Blue Sky Airlines": miscalculation at, 1-2, 3-4; and Six-Stage Evaluation Model, 17, 18, 19

Borg, W. R., 63, 67, 92, 93, 187, 219

Boyer, E. G., 111

Bradburn, N. M., 66

Bradford, J. A., 112

Bray, D. W., 61

Brethower, D. M., 216

Briggs, L. J., 86, 127

Brinkerhoff, R. O., 159, 216

Byham, W. C., 61

241